Beyond
the Crisis of
Masculinity

Beyond the Crisis of
Masculinity

A Transtheoretical Model for
Male-Friendly Therapy

Gary R. Brooks

American Psychological Association • Washington, DC

Copyright © 2010 by the American Psychological Association. All rights reserved. Except as permitted under the United States Copyright Act of 1976, no part of this publication may be reproduced or distributed in any form or by any means, including, but not limited to, the process of scanning and digitization, or stored in a database or retrieval system, without the prior written permission of the publisher.

Published by
American Psychological Association
750 First Street, NE
Washington, DC 20002
www.apa.org

To order
APA Order Department
P.O. Box 92984
Washington, DC 20090-2984
Tel: (800) 374-2721; Direct: (202) 336-5510
Fax: (202) 336-5502; TDD/TTY: (202) 336-6123
Online: www.apa.org/books/
E-mail: order@apa.org

In the U.K., Europe, Africa, and the Middle East, copies may be ordered from
American Psychological Association
3 Henrietta Street
Covent Garden, London
WC2E 8LU England

Typeset in Goudy by Circle Graphics, Inc., Columbia, MD

Printer: United Book Press, Baltimore, MD
Cover Designer: Naylor Design, Washington, DC

The opinions and statements published are the responsibility of the authors, and such opinions and statements do not necessarily represent the policies of the American Psychological Association.

Library of Congress Cataloging-in-Publication Data

Brooks, Gary R., 1946-
  Beyond the crisis of masculinity: a transtheoretical model for male-friendly therapy / Gary R. Brooks.
     p. cm.
  Includes bibliographical references and index.
  ISBN-13: 978-1-4338-0716-9
  ISBN-10: 1-4338-0716-5
  1. Men—Mental health. 2. Men—Counseling of. 3. Masculinity. I. Title.

  RC451.4.M45B754 2010
  616.890081—dc22
                                    2009030800

British Library Cataloguing-in-Publication Data

A CIP record is available from the British Library.

Printed in the United States of America
First Edition

To Everett Adams and Joseph Michael, inspirations and role models

CONTENTS

PREFACE

In most every career, there comes a juncture where professional assumptions and aspirations undergo some sort of major reassessment. Mine came early in my professional life at a Veterans Administration Alcohol Treatment Unit in central Texas a few decades ago. I was there to help eight men confront the myriad issues behind their alcoholism.

This would be my first venture away from the world of psychotherapy as taught in graduate school classes and into the world of psychotherapy as practiced "out there"—that is, in the real world, with the troubled patients who populated my therapy textbooks. And although I was fully prepared to engage these men on the issues that harbored their psychic demons, I quickly discovered through their group conversations a much more threatening demon: these middle-class, wage-earning veterans' vulnerability to a crisis of masculinity that was just beginning to take hold in America.

During those sessions—some of which I detail in the introduction to this work while preserving the anonymity of these men—I became intensely committed to studying, surveying, and introspecting about all aspects of the male experience. Over the past 30 years, I have discovered and consumed the recent body of men's studies scholarship and have contributed my own perspectives to this growing literature. Along the way, I have developed a deep appreciation of how masculinity is a source of direction and purpose in the lives of us men as well as a thorough recognition of how the pressures and strictures of the male gender role are important contributors to men's development of behavioral and emotional problems. Through this recognition, I have developed ideas about how to modify conventional psychotherapy methods to accommodate men's indirect and frequently self-defeating coping styles and their deep-seated resistance to help-seeking in general and to psychotherapy in particular. For those reasons, I am exceptionally excited to offer this volume.

This book is an outgrowth of several trends converging upon the fields of counseling and psychotherapy over the past few decades. First, controversy over the effectiveness of psychotherapy demanded that anecdotal evidence and clinical testimony be replaced with actual empirical evidence. Not long after initiating these studies, researchers discovered that although it was possible to show a generally positive outcome for most people in most therapy formats, more sophisticated questions needed to be pursued: Namely, which types of intervention would be most effective, with which groups of clients, under what circumstances? With the recognition of the need for more sophisticated approaches to therapeutic effectiveness, the age of one-size-fits-all psychotherapy was over.

At the same time that the psychotherapy establishment was facing challenges regarding the scientific grounding of psychotherapeutic practice, it began to encounter major challenges to its politics and philosophical biases. As the women's movement demanded a revision of psychological theory and therapy practices, it became quite apparent that androcentric theories and sexist practices needed to be replaced with those more informed by women's studies and feminist theory. With the discovery of women's perspectives, it then became possible to decipher the unique and critical aspects of the male experience. As gender became recognized as a central organizing variable, therapists realized that the previous assumptions about working with *persons* needed to be supplemented with ideas about work with *woman persons* and *man persons*.

Another force that would come to affect counselors and psychotherapists emanated from the larger medical and public health communities. With challenges to the medical model and limitations of tertiary intervention, mental health practitioners were challenged to develop more interventions to promote health and well-being in a primary prevention model. This development has radically expanded opportunities for mental health professionals to broaden their influence beyond their secluded offices via new roles as consultants, educators, and program developers.

Within graduate schools and training institutions, even the most cherished therapy traditions have also undergone some fundamental shifts. Whereas therapists not so long ago had no difficulty being identified as a practitioner within a well-defined theoretical orientation, most all therapists are now integrating many differing orientations; the eclectic therapist has now become the professional norm. Concurrent with this development, the more scientific branches of the psychotherapy community have urged the development of scientific or technical eclecticism, with the ultimate goal of developing transtheoretical approaches.

Within the world of the men's movement and men's studies, developers of a new psychology of men recognized the need to augment their passionate efforts to identify the hallmarks of masculinity and the male experience with a more nuanced recognition of multiple masculinities as mediated by race, ethnicity, social class, sexual orientation, and physical ability status. As a result of this recognition of diversity among men, therapists now understand the need to account for common experiential threads among all men as well as diverse factors that are unique to each cultural group.

The complexity of integrating diversity within the new psychology of men could seem overwhelming to those already struggling to adjust to the challenges of comprehending gender-based differences. Ultimately, however, the matter has been made more feasible with the appearance of multicultural counseling and therapy models. When most all therapy encounters are recognized to have cross-cultural components, the challenge shifts from rote learning of multiple skills and knowledge bases to a more productive and meaningful process of therapist self-awareness and mutual learning between client and therapist.

I would like to express my hope that this book has met its goal of providing one response to the many substantive shifts in demands on counselors and therapists. It is also my hope that we will continue to find new ways to recognize the many important contributions of men and to meet their needs to incorporate sweeping cultural changes and become higher functioning contributors to their families, communities, and personal well-being.

ACKNOWLEDGMENTS

An ideal editor is one who understands what you are trying to say, facilitates the manner in which you say it, and provides support and encouragement during the entire stressful process. At APA Books, both Susan Reynolds and Peter Pavilionis personify this special kind of editor: I am deeply grateful for Susan's vision and pursuit of this project and for Peter's careful review of the material and for his wordsmithing, which have made this book far better than it otherwise would have been. I would also like to thank two anonymous reviewers for their very helpful comments on an earlier version of this manuscript.

My familiarity with men's studies literature has benefited greatly from the work of Joseph Pleck, Michael Kimmel, Jim Doyle, William Pollack, Ron Levant, and James O'Neil. The theoretical bridge from men's studies to psychotherapy has been built upon the critical contributions of George Albee, Mark Kiselica, Michael Addis, Jim Mahalik, Fred Rabinowitz, Sam Cochran, Chris Kilmartin, Derald Wing Sue, David Sue, James Prochaska, and John Norcross. My capacity to appreciate diversity has been greatly enhanced by my many friends and mentors within the groups supporting the National Multicultural Summit. I have greatly benefited from the opportunity for collaborative writing with Glenn Good, Ron Levant, Louise Silverstein, Doug Haldeman, Don-David Lusterman, Carol Philpot, and Roberta Nutt.

Finally, I remain continually thankful for the support and love from my wife, Patti; my daughters, Ashley and Allison; and my mom.

Beyond
the Crisis of
Masculinity

INTRODUCTION

The *crisis of masculinity* in American society appeared sometime in the early 1970s, in reaction to the Second Wave of the feminist movement. For young adult men across the United States, the most visible sign of the masculinity crisis at this point was the sudden appearance of men's studies programs on select college campuses. For older American men, nothing quite prepared them for the ongoing assault against a lot of the traditional tropes that constituted manliness and a masculine persona in the United States in the mid-1970s.

To say that there were typical categories of responses among all men in American society during that period is to presume a level of activism or reaction among them similar to that of those who were launching such cultural and gender-based criticisms on a daily basis. A large segment of them were defensive, to be sure. Some were more proactive and responsive to the cultural criticism of *hypermasculinity* that permeated American culture. And then some men reacted in self-destructive ways, internalizing an anger born of helplessness and lack of understanding. It's this last segment of troubled men that introduced me directly to the American crisis of masculinity.

Eight men sat waiting more or less expectantly for me on a Monday each week in a room at a Veterans Administration (VA) hospital in central Texas during the mid-1970s. Most were dressed in the denim and boots typical for the truck driving and oil rigging occupations that had intermittently supported them in that part of the country. Two other men, unshaven, bleary-eyed, and seemingly disoriented in their hospital robes and paper slippers, were the newest admissions to this Veterans Administration Alcohol Treatment Unit. The stark overhead fluorescent lighting would have been even more glaring had it not been for the low-hanging cloud of cigarette smoke that blanketed most all 1970s mental health treatment settings. Although overheated and poorly ventilated, the group room was a major climactic improvement for these men, whose very recent winter nights had been spent in colder, wetter, and far less secure environments. A few of the men made note of my presence, but most took greater interest in their coffee and burning cigarettes. As I surveyed the room, I suspected that it was more than the smoking, the lighting, and the room temperature that was causing my uneasiness. What was I doing here? How did I get myself into this odd and totally foreign situation? The simple explanation was that I had needed extra experience away from my graduate school classes and had arranged a special practicum assignment.

I was a 2nd-year psychology graduate student, determined to project confidence and enthusiasm about the transforming powers of psychotherapy. Yet to my surprise, the first therapy session with these men was awkward, and the response to me was underwhelming. Successive sessions were equally unproductive, and my frustration with these men escalated. With no real alternative, I soldiered on with greatly lowered expectations of these men and their possibilities—but with the stubborn conviction about the suitability of my therapeutic approach.

Although my graduate training was still in progress and I realized there was much more to learn, I'd felt fairly confident that my exposure to Rogers, Perls, Ellis, Meichenbaum, Yalom, and the other therapy giants would be quite sufficient. I felt confident of my inherent therapeutic abilities and capacity to bring therapeutic wisdom to these men, all middle-aged military veterans who found themselves in a central Texas VA hospital after repeated failures to negotiate their lives without abusing alcohol.

I was prepared to talk to these men about alcoholism, the counseling process, coping mechanisms—the standard repertoire of approaches I'd been taught and was about to use with these men as I helped them dig deep into their past and present to unearth the various and complex reasons why they drank alcoholically. And yet, as the sessions progressed, I noticed that we were discussing an entirely different (or so I'd thought) subject—one that took hold quite subtly and quickly but came to dominate our weekly hour or so in that VA hospital room. With only a few weeks remaining in my first training assignment, I was challenged by my supervisor to provide a clinical case presentation. With no obvious successes in either my group or individual therapy cases, I took the supervisor's suggestion to present several cases that would offer a broad and subjective portrait of the lives and challenges of these middle-aged, working class, traditional men. Seeking an entree into their experiential worlds, I began one of my final group sessions with an unexpected query: "What does it mean to be a man?"

Initially surprised by the inanity of this question, the group members began describing the obvious—that is, what everyone knows and really doesn't need to waste time talking about.

George: A man is a leader of his family, just like a squad leader in Nam. It's on him.

Harry: Yeah, that's right. A man does what he has to do, regardless of what is.

Jesse: No shit. He doesn't whine or cry or back down. He meets things head on and gets it done.

Ron: Exactly, and if things get tough he keeps it to himself. He doesn't lay his problems on others.

Mike: Absolutely. But don't forget that a man has to set an example. He has to make his mark and be somebody others can look up to.

There may not have been any dramatic surprises in what these men said, but I was immediately struck by what seemed to be occurring. Most obviously, there was a palpable shift in atmosphere as all the men became intensely engaged in offering their personal views and experiences. Even the members previously most detached seemed to become energized in their effort to educate their naive and inexperienced therapist about the harsher realities of real men's lives. In spite of the differences in their life circumstances, they were of a single voice in identifying a code or standard that governed their lives. Sadly, the most compelling aspect of their perspectives on manhood was that each was describing a man they were unable to be—a standard each, in some fundamental way, had been unable to meet.

At that moment, I couldn't help but speculate on the odd nature of masculinity. Although it clearly was a topic with deep relevance to these men, it was one they rarely discussed or questioned. More important, although the topic of masculinity evoked strong reactions in men, it seemed to offer less inspiration than it offered burdensome pressures. At one level, there was obvious pride in identifying with manhood, but at a deeper level there was as much doubt and shame as there was empowerment or fulfillment.

For the first time of that entire training assignment, the allotted group hour was exhausted long before each man had exhausted his contributions.

In retrospect, that session marked a pivotal point in my contact with these men and in my approach to psychotherapy. At the time, I certainly was pleased that things had become more lively and engaging, but I had no real awareness of the revolutionary effect that session would have on my overall approach to therapy with men. In retrospect, I now recognize that the session marked not only a dramatic difference in my therapy methods but also a substantive shift in my philosophy of how to interact with men. On one level, I had stumbled upon a topic of immense meaning to this group of men. Of equal significance, however, I had unexpectedly made an even more fundamental realization: In the unfolding of the discussion of *manhood*, I found myself more enthusiastic and invested than at any other point in my limited clinical experience.

Over the next several days of therapy, as I built upon these new inroads to explicate these men's stories and struggles, I discovered a reservoir of subjective wisdom that I had never previously accessed. Despite my initial assumption of a wide gulf between me and these men, I was struck by the commonalities among us. We had encountered similar challenges and continued to struggle to find a path toward being *good men*—some more successfully than others. Empathy, once only an aspiration, flowed readily as I acknowledged the ways in which I had had access to situational advantages unavailable to them. Although our lives had unfolded in very different ways, I felt a sense of connection I had never known.

The more these eight men talked, the more it became abundantly clear that they were undergoing a crisis of masculinity. Each of the men had a more or less clear idea of how a man is supposed to behave and what general standards he is expected to meet. To a great extent, each of them was failing to meet those standards, and those failures played a consequential role in his self-defeating behavior. But were these men dysfunctional? As alcoholics, they were getting the standard therapeutic treatment; and more than a few in the group—and many, many more men outside the group then and now—may have been prime candidates for the treatment of comorbid psychopathologies, such as hyperaggression, depression, and various other maladaptive behaviors.

But as men, did they not also require treatment for their self-imposed obstacles (and the consequent pain and self-destructive behaviors) to living up to the traditional cultural exemplar? For many in our culture, both professionals and average citizens, it is more comforting to simply see these men as aberrantly dysfunctional because the implication seems more straightforward. Simply put, the view implies that dysfunctional men need to be treated and rehabilitated to become more similar to "real men"—that is, to better meet the code of masculinity and fit more fully into the well-established template for manhood. Of course, there may be critical flaws in such a formulation. Perhaps the matter is far more complex, and the necessary responses to the situation less straightforward, than mental health professionals (and these demoralized men themselves) have previously realized.

First, rather than accepting conventional wisdom, consideration needs to be given to whether traditional masculinity is as "natural" and inevitable as has generally been assumed. Is it possible, for example, that there is more variability across historical eras and cultural contexts than has been recognized? That is, could *masculinity* be as much an artificial construction as it is a biological or evolutionary imperative? Also, is it possible that many aspects of the traditional male code are internally contradictory, making it impossible for most men to meet all its expectations? Furthermore, do the dominant ideas about manhood function as benevolent guidelines that reassure men and enhance their well-being, or, conversely, do they generate insecurity and chronic doubts about whether a man is manly enough? Might they produce self-destructive behavior because they fail to identify when enough is enough in displays of male power and virility? Fundamentally, is the path from boyhood to secure manhood clearly marked, warmly mentored, and collectively celebrated, or is the journey far more enigmatic, traumatic, and emotionally isolating? Finally, does the code of masculinity provide space for adaptation to changing times and social circumstances, or is it so rigid and inviolate that men become reactive to the point of reflexively enacting atavistic demonstrations of manliness?

Because these speculations have critical relevance in efforts to craft a therapeutic approach to a boy or man entering the office of a mental health professional, the matter will receive considerable attention in the pages that follow. It is vital that men like those in the VA group, despite their fully justified labels in the *Diagnostic and Statistical Manual of Mental Disorders*, be understood as more than just pathological men. To employ a familiar metaphor, these men might be similar to the canaries in coal mines, whose greater sensitivity and vulnerability alerted miners of imminent danger from toxic fumes. Perhaps these men, because of a lowered level of coping resources and lack of the sophisticated defensive maneuvers of more advantaged men, are more likely to evidence the unvarnished distress of men struggling to cope with both the inherent contradictions of the traditional male role and the sweeping changes in the demands of contemporary manhood. Perhaps they are only the most obvious representatives of the modern crisis of masculinity.

In the brilliant film *Pleasantville*, William H. Macy portrays George Parker, a middle-aged, 1950s businessman who returns home one evening, just as he apparently has done every evening for many years, to find his wife Betty not there to welcome him. Worse yet, no dinner has been prepared. In an absurdly comic scene, he steps outside into the rain and cries out "Where's my dinner?" Although this behavior is clearly presented as ridiculous, it also evokes a sense of the man's pathos. In response to his disequilibrium, Parker hurries to the local bowling alley to seek the support of his buddies. As he describes his seemingly abandoned home, his bowling buddies react with shock and horror. Initially perplexed by the suddenness of the events, Big Bob, the bowling team captain, rises to announce his detection of a spreading social malignancy, and he calls for a swift and forceful counterresponse: "I think we all know what's going on out there, and thank God we're in a bowling alley. . . . But if we don't do something about this soon, it will get all of us!"

By recreating the world of the 1950s sitcom, *Pleasantville* offers an invaluable glimpse into gender relations before the Second Wave of the feminist movement. George Parker and his bowling buddies are alarmed by the failure of Betty Parker to greet her husband with his dinner, and they are fully receptive to viewing this act as a harbinger of impending changes in male–female relations. In knee-jerk fashion, they demonize the events and begin formulating a strategy to squelch what they consider to be an incipient gender rebellion. Like most reactions based upon limited appreciation of underlying causes and formulated in angry reactivity, the proposed strategies of Big Bob to restore order in Pleasantville turn out to misguided and self-defeating.

In addition to its considerable entertainment value, the most compelling virtue of *Pleasantville* is its capturing of the dominant mind-set of American men in the latter half of the last century. The men of the film, similar to most men of the era, not only sensed the looming changes on the gender landscape but also impulsively latched onto ill-conceived responses that set the stage for a broad crisis of masculinity. Like many crises, this chaotic upsetting of traditional gender expectations is best understood as more than a phenomenon that suddenly appeared out of the blue. That is, this crisis of masculinity needs to be recognized as a function of fundamental flaws in the construction of masculinity, the paradoxical nature of its benefits, epochal revisions to the sociocultural and sociopolitical environment, and insidious processes that have interfered with the recognition of its detrimental effects.

Extreme pressures for men to be strong, aggressive, and fearless leaders have advanced many men's political and economic status, but such status achievement has come at a price that is poorly understood. The power men experience as a group has too infrequently provided them with feelings of empowerment and personal control of their lives. Gone are the unexplored and unsettled frontiers that once offered some men an outlet or escape from certain demands and social responsibilities. Jobs demanding manly strength and stamina, as well as naked, aggressive competition, have been transformed; even warfare has become increasingly automated and more detached from the skills of the soldier as warrior—skills that were once the sole province of men.

Women's empowerment, although potentially a positive force for men as well as for women, has instead been viewed (in varying degrees) by most men as an infringement on the privileges men have customarily received for meeting male duties, such as providing strength and protection in the home and serving as the traditional breadwinner.

The expectation that men should hide or disguise their distress over these vastly changed (and ever-changing) roles and entitlements has caused many men to suffer in silence or else subconsciously channel their emotional pain into multiple self-destructive behaviors. In chapter 1, I detail this pervasive psychic distress among men—distress that ranges from a general yet persistent malaise to three primary areas (the "Big Three") of major problems—violence, substance abuse, and sexual misconduct—that are represented in various ways in the categorizations of the mental health profession's definitive *Diagnostic and Statistical Manual of Mental Disorders* (4th ed.; American Psychiatric Association, 1994).

Under optimal circumstances, men would recognize their distress, accurately attribute its sources, and proactively seek professional help to accommodate more effectively their difficult circumstances. Concurrently, mental health institutions and professionals would comprehend the factors underlying men's dysfunctional behavior, provide outreach to troubled men, and develop therapeutic interventions that are sensitive to men's pain and congruent with their behavioral style. Sadly, this has not taken place. Few men are able to identify the deeper causes of their distress, and many repress or deny their turmoil. Even when the pain is apparent, most men, true to their go-it-alone socialization, have avoided all forms of help in general—psychotherapy in particular.

Compounding this problematic situation, the field of psychotherapy has not accommodated well enough the special needs of men. In an oddly ironic way, this helping profession, historically dominated by male perspectives, has generally missed the boat when it comes to recognizing and addressing the crisis of masculinity. This is not to say that the psychotherapy field had done especially well in meeting women's needs (or the needs of other oppressed groups). However, because of the extraordinary efforts of feminists and women's studies advocates, the varieties of "the female experience" have received greater recognition; therapies have been developed that are more harmonious with the needs of girls and women. Simply put, a similar process is vitally necessary for boys and men; otherwise, the longstanding disconnection between those in a position to help and those needing the help will continue. This is the subject of chapter 2 of this work.

What then is needed to address this conundrum? Most fundamentally, a new paradigm is required for psychotherapy with boys and men. Traditional approaches have been colossally uninformed by an in-depth appreciation of the unique challenges in the lives of boys and men. These approaches have largely failed to appreciate male attribution styles and the implications of indirect solutions to psychic pain. They have insufficiently recognized the inherent problems of the male code's interference with acknowledging distress and admitting the need for help. There has been neither a countering of the distorted public image of psychotherapy processes nor adequate development and presentation of a model of mental health intervention that would be palatable to boys and men. This untenable situation needs to change.

Of all the problematic aspects of traditional therapeutic practice for males, none is more outdated than the customary reliance on tertiary prevention—that is, for too long, therapists have been willing to limit their work with men only to those who come to occupy a seat in a formal therapeutic office setting. To counter this unnecessary restriction in access to needy males, therapists and counselors benefit by thinking more broadly regarding formats and settings for therapeutic interventions with men. In chapter 3, I discuss primary prevention activities for boys and men that seem to offer them a creative avenue to heighten their awareness of how gender role strain affects all facets of their daily life and simultaneously to address their negative attitudes toward formal psychotherapeutic settings. As such, this chapter (as, I hope, this book) is intended also for a nonclinical readership—that is, for men of all ages and backgrounds who have entertained the notion of psychotherapy but who are reluctant to participate in the conventional therapeutic process.

These activities "outside the therapist's office" may include participation in organized programs targeted to common male problems, involvement with men's groups, or exposure to psychoeducational pursuits. Additionally, therapists in certain special settings can utilize their consultation skills and familiarity with men's studies to broaden and enrich already existing programs or establish innovative new programs designed specifically for men.

Of course, such primary preventive interventions and proactive outreach are of little therapeutic consequence if the troubled male and his prospective therapist cannot forge some sort of bond that gets the prospective male client engaged in the therapeutic process itself. In this regard, the therapeutic community is fortunate enough to be able to turn to a line of professional literature on male therapy that has made its appearance recently. This volume builds on that literature, beginning in chapter 4, to offer a transtheoretical model of male-friendly therapeutic interventions for boys and men. This model incorporates insights about stages of change and the challenges inherent in many men's problematic coping with emotional distress. It calls for a certain appreciation of men's reluctance to enter therapy and offers perspectives to advance men from a *precontemplative* stage—that is, a stage in which men are just becoming aware that they have a problem and are thinking about ways to address their peculiarly problematic gender-role strain. In this way, therapists will be able to take full advantage of opportunities presented when a male client is on the threshold of the therapist's office. This process is enhanced by a male-specific diagnostic assessment process to enrich understanding of the client, facilitate therapy engagement, and produce a solid therapeutic alliance.

Therapeutic engagement is only a critical first step. Thereafter, therapists face the substantial challenge of delivering interventions congruent with typically male here-and-now problem-solving styles. To meet this challenge, it is necessary to incorporate established therapeutic wisdom into the expanding knowledge base of the *new psychology of men*. Chapter 5 identifies male-friendly variants of several individual approaches, the all-male group approach, and marital and family therapy approaches. It also describes the new body of work offering special adaptations of therapeutic interventions for boys and adolescent males.

Despite the advantages of examining commonalities among all men, there is also a critical need to consider how race, ethnicity, sexual orientation, and physical ability status intersect with the social construction of masculinity. Much as the Third Wave of feminism has sought to deconstruct prevailing assumptions about femininity, this volume strives to move beyond the hegemonic paradigm of White heterosexual masculinity. In this effort, it attends to the work of leading multicultural experts to provide greater recognition of the oppressions of some men and consider adaptations of therapeutic interventions for work with diverse male populations.

Chapter 6 acknowledges that multicultural competence with male clients involves more than familiarity with the growing literature of the new psychology of men. Beyond their increased knowledge about men, the most effective therapists with boys and men will be those who enhance their intervention skills as well as their personal self-awareness and their skills of inclusive empathy. To facilitate the movement toward greater competence with male clients, this volume encourages therapists to introspect upon the unique assets and possible blind spots they bring into their work with boys and men. In addition to suggesting special intervention skills related to men's preferred interpersonal styles, chapter 6 offers a multicultural schema of sorts for the therapist to isolate the core problems that plague men from the multicultural narrative that in various ways disguises the problems peculiar to all constructs of masculinity. This chapter also explores the issue of the therapist's own self-awareness and self-assessment when dealing with men from wholly different backgrounds—not only in terms of ethnicity and sexual orientation but also in terms of physical ability, education, socioeconomic status, and other salient multicultural therapeutic variables.

Because of the complex therapeutic challenges of work with boys and men, it makes the most sense to draw from the contemporary trend toward eclectic therapy and the transtheoretical integration of approaches. To facilitate this objective, I return to the discussion of the transtheoretical model in chapter 7 of this volume and review the principal elements of James Prochaska and John Norcross's transtheoretical model. The chapter attempts to demonstrate how the model can be integrated with the new literature of male-friendly psychotherapies to offer an organized framework for choosing therapeutic interventions for boys and men.

In sum, this work offers a model of male-friendly psychotherapy that is informed by in-depth knowledge of men's lives and the ambiguous role of power in men's lives. It is broad and catholic in its consideration of modes of intervention, positive and focused on personal enhancement, transtheoretical, sensitive to variations and diversities among men, and proactive in its call for better therapist self-awareness.

1

THE CRISIS OF MASCULINITY

Although women have predominated in the ranks of psychotherapy clients over the years, there has been no shortage of men who find themselves on the receiving end of mental health treatment. Despite the notable differences in susceptibility to variants of mental illness, it has only been within the past few decades that the gender components of the psychopathologies have been highlighted, with previous interventions generally oblivious to the role of gender variables in the etiology of problematic behavioral patterns. This new attention to the manner in which gender socialization contributes to psychopathology is one of the most vitally important legacies of feminism and the women's movement, precisely because of the insistence that the mental health fields recognize the intersections of gender, psychiatric diagnosis, and clinical interventions.

Chesler (1972) presented one of the earliest and most influential indictments of psychiatry for pathologizing and stigmatizing women. Most research has revealed that women have been diagnosed and treated for mental illness at a much higher rate than men, have been far more likely to receive psychotherapy, and have been twice as likely to receive psychotropic medications (Ballou & Brown, 2002; Maracek, 1997). This outcry against the overrepresentation of women in clinical settings, however, does not negate the reality of the extreme distress that propels many men into mental health treatment. The fourth edition of the mental health profession's *Diagnostic and Statistical Manual of Mental Disorders* (*DSM–IV*; American Psychiatric Association, 2000) finally recognized the differential rates of mental disorders, identifying numerous disorders that are far more common among men. For example, the *DSM–IV* notes that men are five times more likely to be diagnosed with alcohol abuse, four times more likely to be diagnosed with illicit substance abuse, and three times more likely to be diagnosed with antisocial personality disorder. In addition, men represent nearly the entire population of those patients diagnosed with paraphilia and the greatest preponderance of those patients diagnosed with combat-related, posttraumatic stress disorder.

TROUBLED MEN IN TROUBLED SETTINGS

The epidemiological data make it quite clear that the men in my Veterans Administration therapy group were not completely anomalous, as there are many avenues for men to enter formal psychiatric settings. Yet these numbers do not tell the entire story, because the medical model approach of the *DSM–IV* is not capable of identifying all the other ways that many men suffer. In describing "the dark side of masculinity," Louise Silverstein and I posited that traditional male role socialization produces a wide range of problematic interpersonal behaviors that are profoundly harmful to society and to men themselves (Brooks & Silverstein, 1995). These dark side behaviors do not align perfectly with the formal psychiatric diagnostic categories because only some of them are the product of formal mental disorders, while others are the cause of a mental disorder, and others do not produce a formal diagnosis at all.

Violent Men

Men's violence is both vilified and celebrated. When displayed as part of a man's beliefs about patriotic duty or his superior athletic ability, violence is considered to be an enactment of true manhood. For example, Fasteau (1975) described violence as "the crucible of manhood," (p. 149) and Doyle (1995) identified the "warrior male" and "epic male" (p. 28) as central to portrayal of exalted men. The recent *Tough Guise* video (1999) illustrated how the need to be viewed as rugged and tough has become critical to young men's lives. At the same time, however, the mental health literature is replete with descriptions of the enormous damage inflicted by violent men. Male violence against women has been estimated to occur in the adult intimate relationships of between 21% and 34% of women (Goodman, Koss, Fitzgerald, Russo, & Keita, 1993). In his thorough review of the problems of men's violence, Katz (1999) noted, "Men's violence against women is a major contemporary social problem that is deeply rooted in our cultural traditions" (p. 21). Male violence against other males is epidemic, with men as the most likely perpetrators and victims of violent death (Stark, 1990). Only recently has male violence against boys (i.e., males under age 18) received needed attention, with data suggesting serious childhood physical abuse inflicted by men against boys as common as one boy in five, and "minor violence" rates as common as 65% of all boys (Lisak, 2001b).

Substance-Abusing Men

It has been noted that "alcoholism and masculinity seem to go hand in hand" (Brooks & Silverstein, 1995, p. 288). Conservative estimates are that men are far more likely than women to experience alcohol problems, and some authors cite a rate of four or five alcoholic men for each woman who abuses alcohol (Dawson, 1996; Grucza, Norberg, Bucholz, & Bierut, 2008; Lemle & Mishkind, 1989). More recent data (Grucza, Norberg, Bucholz, & Bierut, 2008) indicate that the alcohol dependence rate is increasing for women and remaining at the same high rate for men, with age of onset becoming earlier for both genders. Many traditionally male settings, from military units to college fraternities, have been complicit in encouraging men to abuse alcohol. Some older data indicated that the prevalence of full-blown alcoholism may be as high as 1 in 10 men (Heilman, 1973).

Similar to alcohol abuse, abuse of illicit substances is also far more prevalent among men. Diamond (1987) noted that "although addiction does not discriminate against women, it does seem to be a disease that is closely associated with men" (p. 332). According to older Department of Justice figures, more than 85% of drug offenders are male (Stephenson, 1991). More recent epidemiological data from the Substance Abuse and Mental Health Services Administration (2008) indicated that 14.5 million men met the *DSM–IV* criteria for substance dependence or abuse, a figure representing nearly 11% of the male population (the women's rate was approximately 6%).

Sexually Offending Men

Men are more commonly the victims of sexual assault than is generally recognized (Lisak, 2001b), and women are sometimes sexual perpetrators. Nevertheless, women are far more commonly the victims of rapes, and men are far more commonly the perpetrators (Koss, 1993). Prevalence studies of rape and sexual assault are exceptionally difficult to comprehend because of their widely varying estimates of occurrence. For example, Kaplan, O'Neil, and Owen (1993) noted that research studies have varied in prevalence estimates from 5% to 44% of all women. There is an unfortunate perception that those who rape or commit sexual assault are pathological strangers, but the data actually show that between 50% and 88% of rape victims know their perpetrators (Koss & Cook, 1998; Russell, 1982). Date rape is alarmingly common, with estimates at 15% to 30% of all women experiencing this at some point in their lives (White & Kowalski, 1998). Katz (1999) cited research finding that "20 percent of adolescent girls were physically or sexually abused by a date. . . . Nearly one-third of American women report being physically or sexually abused by a husband or boyfriend at some point in their lives" (p. 21). Lest these figures be dismissed as the product of a few deviant men, we need to consider the research finding that 43% of male high school students considered it acceptable for a boy to force sex upon a girl if they had been dating for a long time (Muehlenhard & Linton, 1987). It is probable that most men generally conduct themselves with sexual integrity, but these figures nevertheless suggest that there is something seriously wrong with the way masculinity is constructed and enacted in our culture.

THE PSYCHOPATHOLOGY OF MEN'S EVERYDAY LIVES

It is clear that men have always been represented disproportionately in mental health treatment settings. Unfortunately, because of their aversion to help seeking, men usually have not entered those therapeutic settings until their situations have become desperate (Scher, 1990). It would seem likely, therefore, that the clinical populations of men described above represent only a small percentage of all men, including those men who may be struggling in some aspect of their lives. This notion is entirely consistent with the popular school of thought that contemporary men are now experiencing major upheavals in all areas of their lives and have been challenged to make radical shifts in their relationships with women, their children, their careers, and their physical selves. This perspective has been presented widely by a range of gender scholars who are in agreement that many sweeping changes in the psychosocial landscape of the last several decades have generated a *crisis of masculinity*. Specifically, the cumulative pressures boys and men face to fulfill the mandates of the traditional masculine role—in the midst of a constant social reassessment of both gender paradigms—disposes them to a range of profound mental, physical, and interpersonal problems.

Masculinity and Health

Of all the toxic aspects of the male gender role, the health-diminishing and life-threatening components are the most dramatic. In brief, men live shorter lives than women (by 6 to 8 years) and have higher morbidity from certain illnesses (Arias, 2005). Although some theorists have speculated that these differences are related to inherent biological factors, most researchers (Phillips, 2005; Verbrugge, 1985) have explained the life expectancy data as a function of gender-related behavior. Courtenay (2005) reviewed the extensive body of research on sex differences in physical health and observed, "Men who adopt traditional beliefs about manhood and dominant norms of masculinity have greater health risks than their peers with less traditional beliefs and engage in riskier behaviors" (p. 30). For example, to be consistent with the "The Sturdy Oak" mandate of traditional masculinity, men are far less likely than women to perform routine preventative health behaviors or maintain routine health appointment schedules, and men ask fewer questions when visiting their physician (Courtenay, 2005). Furthermore, men commonly feel less of a need for adequate amounts of sleep, safety measures, and prudent eating habits (Copenhaver & Eisler, 1996; Courtenay, 2005). Despite greater attention being given to the intersection of gender and physical health, the alarm raised by Harrison more than 3 decades ago—"Warning: The male sex role may be dangerous to your health"—remains highly relevant (Harrison, 1978, p. 68).

Masculinity and Corrupted Boyhood

In the past several years there has been a major surge in books calling for attention to the mounting problems of America's young women and men. Following the phenomenal impact of Mary Pipher's *Reviving Ophelia* (1994), a work that articulated the plight of contemporary young women, many other writers have echoed similar concerns about the lives of young men. William Pollack's *Real Boys* (1998) raised alarms about the cultural climate for young men, and he has been joined by several authors with similar concerns (Garbarino, 1999; Gurian & Stevens, 2005; Kindlon & Thompson, 2000). Although there are many differences among these publications, all share the common thesis that socialization pressures and demands of modern life can be toxic to boys' development.

Garbarino (1999) focused on the increased levels of violence among young men as the "Give 'Em Hell" aspect of the traditional male role is supplemented by shifts in cultural climates to abandon and reject young men. The works of Gurian (2006) and Kindlon and Thompson (2000) implicated broad cultural failures in recognizing the special developmental needs of boys and young men. The most recent work in this genre is that of Sax (2007), who identified five factors that he believes drive "the growing epidemic of unmotivated boys and underachieving young men." In a work certain to stir controversy, Sax cited changes in public schools that disadvantage boys: increased use of video games among boys; overdiagnosis of attention-deficit/hyperactivity disorder in boys and young men; elevated levels of environmental estrogens; "devaluation of masculinity," and unavailability of suitable male role models.

At a more disturbing and deadlier level, Kellner (2008) traced the recent spate of school shootings and killing sprees committed by a relatively young male cohort—including Columbine, Virginia Tech, and Northern Illinois University— to "a crisis of out-of-control gun culture and male rage, heightened by a glorification of hypermasculinity and violence in the media" (2008, p. 14). Jackson Katz and Sut Jhally (the writer and director, respectively, of the *Tough Guise* video) located the problem more precisely with the example of the 1999 Columbine High School tragedy, posing a painful rhetorical question that Eric Harris and Dylan Klebold probably posed to themselves—and answered themselves—during the months, weeks, and days leading up to their intricately planned and deadly rampage against their fellow classmates:

> How do you respond if you are being victimized by this dominant system of masculinity? The lessons from Columbine High—a typical suburban "jockocracy," where the dominant male athletes did not hide their disdain for those who did not fit in—are pretty clear. The 17- and 18-year-old shooters, tired of being ridiculed or marginalized, weren't big and strong, and so they used the great equalizer: weapons. Any discussion about guns in our society needs to include a discussion of their function as equalizers. In Littleton, the availability of weapons gave the shooters the opportunity to exact a twisted and tragic revenge: 15 dead, including themselves, and 23 wounded (*Boston Globe*, May 2, 1999, p. E1).

Although the recent publication of a thorough analysis of the Columbine tragedy (Cullen, 2009) challenged the straightforward view of Harris and Klebold as marginalized outcasts seeking revenge against jock culture, the painful reality is nevertheless unchanged: Angry young men remain susceptible to cultural forces supporting gun culture and male violence.

It must be pointed out that although each of these new works focuses on the damages inflicted on young males, they differ in their degree of confluence with the gender role strain perspective. To a large extent, these works are more prone to implicate cultural institutions for failure to recognize or channel young men's essentially different natures and less prone to examine the socially structured aspects of the problems. Others, however, have been more likely to look at contributions of a violent cultural context. For example, Katz (1999) described the "tough guise," a persona he says many young men feel compelled to adopt after exposure to an ever more violent media culture and massive pressures not to appear weak or feminine; Kellner (2008) also pointed to even more destructive hypermasculine reactions to the same violent media culture. Levant (1995) described the "ordeal of emotional socialization," whereby boys are systematically taught to deny and suppress their tender and vulnerable emotions to fit in with the dominant ideas of masculinity. Robertson and Shepard (2008) described the "Boy Code," which contains the dominant messages harshly enforced on boys and young men.

Masculinity and Work

Men's relationship to their work has been the source of both their greatest satisfactions and their greatest disappointments. All explications of the male role cite "work" as a central component of how men define themselves. David and Brannon (1976) referred to this as The Big Wheel component of masculinity, while Doyle (1995) labeled it as "the success element." Brenton (1966) observed that "the American male looks to his breadwinning role to confirm his manliness" (p. 194). In her classic description of the "good provider role," Bernard (1981) noted, "success in the good-provider role came in time to define masculinity itself. . . . Men were judged as men by the level of living they provided" (p. 3).

This merging of masculinity with work success and the good provider role creates multiple pitfalls for men. First, because it is never made clear how much success is enough, men are susceptible to always envying the accomplishments of higher achieving men. Second, many ethnic minority men are disadvantaged by the enormous disparities in opportunities to participate in the workplace with unemployment rates of African-American and Native-American men more than double that of White Americans (Sue & Sue, 2003). Third, as women have entered the workforce, many men have had great difficulty moving from a sole provider role to that of partner in a dual-career relationship (Gilbert, 1993). Finally, men who have made work the central focus of their life energies have major problems when their work connections are ended from unemployment, disability, or even from retirement (Marini, 2005; Sternbach, 2001).

Masculinity and Fatherhood

No problematic aspect of the male role has been more noted than that of the restrictiveness of traditional fatherhood. Some authors have described the lifelong issues created when boys are deprived of emotional connections with their fathers. For example, in *Finding Our Fathers*, Osherson (1986) described how the "unfinished business" of sons with their fathers commonly plays out in adult relationship issues. The major thrust of Robert Bly's mythopoetic retreats is resolving the "father hunger" and the "devastating effects of remote fathers." Also, many authors have described the penalties traditional masculinity exacts on the fathers themselves. For example, Levant & Kelly (1989) and Shapiro (2001) have described how most men's poor preparation for fatherhood has caused such them such difficulty that they miss out on major opportunities for emotional connections with their young children. Furthermore, men have typically had less involvement than women with their growing children, with daily contact estimates varying between 12 minutes (Hochschild & Machung, 2001) and 2 hours (Hossain & Rooparine, 1993). Fortunately, a recent image of "new fathers" has emerged. Pleck (1987) characterized this new father in the following way: "he is present at the birth; he is involved with his children as infants, not just when they are older; he participates in the actual day-to-day work of child care, and not just play; he is involved with his daughters as much as his sons" (p. 93). Unfortunately, multiple logistical and psychological factors have continued to restrict men's fullest participation in the raising of their children (Pleck, 1987, 2007; Pleck & Masciadrelli, 2004).

Masculinity and Relationships With Women

Many volumes have been written on the age-old conflicts between women and men, and this issue can only be briefly touched on here. Despite the fact that some persons view the battle of the sexes as an inevitable outgrowth of biology and evolutionary imperatives (Buss, 1994), many others indict gender politics and socialization as playing a more critical (and more alterable) role in this long-standing state of affairs. Women's studies writers have commonly identified misogyny as a pervasive aspect of patriarchal cultures. For example, Williams (1977) catalogued the dominant historical views of women as falling into four categories: "earth-mother, temptress-seductress, mystery, and necessary evil" (p. 8). The advent of the contemporary women's movement has done a great deal to confront the various permutations of misogyny embedded in the culture, but such confrontation has also inspired reactivity and backlash toward women among some men (Clatterbaugh, 1990; Faludi, 1991).

At a psychological level, virtually all men's studies writers have identified substantial problems in the way men have traditionally been socialized regarding women. The "No Sissy Stuff" mandate identified by David and Brannon (1976) and the "anti-feminine element" (Doyle, 1995) both speak to the demeaning of all that is feminine. Because masculinity has generally been defined by its opposite (i.e., not feminine), many developing boys may have difficulty identifying exactly how they are supposed to appear "manly," but they have a clear idea of what they must not act like: They must not act like girls. Doyle (1995) described this proscription as "Don't be like a girl because . . . well, girls are bad, stupid, inferior, subordinate" (p. 134). In eschewing anything feminine within themselves, young males implicitly learn to have lower regard for women in general.

Further complicating males' relationships with women have been the problems inherent in the socialized differences in relational and communication styles. Tannen (1990) described the differences as women's communication preference for language that emphasizes support and validation whereas men's preference is for advice giving and information sharing. Further, Levant (2003) identified "normative male alexithymia" as an outgrowth of the differential socialization of boys toward emotions and the eventual cause of men's limitations in communication and emotional expression. This alexithymia concept, of course, is relevant to the oft-heard complaint among women that men are inadequate as emotional partners because they are so emotionally walled off and uncommunicative.

A final aspect in this very brief overview is the problem resulting from gender differences regarding sexuality. In their meta-analysis of gender differences in sexual attitudes and behavior, Hyde and Oliver (2000) found that women and men differed significantly in their incidence of masturbation (males having the higher incidence) and their attitudes toward casual sex (with males more likely to endorse this behavior). These findings are highly supportive of the vast body of literature identifying women's and men's sexual attitudes as discrepant and, thus, also harmful to male–female relationships. In describing men's "non-relational" sexuality, Levant (1997) cited research findings that men, compared with women, think about sex more frequently, report more sex partners, purchase more autoerotic materials, and have more permissive attitudes toward casual sex. In my own writing (Brooks, 1995), I described the "centerfold syndrome" as a dysfunctional compilation of attitudes toward women and sexual behavior that are a product of normative male sexual socialization. This syndrome includes compulsive voyeurism, objectification of women's bodies, needs for masculinity validation through sex, and fears of true intimacy.

The foregoing material is certainly not being presented to suggest that healthy relationships between women and men are not possible. Nor is my intention to suggest that most men are lifelong prisoners of the destructive aspects of their socialization toward women. Rather, my intention is to point out that there are many impediments to these healthy relationships, and men's social sexualization is yet another area whereby gender role strain can hamper men's optimal functioning.

Masculinity and Men's Relationships With Other Men

Two extraordinary facts become obvious when one examines the research of gender patterns in friendships. First, most men are quite lonely. Second, most men are highly dependent upon at least one woman for emotional comfort and support.

Men's loneliness is one of their most closely guarded secrets because it often hides behind a facade of social connectedness and public camaraderie among men. Research into friendship patterns of women and men has found that although women and men report similar numbers of friends and similar amounts of time spent in same-sex relationships, there are considerable differences in these patterns. Brehm (1985) found that men tend to have friendships characterized by shared activities, whereas women are more likely to have friendships characterized by interpersonal intimacy and discussion of feelings.

Over the past 3 decades there has been considerable convergence around the idea that men's friendships are limited, relatively superficial, or absent. For example, the well-known study by Levinson, Darrow, Klein, Levinson, and McKee (1978), found participants to be essentially without friends. Rosenberg, Rosenberg, and Farrell (1999) studied 433 middle-class men and found that friendships diminished over time, and those that remained were limited and utilitarian. The diminishing of same-sex friendships in men is closely related to the findings that men generally are lonelier and have lower levels of social support (Ashton & Fuehrer, 1993; Burda & Vaux, 1987).

In a thorough analysis of men's friendship literature, Levy (2005) challenged previous research rooted in sex differences and role theory, offering an analysis based in the concept of *hegemonic complicity* (that is, the degree to which an individual man sees the dominant view of masculinity as salient within the specific situation and social context). Levy offered two differing conceptions of how men practice interaction: friendship and comradeship. In Levy's view, *friendship* is marked by personal intimacy, specificity, reciprocity, and emotional closeness. *Comradeship*, however, differs in terms of lacking specificity, commitment, and emotional honesty. Comrades are easily replaceable, because "one is as good as another" (Levy, 2005, p. 203). In his qualitative research, Levy found that middle-class men who practice hegemonic complicity are far more likely to engage in comradeship than friendship. Therefore, Levy appears to concur with others (Bank, 1995; Dolgin, 2001; Greif, 2009) who have argued that men's friendships need to be understood in a more nuanced way, without demeaning the special positive qualities of men's friendship variants. However, even when the special features of men's friendships are recognized, there appears to be considerable evidence that most men lack emotionally close friendships and have few social supports to assist them through difficult times.

An additional feature of men's emotional isolation is the pattern of men's overdependency on women for emotional support and validation. Pleck (1980) noted that men depend on women for "masculinity validation" and for "expressive power." McGill (1985) studied the intimate relationships of more than 1,000 men and found that most men disclose their innermost thoughts and feelings only to one special woman. This finding is similar to that of Burda and Vaux (1987), who found that male subjects demonstrated a clear preference for females as primary sources of emotional support.

Many possible explanations have been offered for men's emotional isolation from other men, including those suggesting sociobiological factors (Buss, 1994; Tiger, 1969) and those highlighting structural restraints (Cohen, 1992). Most relevant here, however, are those explanations citing the emotional and relational restrictions in the social construction of masculinity. Notable aspects of this construction are the aforementioned prohibitions of emotional expressiveness, fears of vulnerability, and rampant homophobia (Kilmartin, 2007). Entire volumes could be written on the distancing effects of homophobia among men, and most men's studies writers agree with Reid and Fine (1992), who consider it to be "the greatest barrier to friendships among men" (p. 142). It is interesting that there has been some indication that gay men are more likely to develop strong emotional intimacy with their male friends (Nardi, 1992), but gay men also are subject to restrictions from internalized homonegativity and heterophobia (Haldeman, 2001b).

Any description of the dark side of masculinity risks misinterpretation as male bashing or hostility toward men. This is not the intent of this cataloging of the multiple problems inherent in adhering to the traditional masculinity code. Most men conduct themselves responsibly, and certainly there is room for the "positive psychology perspective" presented by Kiselica, Englar-Carlson, Horne, and Fisher (2008). Nevertheless, it is vitally important to note how the treatment of men in clinical settings must be conducted with awareness of the manner in which masculinity role stresses contribute to psychopathology. It is also critical that major attention be given to the immense problems inherent in the structure of the traditional male role and the complex task facing boys and men in negotiating a personal role definition that is enhancing to all. This matter has always been difficult, but there are indications that the issues have reached crisis proportions from the 1950s to the present time.

Betcher and Pollack (1993) wrote, "We live in a time of fallen heroes. The monuments built of men, by men, and for men have tumbled. Men have been brought to earth, their strengths put in perspective by their flaws. . . . The empire seems to be crumbling" (p. 1). Levant and Kopecky (1995) echoed a similar theme when they stated, "American manhood is in crisis— has been for a generation. . . . The social changes wrought by the feminist movement and the influx of women into the workforce have left our traditional code of masculinity in a state of collapse" (p. 1).

There can be little doubt that over the past several decades the concept of masculinity has appeared prominently on the national radar, both in terms of popular consciousness and academic scholarship. Most of that attention has been congruent with the masculinity in crisis perspective—that is, the majority of men have been forced to give up the hope that they can live their lives in a fashion identical to those of their fathers and grandfathers. The blueprints of their masculine heritage will no longer suffice; new and untried models of male behavior will be necessary.

In her popular book *Stiffed: The Betrayal of the American Man*, Susan Faludi (1999) attempted to characterize the troubled national mood of the late 1990s in terms of attitudes toward men and all things male. She noted that "as the nation wobbled toward the millennium, its pulse-takers seemed to agree that a domestic apocalypse was under way: American manhood was under siege" (Faludi, 1999, p. 6). And if there remained any uncertainty after such a bleak assessment, the book's frontispiece makes clear the extent and magnitude of the crisis: "Anyone who reads a magazine, watches a TV talk show, or listens to a radio call-in program has heard the evidence: America is having a masculinity crisis."

ORIGINS OF THE CRISIS

In discussions of this masculinity crisis, most chroniclers immediately attribute the origins to the most apparent source—feminism and the "Second Wave" of the women's movement. Although this movement's First Wave—best represented by the suffrage campaigns of the 19th and early-20th centuries—created disruptions in the social order, the Second Wave had the widest and deepest impact. This phase, the Women's Liberation Movement of the 1960s and 1970s, actively and outspokenly addressed a broad range of inequalities in the public and private spheres. (Feminism's Third Wave, beginning in the 1990s, has continued the push for social justice for all women, but has diversified its focus and does not seem to have generated the same degree of reactivity in men as its predecessor). However, in spite of differences of emphasis, the women's movement and feminism have been consistent in the challenges to patriarchy and male entitlement.

Although there is danger in attempting to reduce the many complex strains of feminist theory to a few simple statements, Freeman's description (1989) seems reasonable:

> The feminist perspective looks at the many similarities between the sexes and concludes that women and men have equal potential for individual development. Differences in the realization of that potential, therefore, must result from externally imposed restraints, from the influence of social institutions and values. The feminist view holds that so long as society prescribes sex roles and social penalties for those who deviate from them, no meaningful choice exists for members of either sex. . . . Only by understanding their [sex roles and restraints] origins

and manifestations can we gain the wisdom to dismantle them and create a more just society. (p. xi)

It is probably unnecessary to note that reactions to the ideology and political activities of feminists have varied widely across the social terrain and have not always been welcomed, even among those persons who seem to have benefited the most from them. Those who have been most troubled by feminism have typically cited the more extreme statements and positions of the most radical elements of the movement, claiming that feminism represents anti-male sentiments and efforts to establish "the new sexism" and a world of female advantage (Farrell, 1993). Those most distressed by feminist ideas have accused the movement of precipitating extreme social problems ranging from damaged boys, emasculated males, and fatherless homes (Sommers, 1995, 2000). Although only a small portion of the broad U.S. population has taken such extreme positions, most all have agreed that the new algebra of relationships has demanded new behaviors from men. For example, most men would need to share power and leadership in relationships, compete with women for positions in the workplace, take on additional responsibilities in their homes, and become more involved in parenting. For most men, these seemingly straightforward changes would become more than a simple recalibration of lifestyles. Instead, it would demand a fundamental reexamination of everything they had been taught about manhood and proper male behavior.

The accommodations demanded by the women's movement alone may well have been sufficient to induce crises in men's lives, but the modern women's movement emerged following 2 decades of transition in American men's struggles to find meaning and purpose in their lives. In his cultural history of American manhood, Kimmel (1996) described the post–World War II era as a time of great restlessness and insecurity as men returned to family life and domestic roles and attempted to replace the heroic images of warrior men with new images based on domestic and working roles. "As the 1950s drew to a close," Kimmel observed, "American men still felt temporary about themselves. . . . Responsible breadwinners and devoted fathers, they were still anxious about overconformity but unable and unwilling to break free of domestic responsibilities to become rebels on the run" (p. 257).

In his analysis of the beginnings of the modern masculinity crisis, Gilbert (2005) contended that problems had resulted when the 1950s census data indicated that women outnumbered men for the first time in American history. "Thus concluded a unique phase of American society—the long history of male majority" (p. 215). Gilbert also noted that Betty Friedan's *The Feminine Mystique* (1963), the hugely influential plea for women's liberation and attention to "the problem with no name," had also expressed grave concerns about the lives of men. He observed that Friedan decried "the feminization of American culture" and wrote that "men had been terribly wounded by contemporary distortions of culture and beleaguered by confusing gender roles" (as cited in Gilbert, 2005, p. 218). Although Faludi's *Stiffed* focuses primarily on the contemporary crisis of masculinity, she actually traced the roots of the crisis to failures in the promises of postwar manhood—the failure of "the unpassed torch." In essence, she claimed that the "national male paradigm" that had successfully made the transition from war to peace time following World War I did not make a similar passage in the decades following World War II.

If the postwar years of the late 1940s and the 1950s set the stage for men's discontent, the radical changes and social movements of the 1960s provided the stimuli for disruption of the secure facade of masculine self-assurance and confidence. The women's movement, the civil rights movement, and the gay rights movement all challenged the hegemony of White, heterosexual men. Kimmel (1996) stated that "the sustained, insisted demands for inclusion by those who have historically been marginalized did not begin in the 1960s, but it then became a permanent fixture in the national social and political agenda" (p. 263).

The demands for inclusion were certainly not universally welcomed by most men, and often they were met with stonewalling or angry reactivity. Nevertheless, in the midst of this tense environment of confrontation and adversarial battling, some men recognized that the feminist movement might actually have potential benefits for men. This realization ushered in an era of men writing about men's lives, not in the conventional hero-worshipping and celebratory way but with a particular passion for heightening awareness of the poorly recognized costs of manhood. Such writing initiated men's studies as new area of scholarship and laid the groundwork for the many variants of the men's movement.

RESPONSE TO THE CRISIS: THE MEN'S MOVEMENT

Rather than attacking feminism as anti-men, many men in the late 1960s and 1970s were inspired by the women's movement to look at ways that sexism also constricts men's lives. In a number of groundbreaking works (Brenton, 1966; David & Brannon, 1976; Fasteau, 1975; Farrell, 1975; Goldberg, 1976; Nichols, 1975), these men described the hazards of being male and the restrictions of the traditional male sex role. These treatises varied in their alignment with the perspectives of feminism, but all called for a degree of *male liberation*. For example, Sawyer (1970) stated that "male liberation calls for men to free themselves of the sex-role stereotypes that limit their ability to be human" (p. 170). Clatterbaugh (1990) described a group of "profeminist men" who "concluded that American society is sexist . . . that men's lives too are greatly affected by this system of male dominance and that men are competitive, emotionally isolated from one another and their families, and overly involved in work and sports" (p. 37).

A tangible outgrowth of the earliest men's studies writings was the appearance of several strains of social activities or phenomena that can broadly be considered to represent a "men's movement." The movement was similar to the women's movement in terms of its commitment to countering sociocultural pressures constraining people's lives, but it was far less cohesive in organization and ultimately quite variegated in philosophy. Clatterbaugh (1990) categorized the men's movement as generally consisting of mythopoetic men, reactionary men, conservative men, and profeminist men. (This categorization is admittedly a major simplification of Clatterbaugh's work.)

The mythopoetic men's movement has probably been most associated with the activities of poet Robert Bly and others adopting this spiritual perspective, such as James Hillman, John Rowan, and Michael Meade. These mythopoetic leaders drew from mythology, Wiccan traditions, and Jungian ideas of masculine archetypes to identify and repair the "wounds" inflicted on men by modernity. Bly, for example, argued that boys' separation from their fathers after the shift from agricultural to industrial economies created deepseated feelings of "father loss" (Bly, 1990). Similarly, the "feminized" modern culture was thought to have precipitated men's loss of touch with the "wild man within." To combat these trends, Bly conducted wilderness retreats, men's sweat lodges, and drumming rituals "to help men rediscover deep unconscious patterns. . . . These patterns are best revealed through a tradition of stories, myths, and rituals" (Clatterbaugh, 1990, p. 11).

A more recent variant of this spiritual perspective is Promise Keepers, a national organization of Christian men. This group has viewed itself as committed to helping men counter emotional isolation from one another, replacing lost spirituality in men's lives, restoring men's leadership role in the family, and countering the damages they view to be created by men's abdication of family leadership (Newton, 2005).

A second major variant of the men's movement has been one that takes a strong reactionary stance to the activities of the women's movement. This antifeminist perspective sees men as having become new victims of sexism and advocates the need for a men's rights perspective (Doyle, 1976). The men's rights group has challenged the notion that women are the more victimized gender and has called for what it considers to be greater social justice toward men. In this regard, they have lobbied for revisions of laws in the areas of child custody, divorce, and domestic violence, which they view as commonly oppressive toward men.

A third group—a somewhat amorphous collection of theorists identified by Clatterbaugh (1990) as "the conservative perspective"—rejects the idea that men's behavior is governed by social forces or through environmental factors. Instead, masculinity is viewed as a product of relatively immutable biological and evolutionary forces. As a result, persons from this perspective consider men's movement calls for cultural change to be misguided and ultimately futile because biological and evolutionary tendencies cannot be changed appreciably by social movements.

Yet another men's movement group has been highly empathic to feminism, viewing it as a critical stimulus for the study of men and masculinity. Those adhering to this view—profeminist men—see no conflict between the political and social activities of the women's movement and the interests of men. All of these activities are seen as important steps in identifying and challenging aspects of the broader culture that are oppressive to both women and men. These profeminist men developed a national organization, the National Organization for Changing Men—later adopting the name National Organization of Men Against Sexism—and, beginning in the mid-1970s, have held an annual Men and Masculinity conference. Their view of their mission has been the one most consistent with the male liberation perspective noted previously—that is, it focuses on men's consciousness-raising and collaboration with feminists to deconstruct sexist social institutions.

Philosophical Variations in the Men's Movement

In reviewing the reactions to the crisis of masculinity reflected in the various branches of the men's movement, one can surmise that these branches embrace different underlying phenomenologies or philosophies about men's troubles. At their core, profeminist men differ radically from other men's movement groups in terms of their view of the fundamental bases of male behavior. This difference, commonly described as a conflict between essentialism and social constructionism, is critical in making sense of the varied writings in the field of men's studies (and ultimately a major factor in any consideration of providing help for men).

Essentialism is a broad term that can be utilized to capture the core ideas of those who view the behavioral differences between women and men to be deeply rooted in their intrinsic natures. Gender differences in social roles are viewed as secondary to innate factors. Brooks (1997) noted that "whatever root cause is cited—evolution, genetic makeup, brain structure, hormones, or God's will—the essentialist position holds strongly to the idea that women and men are fundamentally very different" (p. 37). Because of the inherent conservatism of this position, essentialists are not welcoming of feminism, as it is considered by many to represent a challenge to the natural order of things. Hence, many of these moral conservatives rail against feminism as an effort to demean men, elevate women, and expose the damages of male nature unmitigated by women's civilizing influence (Clatterbaugh, 1990). Other essentialists—namely, the biological conservatives—are minimally concerned about feminism, dismissing it as insignificant in the face of fundamental sex differences based in biology and centuries of evolution (Buss, 1994). From this perspective, social movements are doomed to failure if these essential and substantial differences are ignored. Also, psychotherapy that is anchored in essentialism has a profoundly conservative mission to preserve the status quo and reinforce traditional gender values.

Social constructionism is fundamentally different from essentialism in terms of its view of the underlying causes of male and female behavior, its ideas about the stresses experienced by contemporary women and men, and its formulas for redressing the many and frequently different experiences of distress manifested by women and men. Many varied and nuanced perspectives are somewhat oversimplified by the social constructionism label, but all are similar in one respect: a rejection of the idea that biology and evolution are supreme in governing the behavior of women, men, boys, and girls. Although biology and evolution are recognized as playing a role in the unfolding of gender, much more importance is attached to the ways that the behavior of women and men is shaped by social roles that vary over time and context. "Differences between women and men occur because social roles are constrained by different ideals and stereotypes" (Clatterbaugh, 1990). Consistent with this perspective, Wood (1994) noted that "gender is a social, symbolic creation. The meaning of gender grows out of a society's values, beliefs, and preferred ways of organizing collective life. A culture constructs and sustains meanings of gender by investing biological sex with social significance" (p. 21).

In applying the constructionist perspective to men, Kimmel and Messner (1989) stated that

> the important fact of men's lives is not that they are biological males, but that they become men. Our sex may be male, but our identity as men is developed through a complex interaction with the culture in which we both learn the gender scripts appropriate to our culture, and attempt to modify those scripts to make them more palatable. (p. 19)

From the social constructionist perspective, the women's and men's movements are vital in bringing social roles into the forefront of public discussion, with the objective of examining both their benefits and destructive effects. Times and cultures change, so social roles must be continually discussed and negotiated. Within this perspective, psychotherapy is viewed much more critically, as it is seen as both a possible source of personal liberation and, sometimes, an agent of social oppression.

The Men's Movement in Academia: Men's Studies

Much as the energy of feminism and the women's movement eventually came to be represented in the academy by women's studies programs, the momentum of the men's movement pushed some of its variants onto college campuses as well. The first men's studies courses began appearing in the late 1970s and early 1980s, but they did not develop into the level of a discipline until the 1990s (Urschel, 2000). Although the earliest works addressing men's pain and distress were varied in their philosophies and politics, most men's studies scholarship has been more congruent with the philosophies of the social constructionists. In general, men's studies scholars have endeavored to elucidate the components of the traditional male role, sometimes referred to as *masculinity ideology*. Pleck (1995) noted that "masculinity ideology refers to beliefs about the importance of men adhering to culturally defined standards for male behavior. . . . [It] conveys the individual's endorsement and internalization of cultural belief systems about masculinity" (p. 19). This recognition of masculine ideology has been seen as a critical first step toward helping men deconstruct that male role ideology, allowing them to begin countering its more restrictive aspects.

ARTICULATING THE MALE GENDER ROLE

To be sure, there is much variability in how men operationalize cultural pressures, yet there is considerable overlap in the understanding of masculinity ideology and the traditional male role. Pleck (1995) observed that "within the diversity of actual and possible standards about men and masculinity in contemporary U.S. culture, there is a *particular* constellation of standards and expectations that individually and jointly have various negative consequences" (p. 20). A brief overview of some men's studies writing about these standards and expectations is helpful here.

In presenting one of the earliest and most commonly cited descriptions of the male gender role, David and Brannon (1976) identified four major components. They labeled the first as "No Sissy Stuff," meaning that men should never display any "feminine" behaviors. They called their second component "The Big Wheel," referring to the mandate that men are expected to seek success and status. Third, "The Sturdy Oak" reflects the pressure on men always to project toughness, confidence, and self-reliance. Finally, the "Give 'Em Hell" component is one that disposes men to act aggressively and sometimes violently.

Over the 2 decades following David and Brannon's (1976) categorization of masculine ideology, other men's studies scholars have offered additional perspectives. For example, Solomon's (1982) overview of the male gender role added *homophobia* and *sexual dysfunction* to David and Brannon's typology. O'Neil (1982) described "The Masculine Mystique" as consisting of 15 values that men should endorse. Doyle's (1995) review of writing on the male gender role described elements—the antifeminine element, the success element, the aggressive element, the sexual element, and the self-reliant element—that are very much in line with previous characterizations.

Based on the theoretical work of these men's studies scholars, others have taken the next step to measure empirically and to categorize attitudes about masculinity. In their review of the state of development of instrumentation to measure masculinity ideology, Thompson and Pleck (1995) highlighted 11 measures that are either *prescriptive* (i.e., beliefs about what men should be like) or *descriptive* (i.e., beliefs about what men actually are like). In the years following Thomspson and Pleck's overview, three masculinity measures have inspired considerable research. The most commonly used measure has been the Gender Role Conflict Scale (GRCS; O'Neill, Helms, Gable, David, & Wrightman, 1986), although the Conformity to Male Norms Inventory (CMNI; Mahalik et al., 2003) and the Male Role Norms Inventory (MRNI; Levant & Fischer, 1998) have also been widely used. Exhibit 1.1 shows the consensus regarding the components of masculine ideology.

Problematizing Masculinity: The Gender Role Strain Paradigm

Special attention must be given here to Pleck's (1995) proposal of a "gender role strain paradigm," which was offered as a thoroughly different way of thinking about men and their behavior. Previously, masculine behavior had been thought of as the outgrowth of inevitable and invariant processes producing sex-typed personality traits that reside within individuals. The psychological health of men and boys was thought to be dependent on successful incorporation of these essential sex-based traits and the simultaneous development of a solid and secure male identity. This conceptualization, referred by Joseph Pleck (1995) as the *gender role identity paradigm*, theorized that young men would develop serious psychological problems without a sound gender-based identity. Contrary to this view, however, the gender role strain paradigm has presented a vitally important new view of gender roles. Here, masculine behavior is considered to be shaped by prevailing gender ideologies that vary over time, are sensitive to social context, and are inherently contradictory. Most important, this model proposes that a considerable portion of men's problems are the result of the impossibility of fully meeting the extreme demands of masculine ideology. Traditional gender roles are seen as

EXHIBIT 1.1
Three Masculinity Measures

Gender Role Conflict Scale (O'Neill, Helms, Gable, David, & Wrightman, 1986)
1. success, power, competition
2. restrictive emotionality
3. restrictive affectionate behavior between men
4. conflicts between work and family relations

Conformity to Male Norms Inventory (Mahalik et al., 2003)
1. winning
2. emotional control
3. risk-taking
4. violence
5. power over women, dominance
6. playboy-ism
7. self-reliance
8. primacy of work
9. disdain for homosexuality
10. status seeking

Male Role Norms Inventory (Levant & Fischer, 1998)
1. avoidance of femininity
2. fear and hatred of homosexuals
3. extreme self-reliance
4. aggression
5. dominance
6. nonrelational sexuality
7. restrictive emotionality

---

inherently patriarchal in their upholding of gender-based power structures, but they are also recognized as ultimately restrictive and harmful to both men and women.

Kimmel (1994) referred to this situation of gender role strain as "a paradox in men's lives in which men have all the power, yet few individual men feel powerful" (p. 135). In other words, most men see themselves as falling far short of the idealized "real man." As a result, many men cope with this discrepancy between the impossible masculinity ideals and the realities of their own self-perceptions through adoption of a range of self-defeating "macho" behaviors. As noted before, many men's studies authors have implicated gender role strain as a factor in men's violence, substance abuse, and sexual misconduct. Fortunately, most men are better able to manage gender role strain and never resort to these more extreme compensatory behaviors. Nevertheless, there is mounting empirical evidence that the degree of gender role strain is closely related to some major restrictions in the lives of boys and men—the psychopathologies of men's everyday lives discussed early in this chapter.

2

HOW PSYCHOTHERAPY HAS FAILED
BOYS AND MEN

In the previous chapter I described the *dark side of masculinity* as a series of highly adverse consequences of traditional masculinity social-ization. Of course, not all men experience these negative consequences; many men integrate their gender role mandates into the most positive man-ifestations of manhood. Nevertheless, all men must struggle with the more restrictive components of male gender role strain, and all men must find ways to cope with the rapid shifts in cultural expectations of them. Although there can be some controversy about whether the problems of modern men fully constitute a *crisis of masculinity* (Gilbert, 2005; Heartfield, 2002; Horrocks & Campling, 1994), it would be hard to be unimpressed with the aforementioned literature showing the multiple ways that men have been restricted in their optimal functioning. Sadly, these restrictions have been exacerbated over time by one pernicious aspect of traditional masculinity: the expectation that men should endure their hardships alone and should ardently avoid most all forms of help seeking.

This "go-it-alone" issue is problematic enough by itself, but it becomes even more injurious in the context of men's special apprehensions about psy-chotherapy. This chapter attends to the broad issues of men's troublesome relationship with the help-seeking process in general and also seeks to explain why men are especially averse to psychotherapy in particular. Furthermore, an argument is made that the psychotherapy establishment, despite being historically dominated by men, has largely failed to develop models of psychotherapy that are more harmonious with men's unique ways of experiencing emotional pain and coping with their psychic distress.

MEN AND HELP SEEKING

Popular culture is replete with examples of the widely endorsed stereotype of men who will go to extraordinary lengths to avoid asking for directions or otherwise seeking help. The prevalent jokes about men who drive aimlessly for hours to avoid asking for directions and the cinematic images of the bleeding combatant dismissing his injuries as "just a flesh wound" are only two representations of this commonly accepted "truth" about men. Usually dismissed as a relatively innocuous idiosyncrasy, this phenomenon is actually more serious when the deeper implications of men's broad avoidance of help seeking are recognized.

The obstacles of overcoming men's resistance to help seeking are formidable, and the failure of therapists and many men to connect is all too common. Such a failure is illustrated by my early-career interactions with Phil, a 37-year-old, married auto parts manager. His first therapy appointment had been scheduled by his wife, who reported concerns that he had been increasingly irritable and uncommunicative over the previous several months. Phil missed the first appointment but arrived exactly on time for the second. As the session began, the therapist said little, hoping Phil would provide some ideas of his therapy objectives. After a brief silence, Phil broke the ice:

Phil:	Well, doc, what'll it be? My childhood or my feelings?
Therapist:	Do you have a preference?
Phil:	Neither one's very interesting.
Therapist:	You don't seem very pleased about this.
Phil:	No, I'm quite fine.
	(Silence)
Phil:	Gonna ask me some questions?
Therapist:	Would you like me to?
Phil:	Hey, you're the expert.
Therapist:	And how do you feel about that?

Phil:	Just great.
	(Silence)
Phil:	So is this how it's gonna be?
Therapist:	How would you like it to be?
Phil:	This is fine.

After 30 minutes of relatively terse interaction and little rapport development, the final sequence took place.

Phil:	So have we accomplished anything?
Therapist:	What are you thinking we should accomplish?
Phil:	Beats me.
Therapist:	Our time seems to be up. Should we set our next appointment for the same time next week?
Phil:	How about I call you?

Phil never called for another appointment, of course. Unfortunately, encounters like this one with Phil are not rare, as men actually do go to great lengths to avoid admitting a need for help. In their comprehensive review of men and help-seeking, Addis and Mahalik (2003) reported that "a large body of empirical research supports the popular belief that men are reluctant to seek help from health professionals" (p. 5). These authors cited research showing that whether the problems are related to substance abuse, depression, physical disabilities, or life stresses, men are less likely than women to seek professional help. These gender differences have been found to hold across racial and ethnic groups and apply to men across the lifecycle. In terms of their physical health, men have been found to be less diligent in seeking routine preventative health care and far more passive when interacting with health care professionals (Courtenay, 2000).

Men experiencing emotional distress are much less likely than women to be found in the office of a psychotherapist. Numerous studies have demonstrated that men seek psychotherapy and other professional mental health services much less often than women (Gove, 1984; Greenley & Mechanic, 1976; Vessey & Howard, 1993). Kessler, Brown, and Boman (1981) found that women sought psychiatric help at a higher rate even when the severity of the problems is equivalent. Further, men have been found to have greater difficulty recognizing their emotional problems, whether the population studied is medical students (Dickstein, Stephenson, & Hinz, 1990), college students (Gim, Atkinson, & Whitely, 1990), or university faculty and employees (Carpenter & Addis, 2000).

WHY MEN HATE PSYCHOTHERAPY

The lower rates of psychotherapy participation among men can be viewed in various ways: Either women participate excessively or men participate too little (or both). The former explanation is not entirely inconsistent with feminist critiques of mental health practices of the late 20th century (Broverman, Broverman, Clarkson, Rosencratz, & Vogel, 1970; Chesler, 1972), whereby women who were unhappy and dissatisfied were considered susceptible to being labeled as mentally ill and pushed into treatment. Of this process, Maracek (2001) noted that "feminists protested the power of the mental health establishment to enforce the status quo by labeling nonconformity and dissent as mental illness" (p. 303). From this perspective, avoidance of mental health treatment and its stigmatic label can be considered as advantageous to men. Obviously, this point of view applies when one considers the multiple environments in which a mental health diagnosis (or participation in therapy) incurs major penalties—for example, the military, politics, and business settings. Furthermore, there are ways in which men's common postures of invulnerability and emotional stoicism have provided them with interpersonal advantages. For example, Sattel (1976) described men's emotional inexpressiveness as frequently representing deliberate efforts to gain relationship leverage and maintain male power bases.

On the other hand, those who believe that psychotherapy has potential benefits for men would, of course, see men's underrepresentation in therapy as harmful to men. This point of view would be especially salient to those who believe that there is a crisis of masculinity and that all men are subject to some degree of gender role strain. Therapy avoidance is not only a missed opportunity for adaptive coping, but also is a major factor in the maladaptive coping mechanisms so commonly seen in men. Men's denial and suppression of their inner conflicts have been seen as major potentiators of many self-defeating behaviors, such as alcoholism (Marini, 2005), violence (Long, 1987), and sexual acting out (Brooks, 1997). Rabinowitz and Cochran (2002) noted that many of these problems "are commonly associated with . . . a male tendency to externalize psychological distress through action, distraction, and compulsive acting out" (p. 14).

If one grants that underutilization of mental health services, despite its occasional benefits, is ultimately harmful to men, then it is important to examine the many factors that contribute to this therapy avoidance dynamic. This phenomenon can be attributed to four interlocking factors: dominant portrayals of psychotherapy in media, conflicts between the demands of traditional male role and those of the ideal therapy client, perceptions of triangulations against men, and the poor adaptation of therapy models to men's help-seeking styles (Brooks, 1998).

Portrayals of Psychotherapy in the Media

Few institutions receive more negative media attention than does the institution of psychotherapy. From the earliest images of the emotionally distant classical Freudian analyst (e.g., *The Three Faces of Eve*), through the era of the ineffectual and bumbling therapist of the 1970s (Bob Newhart) and the pompous, effete therapist of the 1980s and 1990s (*Frasier*) to the more complex characterizations of the last several years (e.g., *The Sopranos* and *In Treatment*), psychotherapy has received considerable media attention. Whereas it might seem that this attention would heighten the desirability of entering therapy, the consensus is that media images have been more harmful than helpful. Sleek (1995) observed that "the media isn't always kind to mental health providers. . . . Hollywood often portrays mental health professionals as guilty of ethical misconduct—or worse." (p. 7). A recent *New York Times* review of the HBO series *In Treatment* compared that series with other television efforts in this area and noted that "the therapist with an issue has become almost a television cliché, a white-coat version of the whore with the heart of gold" (Stanley, 2008).

In their comprehensive study of psychotherapy and film, Wedding and Niemiec (2003) described several distortions common in most movies. For one, therapy has been more commonly portrayed as classical psychoanalysis, despite the relative infrequency of this therapy modality. The stereotypical view of patients engaged in interminable sessions, futilely seeking to overcome childhood demons does little to elevate popular opinions of therapy (particularly when Woody Allen is the patient).

Schneider (1987) offered a typology of film therapists that included three categories: Dr. Wonderful, Dr. Evil, and Dr. Dippy. Wedding and Niemiec (2003) expanded the typology to include eight core representations of therapists common in films: learned and authoritative, arrogant and ineffectual, seductive and unethical, cold-hearted and authoritarian, passive and apathetic, shrewd and manipulative, dangerous and omniscient, and motivating and well-intentioned. Obviously, the depictions of psychotherapists are quite mixed, yet they are predominantly rather unappealing to the mass consumer.

In addition to the distorted and generally unflattering media images of therapists, the therapy process itself has been misrepresented (Gabbard & Gabbard, 1999; Orchowski, Spickard, & McNamara, 2006), and clients commonly have been portrayed inaccurately, with movies frequently resorting to burlesque caricatures of therapy clients (e.g., *Analyze This*, *What About Bob?*).

Most critics of the media and psychotherapy appear more or less in agreement that there have been major problems with the manner in which all therapists and clients have been represented. As yet, however, no systematic research has been conducted to explore whether there have been differences in the ways in which women and men have been portrayed, either as therapists or as therapy clients. A critical issue to be resolved is whether media representations encourage or discourage troubled women and men from seeking professional help. For our purposes, the critical question is whether the media have caused men in the general public to think of therapy offices as inhabited by men they respect or by men they see as unappealing. Despite the occasional presence of traditionally "manly" men as clients (e.g., Tony Soprano) and admirable male therapists (e.g., Judd Hirsch's character in *Ordinary People*), most men would be much more likely to view the therapy office as populated by "a steady stream of wimps, losers, and social misfits" (Brooks, 1998).

Psychotherapy and Male Socialization

There are many varieties of psychotherapy, just as there are many ways in which men accommodate to the demands of the traditional male role. Nevertheless, there are several common elements in virtually all forms of the "talking cure," and as noted earlier, there has been remarkable consensus on how men are expected to lead their lives. Most unfortunately, the behavioral and emotional qualities of "ideal" psychotherapy clients are radically different than the qualities of "real men." For example, conventional psychotherapy is best when the client is able to self-disclose, relinquish control, recognize and express feelings, experience vulnerability, introspect, confront pain and relationship conflict, admit failure or ignorance, and manage nonsexual intimacy. Unfortunately, traditional masculine socialization teaches men to hide private experience, maintain control, maintain stoicism, present self as invincible, favor action over introspection, avoid relationship conflict, and sexualize intimate relationships. With this in mind, we can see how difficult it would be to create an environment that could possibly be any more uncomfortable for men's most preferred ways of being.

In a previous book, *A New Psychotherapy for Traditional Men* (Brooks, 1998), I offered an overview of relevant men's studies scholarship that reveals many of the antagonisms between core values in therapy environments and the socially constructed values of masculinity (Brooks, 1998).

Dominance, Power, and Interpersonal Control

Few things unsettle men more than feeling out of control. Men are taught that manliness is associated with control over one's environment, one's loved ones, and one's emotions. Men are taught to take charge of situations and always remain in the driver's seat (both figuratively and literally). O'Neil (1982) identified "control over women" as a critical component of the traditional male role. Scher (1990) described two primary precepts of masculinity as "to be unlike women and to be in control" (p. 322).

Intertwined with matters of dominance and control are issues related to projection of an image of personal power. Men recognize that patriarchy has historically granted entitlements and privileges to men as a group, and, as a result, they equate manhood with the exercise of social and political power. Yet despite the advantages enjoyed by men as a group, most men do not feel in control of their lives and do not feel powerful on a personal level. McLean (1996) described this as a type of disconnection between social and psychological levels, noting "one of the central paradoxes of masculinity is that while men, as a group, clearly hold the reins of power, the majority of men experience themselves as powerless" (p. 19).

In light of men's needs to be in control and the paradox of their experiences of powerlessness, it should not be surprising that they resist psychotherapy. For most men, therapy offices are viewed as places where others are in charge and clients are in a one-down position. Even short-term abdication of power and control is repugnant to most men, because few see this as ultimately leading to greater emotional mastery and personal power.

Competitiveness and Hierarchical Thinking

Throughout their lives, men are taught to evaluate their worth in relation to other men. Qualitatively different than conceptions of femininity, ideas about masculinity are rooted in hierarchal frameworks whereby manhood is not seen as an inevitable outgrowth of physical maturation, but as a challenge to prove one's masculinity through performance and accomplishments. In boyhood, the male peer group pressures boys to prove themselves through competition and, when necessary, through fighting (Tolson, 1977). Anthropologist David Gilmore described near-universal "male rites of passage" requiring boys to undertake rigorous and dangerous activities before being accepted into the circle of adult men. But this acceptance is only temporary because males are expected to prove their worth continually through competition and climbing the rungs of various status ladders. McLean (1996) captured this dynamic when he noted that "all the institutions within which men lead their lives are implicitly or explicitly hierarchical. . . . They all encourage striving for success, which may involve stepping on the shoulders of one's friends and associates" (p. 25).

Because men are taught to view life as a demand for performance, inter-actions with other men become infused with performance anxiety and stripped of the potential for mutual comfort and support. It is easy to see how a hier-archical worldview interferes with men's willingness to consider psychother-apy. Therapy is not only time consuming and expensive (causing men to fall behind other men in acquiring money and status), it also can be seen as evi-dence of personal failure and competitive disadvantage. Not surprisingly, competitive men on the fast track are more likely to consider coaching, with its promises of expert advice, direct assistance, and potential upgrading of performance.

Emotional Inexpressiveness

Of all its troublesome stereotypes, none hinders the image of therapy more in men's eyes than that of therapy as primarily a place for "getting in touch with one's feelings." Traditional men are well documented as devaluing the benefits of exploring their deeper affective lives and unskilled in expressing any emotions except anger. For example, Ron Levant described most men as programmed to experience some degree of alexithymia, in that they are compromised in the ability to access, label, and express feelings (Levant, 2003). Balswick (1988) wrote extensively about the problems of "the inexpressive male," and, as noted previously, a lack of emotional facility is a major aspect of all measures of traditional masculinity. Although it would certainly be an exaggeration to claim that all men are alexithymic or lack capacity for emotional expression, it is nevertheless true that restricted emotionality is an aspect of the traditional male code and that men who are openly expressive risk censure from self or others.

Although some have viewed men's emotional style as a deficiency, others have described it more in terms of a preference. For example, Deborah Tannen's (1990) psycholinguistic research has emphasized that women and men approach interpersonal communication differently, with men less interested in emotional connection and more focused on exchanging infor-mation, giving advice, describing accomplishments, and issuing challenges. Regardless of the factors contributing to men's views of interpersonal com-munication and the benefits of emotion-focused activities, it seems quite likely that psychotherapy would be viewed with minimal interest by most traditional men.

Sexuality and Intimacy

An abundance of research has demonstrated that women and men are quite different in the ways they think about and enact their sexuality (Buss,

1994; Hyde & Oliver, 2000). To simplify a complex area of research, women are more likely to integrate their sexual needs with their emotional needs, whereas men are more likely to separate the two. In fact, many men's studies writers have considered men's nonrelational sexuality to be a major aspect of men's profound difficulties with emotional intimacy (Brooks, 1995; Levant & Brooks, 1997). Men have fewer relationships characterized by overt displays of deep emotional connection (Wood, 1994) and are more likely to have become anxious or dysfunctional when situations call for emotional intimacy without sexuality. In my book describing the centerfold syndrome, attention was given to this conundrum for traditionally social-ized men: "As young men are learning to wall themselves off from too much emotional intimacy in sex . . . They also are taught to sexualize all feelings of emotional and physical closeness. As a result they cannot experience nonsexual intimacy" (1995, pp. 10–11).

To the degree that men develop this conflict between their needs for emotional closeness and their compulsion to sexualize intimacy, they will obviously have enormous difficulty with the face-to-face nature of most psy-chotherapies. We could anticipate that heterosexual men would tend to sexualize relationships with female therapists and be subject to extreme homophobia with male therapists (whereas gay men have similar issues with differently gendered therapists).

Perceptions of Triangulation and Disadvantage

From its European origins to the offices of American counselors and therapists, the institution of psychotherapy has been largely controlled by men. Because women have always been more populous as clients, the male therapist–female client dyad was by far the most common and predominant template. Pollack and Levant (1998) put it this way: "Traditional psycholog-ical therapies were historically designed by *male* doctors in order to treat *female* patients" (p. 3). Largely unchallenged for many decades, this arrange-ment began to be sharply criticized in the early 1970s. Phyllis Chesler's *Women and Madness* (1972) was the earliest voice in a sustained outcry against the patriarchal nature of therapy and the manner in which it perpetuated women's oppression: "The institution of psychotherapy can also be viewed as a form of social control" (p. 105).

The many feminist objections to traditional models of therapy have been thoroughly addressed in the psychological literature (Worell & Johnson, 2001; Worell & Remer, 1992). Most fundamentally, the objections have been to the oppressive nature of dominant models of the mentally healthy woman and how therapies have typically attributed women's distress to intrapsychic causes rather than social inequalities. Further, therapies were seen as having disadvantaged women "by actively or passively supporting asymmetrical gender and power arrangements that maintained the interpersonal and societal status quo" (Rice & Rice, 1973).

Since the mid-1970s, feminist theorists have made extraordinary efforts to reshape traditional psychotherapies into a variety of feminist therapies that are more harmonious with women's experiences and less likely to contribute to women's oppression. Although there are many variants of feminist therapy, Wyche and Rice (1997) identified three themes that have been common to all: conceptualizing gender as a salient variable, recognizing sociocultural factors as critical in addition to an intrapsychic perspective, and making personal empowerment a goal of psychotherapy.

In forcing the mental health field to recognize gender as a salient variable, feminist therapists provided an avenue for discussion of how men have fared with traditional models of psychotherapy. As a result, many men's studies writers have noted that whereas men have enjoyed some advantages because of androcentric theoretical biases in mental health theory and practice, there have been ways that men have also not fared well in relating to the institution of psychotherapy. As noted by Pollack and Levant (1998), "this traditional treatment arrangement that has proven unworkable for women is equally unmanageable for men" (p. 3).

One outcome of the power shifts in the mental health fields may be reflected in the problem of the *triangulations* originally identified by Chesler (1972). As she contended, women had been harmed by triangulations when the male-dominated culture at large colluded with the male-dominated mental health fields to silence women's voices. In some ways, however, a shift may have taken place over the past few decades as more women have entered mental health practices and more men have come to view psychotherapy as "a woman's thing." Not only have women continued to be far more numerous in therapy clients' chairs, they have also become more likely to occupy the chairs of therapists. In addition, public interest in general mental health topics is much higher among women, as women are the predominant consumers of self-help books and all other mental health–related media such as magazines and television programming (Blackmon, 2004; Hammand, 2008; Simonds, 1992).

Such an embrace of mental health issues may be a mixed blessing for women, but in the eyes of many men this represents an ominous trend. For many men, there appears to be a strong alliance between women as a group and the entire mental health industry. Also, as women in heterosexual relationships have gained a greater say in relationship decisions, greater leverage can be applied to a male partner who is resisting any form of professional help. It is quite common for men to enter therapy believing that they are facing an intimidating alliance between their partner and the therapist.

How Therapists Have Treated Men

Round pegs don't fit into square holes (and any attempt to make them fit will damage the peg and frustrate the operator). Despite the obviousness of this old adage (and its corollary), psychotherapy has been exceptionally slow to recognize the poor match between its most hallowed practices and the needs of the many cultural groups. Psychoanalysis, the earliest and "purest" form of therapy, demanded exceptional qualities and sacrifices from its patients, and over the years classical psychoanalysis has been a treatment for only a highly select few. For most of the 20th century, most people seeking counseling and therapy came from middle-class and majority culture backgrounds: "The professional literature paid little attention to the needs of people who didn't fit that mold" (Seligman, 2006, p. 20).

By the 1970s, the psychotherapy field began to recognize the problems inherent in its ethnocentricity and middle-class bias. Some practitioners felt that the problems could be rectified with programs to "educate" the therapy-naïve general population about proper attitudes and behaviors in therapy. In that vein, pre-therapy training programs appeared as remedial endeavors to make potential clients more amenable to the ways of traditional therapy (Gauron, Steinmark, & Gersh, 1977; Moody, 1984). Although these efforts demonstrated modest success, they came to be recognized as having a somewhat misguided emphasis by putting the burden on clients to adapt to the customary habits of therapists and not doing enough to accommodate a diverse clientele with culturally appropriate therapy practices. Ultimately, mental health practitioners began to recognize that new and expanded psychotherapy models, customized to the needs of special populations, would be needed.

Feminist therapies, among the first of these new therapy models, challenged the sexism and gender blindness of virtually all established therapy approaches (Brown & Harris, 1978; Rawlings & Carter, 1977). Soon thereafter, the mental health field was pressed to expand beyond attention to gender alone and to develop approaches more suitable for work with all forms of diversity. For example, David and Derald Wing Sue have criticized the ways in which traditional therapies have attempted to operate in a "cultural vacuum isolated from the larger social-political influences of our society" (1990, p. 6). Consistent with this push for multiculturalism, there has been recognition that the culturally competent therapist is one who is thoroughly aware of his or her own cultural background and is attuned to the ways that contact with a client from a differing background is a type of cross-cultural counseling.

At first blush, this development would seem to have little relevance to therapy with men. After all, feminists highlighted the androcentric, male-dominated aspects of most all mental health practices, noting that all psychology has actually been the psychology of men. Nevertheless, in their call for greater attention to the unique aspects of women's lives, feminist scholars also laid the groundwork for the study of men's lives as well. Of this, Levant and Pollack (1995) noted that "feminist scholars . . . have rewritten the canon on women's development. In the same spirit, men's studies scholars . . . have begun to examine masculinity not as a normative referent but as a complex and problematic construct" (p. 1).

With this growing recognition of masculinity as a social construct that offers both advantages as well as complications in the lives of boys and men, it has become possible to recognize the sizable problems experienced by males in general, as well as by those men who are potential participants in psychotherapy in particular. Despite the historical predominance of men as social, political, and economic leaders, psychotherapy has simply not treated most males as well as it should. Brooks (1998) noted that "when we consider preferred interpersonal styles and processes, there is considerable utility in thinking of the cultures of psychotherapy and traditional men as different. *To some extent, psychotherapy with traditional men is always a form of cross-cultural counseling*" (p. 65, emphasis in original).

In a similar vein, some observers (Heesacker & Prichard, 1992; Wilcox & Forrest, 1992) have argued that therapy has been too reliant on "feminine" modes of intervention, and that newer modes of therapy more congruent with "masculine" styles must be developed. With regard to boys and young men, Kiselica (2003, 2005) has been particularly outspoken. He has repeatedly noted how the usual emphasis on introspection and verbalization of inner thoughts and feelings is "incompatible with the relational styles of many boys and with their conceptions about the helping process" (2005, p. 17). To counter this incongruity, Kiselica has joined many others (Brooks, 1998; Good & Brooks, 2005; Pollack & Levant, 1998; Rabinowitz & Cochran, 2002) to call for the development of "male-friendly" psychotherapy processes.

DEVELOPING MALE-FRIENDLY PSYCHOTHERAPY FOR BOYS AND MEN

If most men hate psychotherapy, and if the institution of psychotherapy largely has been unfriendly to men, the question naturally arises among therapist and potential male client alike, What would male-friendly psychotherapy look like? In some ways, such therapy might simply be one that explores the extensive body of feminist scholarship and imports its carefully articulated recommendations for work with women and girls into modalities that work specifically for boys and men. In fact, many authors have more or less suggested such a course by calling for consideration of gender as a significant mediating variable in work with *all* clients (Goldner, 1988). In this vein, there have been calls for a therapeutic paradigm that has variously been described as nonsexist and gender-neutral (Brickman, 1984), "gender-sensitive" (Philpot, Brooks, Lusterman, & Nutt, 1997), and "gender-aware" (Good, Gilbert, & Scher, 1990).

Although this line of thinking is appealing and a step in the right direction, it is insufficient for therapy with women as well as for therapy with men. In their differentiation between nonsexist and feminist therapies, Worell and Johnson (2001) noted that the latter variety not only avoids gender stereotyping and reinforcing of role restrictions but also stimulates personal empowerment of women to be able to challenge social restrictions rather than merely accommodate them. Thus, although all feminist therapies are nonsexist, gender-aware, and gender-sensitive, they are much more than that because they have an additional agenda for their clients.

In a similar, yet very different way, male-friendly psychotherapy is also much more than nonsexist psychotherapy. Like feminist therapy, it also calls for profound awareness of sex-based discrepancies in access to power and commitment to assisting clients to overcome them. The difference is found in the nature and location of the disadvantage. For women, the disadvantages have been in the culture at large. For men and boys, the disadvantage has been in the culture of psychotherapy. In spite of their history of considerable power and privilege in so many spheres, men have participated in the creation and perpetuation of an institution that is purported to be available for their assistance, yet one that all too rarely they access or fully use. As a result, to ameliorate the disadvantage for men vis-à-vis the world of psychotherapy, therapists must go well beyond gender neutrality. We must radically alter and broadly expand the conventional ways we think about therapy if there is a hope of making it appealing to men. Therapists must develop a comprehensive and integrated model of psychotherapeutic intervention with men and boys that will alter its image, available formats, internal structure and processes, acceptable content, objectives, pacing, delivery sites, and breadth of relational styles. In undertaking such a reassessment, we will encounter our own phenomenology regarding men, assessing whether or not there is a need for what Sue and Sue consider to be "Competency One"—that is, the need for therapist awareness of one's assumptions, values, and biases (Sue & Sue, 2003, p. 18).

Fortunately, some of this work has already begun (Brooks & Good, 2001; Good & Brooks, 2005). In the following pages, I catalog that work, organize it into a framework, and provide a model for therapeutic intervention for males. This model of male-friendly psychotherapy has several distinguishing characteristics: It is informed by in-depth knowledge of men's lives;

attuned to political issues and the ambiguous role of power in men's lives; broad and catholic in its consideration of modes of intervention; positive and focused on enhancement; eclectic, integrative, and transtheoretical; sensitive to a variety of diversities among men; and demanding of therapist self-awareness.

In chapter 3, I present the first component in a broadened conceptualization of therapeutic interventions for men: consciousness-raising out-of-office activities that seek to prevent the development of maladaptive coping behaviors as a result of male gender role strain and engage men in the psychotherapeutic enterprise to address any such behaviors that have already become manifest to varying degrees in the repertoire of cognitive skills among psychically troubled men.

3

THERAPEUTIC INTERVENTIONS OUTSIDE THE THERAPIST'S OFFICE

John was a 52-year-old, married, Mexican American psychiatric case aide at a Veterans Administration (VA) hospital. After many years of working as a VA custodian, he had managed to acquire enough college credits to become eligible for his current position, which he considered to be a step toward his ultimate goal of becoming a licensed addiction therapist. As part of his work toward his degree, he took a night class on multicultural issues at the local community college. He became intensely invested in the class, especially moved by the readings on men and masculinity studies. As the oldest of nine children of an authoritarian father, he had struggled to make peace with the man before his death 2 years earlier. John sought out his professor after class and pleaded for extra readings about ethnicity and fatherhood issues. The professor provided him with several articles and books and also encouraged him to write his final autobiographical class assignment on the topic. John wrote a passionate and emotionally moving final paper and included a personal note of thanks to the professor for a life-changing experience. Stimulated by this response and aware that John was deeply troubled by estrangement from his oldest son, the professor suggested that John consider attending a father–son retreat scheduled the next month and sponsored by the city's ministerial alliance.

The professor heard little more from John until 6 months later, when he received a lengthy letter describing the retreat and immense changes it had precipitated in his relationship with his son. Not only had the retreat caused them both to recognize the pain from their mutual estrangement, but it had also inspired John to initiate similar retreats within his own church's men's group. As an additional outgrowth of the experience, John noted that he had become far more attuned to father-hood issues in his clinical population of middle-aged and older veterans in recovery from substance abuse. He concluded his letter with an open offer to provide a guest presentation to the multicultural class at any time in the future.

In the previous chapter, I argued that the gulf between many traditional males and therapists can be creatively addressed if therapists become more embracing of the many modes of therapeutic change beyond the most conventional ones. That concept is illustrated by this vignette of John, a man who managed to reshape critical aspects of his life on the basis of an initial serendipitous contact and several self-guided explorations and psychoeducational experiences. Although John's story may not be the most common one of all men struggling with the aforementioned crisis of modern masculinity, it is also not rare. Most observers of the contemporary men's movement have encountered similar stories, and many have had personal experiences of change without formal mental health intervention. Others would argue that John was not really suffering any gender role strain and pain—certainly not any of the Big Three psychopathologies stemming from a masculinity-related identity crisis—and that even if he were, such psychoeducation, men's groups, retreats, and so forth are no substitute for the kind of intense work required between a therapist and client to work out the latter's deep-seated problems. Such a perspective takes a narrow view of therapeutic change and the vast social resources a therapist can rely on to get reluctant male clients into an engaged therapeutic setting.

The broader view of therapeutic change encompasses these vast social resources in the therapist's encounter with men as potential clients or as just vulnerable men. In the first instance—men as potential clients—the therapist uses *proactive outreach* to get a mildly troubled man to become more aware of distinct risk factors in his masculinity construct by joining the potential client in out-of-office settings or groups as a "fellow traveler" in the male gender role journey (O'Neill & Carroll, 1988). In essence, the therapist participates in the out-of-office group as another member, yet one with expertise in how masculinity typically manifests itself and how it is affected by the group's setting.

In the second instance—men as vulnerable individuals—the therapist assumes a *primary prevention* role, helping to establish support groups themselves or consulting with the leaders of setting-specific venues on how they can tailor their regular group discussions and activities toward an enhanced awareness of male gender role strain as it relates to the setting or to the group's common purpose.

In both instances, the emphasis is on consciousness raising and enhancing the lessons of the gathering in terms of masculinity's assets and risk factors within the specific setting, whether the gathering is about work-related issues, relationships, spirituality, health, or other life endeavors that engender discussion of common concerns and desires in an informal setting. Primary prevention puts the male-oriented therapist in a consulting role with the organizers or leaders of the out-of-office group or activity; the consultative role centers on the degree to which the activity or group addresses men's issues and whether the activity/group offers male members any resources to augment their coping skills, if necessary, as a result of their expanded awareness. Proactive outreach envisions a more direct, empathetic involvement with the members of the group/activity as the therapist seeks a mutual benefit from membership in the out-of-office venue. It assumes a more direct involvement with fellow members of the group or activity as the therapist forges a common empathetic bond with those who manifest varying degrees of male gender role strain. The male-oriented therapist thus has a good vantage point to assess those men who gain more awareness of both their peculiar gender role strain and the need for some more direct intervention in terms of exploring their feelings in a formal therapeutic setting.

Whether as a consultant to or a member of the out-of-office group or activity, the therapist undertakes an intervention. Indeed, much of the debate over primary prevention centers on the degree to which an intervention is necessary. However, the distinction between primary prevention and proactive outreach is an elusive one. In fact, proactive outreach can be considered a modality within the primary preventive paradigm; the distinction is really one of degree, depending on the extent of the therapist's participation in the out-of-office group or activity and the degree of intervention.

For this book's purposes, proactive outreach is subsumed within the modality of primary prevention, and I discuss out-of-office interventions under the latter, broader rubric. The following vignette, which relates the story of a colleague and his professional network of fellow therapists, demonstrates the easy and purposeful characterization of proactive outreach as part of the broader modality of primary prevention.

> Howard, a 64-year-old psychologist colleague, was emotionally devastated when his wife was diagnosed with rapidly advancing Alzheimer's disease. As he described his overwhelming sense of loss, his fears, and his resentments, we realized the need for a support group for male partners of spouses with debilitating illness. By specifically targeting male

partners, the group provided opportunities for men to explore the male-specific aspects of their struggles with the caregiving role and the general lack of adequate social support systems. Similar group activities have been organized by other mental health professionals to help men cope with physical loss from testicular cancer, survive an HIV positive diagnosis, cope with a partner's mastectomy, or manage the trauma of divorce. Some participants in these activities experienced a beneficial lowering of their resistance to help seeking and ultimately sought a formal psychotherapy relationship. Most others, however, never felt that need but nevertheless felt a deeper connection with other men and a desire to reach out and advocate for other men in potential distress.

Zur (2008) has presented a compelling argument that interventions that take place "beyond the office walls" or "out-of-office" may be especially helpful in a range of situations. Most relevant here is Zur's (2008) contention that outside-the-office interventions are particularly appropriate for culture-sensitive therapists, that is, those wishing to "emphasize flexibility and respect for clients' tradition, culture" (p. 8). Zur does not specifically address the issues of therapy with males, yet the material I presented in chapter 2 of this volume should make it clear that clients raised in traditional male culture might benefit substantially from this type of therapeutic flexibility and cultural respect.

To some extent, therapists' willingness to consider outside-the-office interventions is tied to therapeutic orientation. As Zur (2008) pointed out, family therapists and humanistic therapists are far more comfortable with this type of therapeutic activity than are analytically oriented practitioners. However, an additional factor may be the degree to which a mental health practitioner is willing to consider primary prevention as a valid therapeutic focus.

To be sure, out-of-office interventions allow the therapist the opportunity to address the psychopathology of men's everyday lives early and preventively—that is, before the troubling malaise of male gender role strain turns into more pernicious and maladaptive coping mechanisms, such as substance abuse, violence, and sexual predation.

PRIMARY PREVENTION IN MENTAL HEALTH

George Albee, who is generally considered to be one of the founders of the primary prevention movement in mental health, noted that "you can't stop an epidemic by treating one person at a time. Taking preventive actions before the epidemic occurs is the only way" (quoted in Bloom, 2008, p. 107). Within counseling psychology, concepts of primary prevention have been proposed as one aspect of a tripartite model consisting of primary, secondary, and tertiary approaches. Conyne (1987) considered *primary prevention* as intentional programs that target groups before problems develop to allow members of those groups to continue functioning in healthy ways. *Secondary prevention* focuses on populations showing early-stage problems to inhibit development of more serious difficulties. *Tertiary intervention* would be reserved for persons who have already developed a pathology or disorder.

According to Bloom (2008), the primary prevention model comprises three essential elements: prevention of predictable and interrelated problems, protection of existing states of health, and promotion of psychosocial wellness for identified populations of people. Based on a social learning model (as opposed to a medical model), preventive interventions typically call for teaching and psychoeducation to "prevent some problem from occurring [and] . . . substitute something positive in its place" (Bloom, 2008, p.110).

As these descriptions of prevention levels illustrate, the model was primarily developed for practical reasons without specific reference to male or female therapy populations. That is, it was generally seen as more efficient and cost-effective to intervene at a broad level with all persons before problems become more ingrained and intractable. However, some gender specificity may be appropriate. When we consider the historical antipathy of boys and men for the institution of psychotherapy, the issue of primary preventive interventions becomes even more relevant. That is, if males have been raised and reinforced to act in a therapy-avoidant manner (and male user-friendly therapies have been largely undeveloped), it would seem to make great sense to intervene as early as possible by tapping a therapeutic resource that is geared toward men's seemingly innate camaraderie and team orientation, a resource that is typically outside the formal office setting.

In fact, Mark Kiselica, a leading proponent of new therapy approaches for boys and adolescents, long ago made very strong arguments for greater attention to preventive mental health. On one hand, he has been highly critical of the counseling psychology field in general for abandoning its emphasis on prevention in favor of more remedial intervention (Kiselica & Look, 1993). That critique was echoed by others within counseling psychology, as they expressed concern that the overall move from a primary to tertiary prevention emphasis would deprive the counseling field of its distinctiveness from clinical psychology (Sprinthall, 1990; Weikel & Palmo, 1989). Later, however, Kiselica sharpened his critique by describing the unique advantages of preventive interventions in work with young males. Specifically, he and his colleagues have presented an approach to positively influence the "developmental trajectory" of young men and build strengths of emotional competence, resiliency, and "positive masculinity" (Kiselica, Englar-Carlson, Horne, & Fisher, 2008).

Given that some primary prevention activities are directed at "untoward environmental factors [that are] the cause of the problems" and they require "collective action, sometimes at an international level" (Bloom, 2008, p. 109), many clinicians might recoil from these nontraditional traditional ideas and dismiss most primary prevention as inappropriate for their practices. In addition, if one were to leave the more narrow and familiar confines of the therapy office, major attention needs to be given to ethical and legal issues, such as potential boundary crossings, problematic dual relationships, and confidentiality violations (Zur, 2008). This matter, of course, is not problematic when the therapist is not an actual participant in an activity and only recommends that a male client participate in a male-oriented consciousness-raising group. Most of the outside-the-office activities described in this chapter do not require therapist participation, or they simply call for a therapist to function within a professional role in a nontraditional setting. However, even in the cases in which therapists might adopt more flexible roles, ethical and appropriate professional standards can be comfortably maintained. In this regard, Zur (2008) described a number of important considerations related to out-of-office interventions, and even went so far as to present an argument for them as more ethical than standard practices. "Clinically-driven, out-of-office interventions are clearly within the standard of care . . . and are neither unethical per se nor lead to exploitation or harm. Some argue that not leaving the office, even when it is clinically indicated, is unethical and immoral as it deprives clients of the best possible care" (Zur, 2008, p. 12).

Many preventive activities have recently been identified that could easily suit many therapists wishing greater facility with male populations. These primary prevention activities could have more than the straightforward benefit of broadening intervention modalities, and in situations in which therapists are actual participants, such involvement could be a vital first step to generate positive contacts between men and therapists. This level of involvement may break the ice, bridge gaps, shatter negative therapist stereotypes, and further the process of empathic connection. Thus, out-of-office activities not only provide a venue for men's self-awareness and consciousness raising, but such activities beyond the walls of a therapist's office also serve to at least make additional therapy in an office setting more appealing by getting the male client to become aware that many other men share the same types of problems.

Perhaps the most compelling argument for the utility of primary prevention can be located in the parallel line of paradigm development in the area of "process of change" and "stage of change" (Prochaska & DiClemente, 1982; Prochaska & Norcross, 2007). This model (described more fully in chapter 7 of this volume) has been exceptionally valuable across all psychotherapies because of its recognition that interventions will frequently succeed or fail depending on whether the client's readiness to change is taken into account. At the earliest point of readiness (i.e., precontemplation), clients are generally unaware of the need to change any aspect of their lives, and "they usually feel coerced into changing. They may even demonstrate change as long as the pressure is on. . . . Once the pressure is off, however, they often quickly return to their old ways" (Prochaska & Norcross, 2007, p. 515). Under certain circumstances, individuals move from the precontemplation stage to the contemplation stage, in which they have become more aware that a problem exists but have not yet made a full commitment to do something about it.

In the section that follows, I describe numerous outside-the-office interventions that represent the fortuitous confluence of several trends in psychotherapy. To some extent, they can be thought of as a more elaborated form of the past pretherapy training groups designed to help unsophisticated clients use therapy more effectively (Gauron et al., 1977). In most ways, they are certainly syntonic with the recommendations of primary prevention advocates and a clear accommodation to the process-of-change theories. In fact, Prochaska and Norcross (2003) made special reference to this needed development in their projections about the future of psychotherapy over the next decade. After conducting a Delphi poll with "preeminent authorities on psychotherapy," they identified 12 emerging themes for psychotherapy, 1 of which was "proactive outreach to entire populations" (Prochaska & Norcross, 2007, p. 552). They noted, "psychotherapy has traditionally taken a narrow and passive approach to patient populations . . . therapists wait for individual patients to seek their services" (Prochaska & Norcross, 2003, p. 552). To correct this restricting pattern, Prochaska and Norcross recommended "proactive outreach" to offer therapeutic services to entire populations. They also noted, "when our field has evaluated the efficacy of psychotherapy, we have implicitly ignored the majority of populations we fail to serve" (2007, p. 309).

PRIMARY PREVENTION FOR BOYS AND ADOLESCENT MALES

Numerous men's studies authors have addressed the mismatch between the psyche of young men and the demands of the psychotherapy office (Kiselica, Englar-Carlson, & Horne, 2008; Levant, 2001a) and have called for creative adaptation of traditional intervention methods. In chapter 5, I describe many of the creative recommendations for altering within-office therapy methods. However, in this section, I describe the many out-of-office interventions that have appeared over the past 2 decades. Although these programs tend to be developed for both male and female youth (i.e., they are gender-blind), the following are those that have targeted behaviors that have been especially problematic for boys and male adolescents.

Violence Prevention

An abundance of prevention programs have been developed to combat the pernicious influence of violence in young people's lives. In their review of preventive interventions with school-age youth, Vera and Reese (2000) noted that violence prevention has become a priority of the federal government, and this awareness has stimulated development of multiple programs with components to address the person-centered and environment-centered risk factors. For example, the FAST Track program (Bierman et al., 1999) is a school-based initiative that has demonstrated reductions in aggressive behavior through the teaching of conflict resolution skills. Bullying behavior has been the target of a multistrategy intervention program developed by Orpinas, Horne, and Staniszewski (2003). Positive Adolescents Choices Training (http://www.researchpress.com/product/item/4800/#4805) is a skill-based prevention program focused on aggression and violence in African American familial and peer relationships. Similar objectives are included in the Across the Ages program and the Providing Alternative Thinking Strategies (PATHS) program (Portwood & Waris, 2003).

Healthy Sexuality, Sexual Violence, and Pornography

Because of the wide range of problems inherent in reaching sexual maturity and developing sexually healthy lifestyles, many preventive programs have appeared to curb problems that are all too common among young men. Vera and Reese (2000) described a range of prevention programs designed to help young men and women avoid sexually transmitted diseases and unwanted pregnancies. Many leaders in the profeminist men's movement have created ambitious consciousness-raising and psychoeducation programs to help young men recognize the complexities of sexual violence and rape prevention (Flood, 2006; Keel, 2005). The CASA House Peer Education Project (Imbesi, 2007) is a pilot project in Melbourne, Australia, designed to help adolescent youth recognize and counter factors involved in sexual violence. In college and church settings across the United States, programs have been developed to help young men speak out about dangers of pornography and sexually compulsive behavior (Jensen, 2005; Kimmel, 1990).

Promoting Competence and Building Resilience

All primary prevention theories indicate that effective programs must have components that not only focus on addressing vulnerabilities and deficiencies but also emphasize building on strengths to develop positive behaviors that make problems less likely to occur. In this vein, Arbona and Coleman

(2008) described the area of resilience research, which has the principal objective of discovering "to what extent resilience, as a protective process, can be enhanced through education, prevention, and counseling interventions" (p. 496). Danish and Forneris (2008) described developmental approaches to promote "competency across the life span" (p. 500). In particular, they identified the Life Developmental Intervention (LDI), which aims to "develop capacity and competence in life planning that enables individuals to encounter and successfully manage both routine and unexpected life events" (Danish & Forneris, 2008, p. 503).

Within the LDI model, Danish and Forneris (2008) have developed a number of specific programs. For example, the Going for the Goal program is designed to teach adolescents a sense of personal control and confidence about their futures. The Sports United to Promote Education and Recreation program attempts to extract positive lessons from sports participation to teach "goal setting, problem-solving, overcoming roadblocks, and seeking social support" (Danish & Forneris, 2008, p. 509). As the titles of the programs indicate, the Goals for Health and the Bridge to Better Health programs focus on enhancing physical health behaviors.

Although these resilience building programs have been developed for children and adolescents of both genders, they seem to have great merit for young men who have been observed to have few resources for negotiating male lifecycle transitions. Throughout the men's studies literature, considerable attention has been given to how contemporary culture lacks sufficient transition rituals and rites of passage for young men and how most young men desperately need guidance from male mentors (Bly, 1990; Jolliff & Horne, 1999; Sax, 2007).

Before leaving this section, a comment seems warranted regarding the evolution of primary prevention programs. The massive *Encyclopedia of Primary Prevention and Health Promotion* (Gullotta & Bloom, 2003) catalogued primary prevention programs for children, adolescents, and adults in more than 150 areas for enhancement of physical, emotional, and spiritual well-being. For the therapist hoping to discover creative ways to intervene with boys and men, this resource clearly provides an enormous range of potentially useful avenues. As yet, however, this field appears to be very broad and generic in its focus, with only a minimal amount of attention to diversity issues. Many of the programs seem targeted toward both genders, regardless of the evidence of differential risk (i.e., sexual assault, adolescent risk-taking). Although there has been some attention to the special issues of African Americans (Sellers, Bonham, Neighbors, & Amell, 2009; Watkins & Neighbors, 2007), there appears to be relative inattention to the risks inherent in racial and ethnic minority status and disability status. Although the seemingly comprehensive encyclopedia of Gullotta and Bloom (2003) mentions the existence of

GLSEN, a nationwide network of support groups and initiatives to lessen homophobia in high schools (http://www.GLSEN.org), there is no identification of any face-to-face program specifically developed to enhance self-esteem and heighten resiliency in gay/lesbian/bisexual youth. Kiselica, Mule, and Haldeman (2008) noted that, fortunately, "several healthy websites are available that can help a boy learn about the gay culture and answer important questions he might have about his sexual identity" (p. 257). Among these are sites managed by Outproud, The National Youth Advocacy Center, and the GLBT National Help Center.

PRIMARY PREVENTION FOR MEN

By and large, the primary prevention model (including its proactive outreach modality) has not been popular among adults, perhaps because of the apparent advantages of working with young men through early life interventions and facilitating developmental transitions. Nevertheless, over the past few decades some models of preventive, outside-the-office interventions for men have been developed. Although primary prevention with adult men may be somewhat more difficult because of their more solidified habits and role patterns, it may be facilitated by the fact that older men can be found in a relatively wider range of settings. Most primary prevention interventions with young males have been school-based, whereas interventions with older males have been proposed for multiple settings: business/industry/work environments, doctors' offices, universities and fraternities, churches, civic organizations, rehabilitation clinics, and senior centers. In the following section, I first describe a number of outside-the-office therapeutic interventions that have not been setting-specific. I then note some of the interventions that have been conducted in specific settings where mental health professionals have access to men who might otherwise never come into contact with a psychotherapist.

The Men's Movement and Men's Gatherings

There is no way of accurately quantifying the impact of the men's movement on the lives of men over the past 4 decades. In fact, any effort to fully describe, analyze, and differentiate the myriad philosophies, political positions, and representative activities would far exceed the scope of this book. Most observers have agreed that, unlike the case of women's movement, there really is no single men's movement. Instead, there has been a very wide assortment of groups and activities with the single commonality of recognizing that men's experiences are different from women's and that men need to unite to improve their life circumstances. The most generally recognized variants of the men's movement have been men's rights activists, the mythopoetic men, profeminist men, and the religious men's groups (Clatterbaugh, 1997; Newton, 2005). At their most basic level, these activities have shared the common thread of consciousness raising, one of the primary elements of the early women's movement (Kravetz, 1978). Although the men's movement received peak attention during the early 1990s, when millions of men participated in some form of male-focused public events, many of these activities have continued. For example, in a 2005 article in the *Boston Globe*, Paul Zakrzewski noted, "Robert Bly may have retreated to his sweat lodge, but the reconsideration of masculinity and fatherhood he helped initiate hasn't ended."

To be sure, there continue to be many opportunities for men to encounter other men in contexts that promote reflection about their lives. For example, Andronico (2001) described the value of the Somerset Institute's Modern Men's Weekend, a variant of Bly's mythopoetic weekends. The ManKind Project (http://www.mkp.org) is an organization of 38 interdependent worldwide centers providing men's retreats for more than 30,000 men annually. Promise Keepers continues to hold annual conferences and claims that hundreds of thousands of men attended their Stand in the Gap gathering in Washington, DC, in 1997 (http://www.promisekeepers.org/faqs/faqs-general-information/what-was-stand-in-the-gap-all-about). On a smaller scale, the National Organization for Men Against Sexism continues to hold annual Men & Masculinity conferences with multiple task groups committed to a profeminist agenda.

Variously known as adventure therapy, wilderness therapy, outdoor therapy, camping therapy, outdoor pursuits, and risk education (Zur, 2008), outdoor/adventure therapy is one of the more well-known men's gatherings activities of late. Although it shares many therapeutic dimensions of Bly's wilderness retreats, outdoor/adventure therapy is not expressly geared toward men; yet it does attract a significant male participation because of its physicality and somewhat controlled tests of endurance. Such therapy is also distinguished from recreation or physical fitness, in that "it is geared specifically to eliciting therapeutic change . . . and, like most clinical interventions, is designed for the purpose of changing one's affect, behavior, and/or cognition" (Zur, 2008). Vision quests are perhaps the best representations of all three dimensions of outdoor/adventure therapy for men: the therapeutic, the spiritual, and the masculine. One men's center in California's San Francisco Bay area bills its semiannual vision quest as "a transformational wilderness experience . . . designed for men in transition, men seeking to find themselves as men, heal their relationships with their families, and find their higher power" (http://www.mensgroups.com/_p_quests.htm).

These men's movement activities are exceptionally divergent. For some men, these encounters will do little more than fuel bitterness toward women and rage at perceptions of mistreatment of men in the courts and within the nation at large. For other men, they will stimulate spiritual awareness and intense recommitment to traditional male social and family roles. For many, however, participation can initiate a self-guided process of personal growth (as described in the aforementioned case) or stimulate a curiosity about the potential benefit of psychotherapy. In addition, as I note later, many men's movement activities can serve as a vital supplement to processes occurring within the psychotherapy office.

Psychoeducation

Interventions providing information to men (and their loved ones) about masculinity, gender roles, and gender role strain can take place in more formal educational settings, as well as outside those settings, through primary-prevention psychoeducational programs. Similar to the process whereby many women first became part of the women's movement through women's studies courses, many men are being offered opportunities for greater self-awareness through formal men's studies courses. These courses are not as numerous as women's studies courses, yet they have shown a steady rate of increase and acceptance in academia (Urschel, 2000). It is ironic that these men's studies courses were initially more populated by women, yet many men have taken advantage of them as a mechanism for greater self-awareness.

Given the phenomenal growth of women's studies and self-help literature over the past several decades, it should not be surprising that there has been a corollary upswing in writing about men's lives. A visit to any bookstore or an Internet search with a *men's studies* keyword will uncover a massive array of literature about the challenges of modern manhood. This development is not as positive as it might seem, because most of the reading is being done by women and relatively few men. Nevertheless, self-help books/courses and bibliotherapy remain viable options to heighten some men's level of awareness and precipitate more therapy mindedness. Prochaska and Norcross (2003) described *self-help* as a "massive, systemic, and yet largely silent revolution in mental health today . . . the percentage of people engaging in self-help activities are now at record highs" (p. 553). Furthermore, these two psychologists argued that self-help activities have not only been demonstrated to be effective but are also commonly used as an adjunct by a high percentage of therapists.

As valuable as these men's studies programs and self-help resources have been, they unfortunately reach only a relatively small sector of the entire male population. Thus, significant cultural change requires a far broader scope of outreach and primary prevention activities. A central component of these primary prevention programs in mental health has been promotion of strengths and positive health behaviors, and a central tool of those enterprises has been psychoeducation. Bingenheimer, Repetto, Zimmerman, and Kelly (2003) noted that "a third class of health promotion technology is mass communication. . . . The purpose of health promotion efforts using mass communication techniques is to convey basic information or a persuasive message to a large number of people" (p. 21). Well established as a major component of mental health promotion, psychoeducation may be especially important for men, because men have often been observed to benefit most from interventions with more of an educational or cognitive orientation (Levant, 1990; Mahalik, 2005a).

In terms of psychoeducation for men, no model has been more carefully articulated than that of James O'Neil's (1996) gender role journey workshop. In his workshops, O'Neil has used a composite of lectures, group awareness exercises, and media exposure to increase participants' awareness of gender role restrictions, intergender conflicts, and sexist behaviors. At its theoretical roots, O'Neil's *gender role journey* metaphor is quite congruent with other models of identity development for racial and ethnic minorities (Cross, 1995; Helms, 1995) and for gay, lesbian, and bisexual individuals (Reynolds & Hanjorgiris, 2000). In this variant, the objective is to create an accepting and benevolent atmosphere in which individuals can move through phases of awareness and integration. O'Neil envisions the process as producing a shift from complete nonintrospective acceptance of traditional gender roles (and rejection of alternative roles) thorough ambivalence, anger, and activism into a final phase of "celebration and integration of gender roles" (O'Neil, 1997, p. 197). Although O'Neil described his workshops as more or less freestanding from formal psychotherapy, it is easy to see how their consciousness-raising aspects would dovetail with it by facilitating many men's transition from precontemplation to a greater consideration of entering therapy.

More focused than O'Neil in his broad work with the gender role journey, Ron Levant has developed group psychoeducational programs to combat "normative male alexithymia" in expectant fathers (Levant & Kelly, 1989) and for nonclinical populations of men in general (Levant, 2003). Typically integrated with individual and marital therapies, Levant's model nevertheless can be utilized in a proactive outreach format in a range of settings.

As promising as these primary-preventive, out-of-office activities have been, they nevertheless have been quite modest in their scope and impact upon the overall male population. In this regard, Rochlen and Hoyer (2005) asserted that the capacity of the mental health fields to reach men will be realized only if there is an embrace of social marketing frameworks. These authors have reviewed efforts to develop brochures describing counseling services and discovered that "traditional" men respond more favorably to alternative services, that is, classes, videotapes, and other structured interventions (Rochlen & Hoyer, 2005, p. 677). In commending social marketing activities, Rochlen and Hoyer made special note of two broad public awareness campaigns. The

Real Men, Real Depression campaign was developed by the National Institute of Mental Health (NIMH) and launched in 2003 to inform men about the prevalence and characteristics of depression in men. A second initiative, Tackling Men's Health, which also addressed men's physical and mental health, was launched by the National Football League.

Both of these initiatives were carefully structured to overcome men's reluctance to admit problems and to seek help, partially through the use of language more consistent with traditional men's lives and through first-person testimonials for men in traditional occupations. It is impossible to know the full impact of these campaigns, but NIMH officials have estimated that "more than 345 million people have encountered information about men and depression through its media campaign" (Kersting, 2005, p. 66). Obviously, therapists wishing to affect men's lives will benefit from familiarity with the utility of public awareness interventions as well as being creative in integrating them with their practice activities.

Setting-Specific Interventions

Up to now, this chapter has focused on creative ways to overcome men's aversion to psychotherapy by implementing proactive outreach through men's movement events, psychoeducational activities, public awareness campaigns, and social marketing efforts. An additional approach to the therapy-aversion problem is found in the old concept of "bringing the mountain to Mohammed" as exemplified by Zabos and Trinh (2001). These professionals utilized this idea in bringing mobile dental services to ethnic minority community members with HIV/AIDS. For this book's purposes, the emphasis would be on taking male-friendly therapeutic interventions to settings commonly inhabited by men.

To some extent, this approach is rooted in the mental health consultation model described by Zins and Erchul (2002) as a "method of providing preventively oriented psychological and educational services in which consultants and consultees form cooperative partnerships and engage in a reciprocal, systematic, problem solving processes . . . to enhance and empower consultee systems, thereby promoting clients well-being" (p. 625). The mental health consultation model allows for outside experts to help caregivers within systems find more effective ways to work with their clients. This consultation model is seen as having three primary applications for ways to reach men: (a) consulting with nonmental health professionals to better recognize men's unique manner of seeking (or avoiding) help and identifying problems men tend to hide; (b) creating credibility and finding the opportunity to work freely as a gender-informed provider of programmatic and individual interventions in nontraditional treatment settings; and (c) helping established providers in mental health treatment settings to recognize the "maleness" of male clients' problems—that is, to see men's adjustment problems in a gender context. Some possible applications of this model are described here.

Health Care Settings

Despite their general aversion to seeking any form of professional help (Addis & Mahalik, 2003), men are nevertheless far more likely to appear in a medical office than a psychotherapy office. Therefore, as Courtenay (2005) pointed out, "any contact a health professional has with a man provides an important opportunity. . . . Health professionals whose responsibility it is to counsel men in medical settings are in a unique position to assist men" (pp. 31–32). Unfortunately, these opportunities have been grossly undervalued. A considerable body of research has demonstrated that communication between male patients and health professionals is highly problematic, with men spending much less time than women in physicians' offices, asking fewer questions, and receiving briefer explanations of their conditions (Courtenay, 2000, 2005).

Because of the shortcomings in the provision of health care information and services to men, Courtenay developed a practice guideline for health professionals who work with men (Courtenay, 2005). The guideline elements are represented by the acronym HEALTH—Humanize, Educate, Assume the worst, Locate supports, Tailor plan, and Highlight strengths. In essence, the plan calls for recognizing men's unique health issues and problems in allowing themselves to access needed care. Although the primary emphasis of HEALTH is on improving men's physical health status, its psychoeducational components emphasize the biopsychosocial model (Engel, 1980), which allows men to see the intersection between their bodies and their emotional well-being. In his work within the health care system, Courtenay exemplifies the possibilities of the consultation and proactive outreach models whereby a men's studies perspective is introduced into a setting to customize approaches to male clients. These alterations create more compassionate and empathic encounters, and thus are not only likely to improve men's healthcare but are also likely to have psychotherapeutic benefits as well. Some of the men who benefit may go no further in a therapy journey, but many others may be empowered to make further moves toward formal therapy.

Business and Industry Settings

Corporations and business settings have long been the sites where men play out the "Big Wheel" component of the traditional male role (David & Brannon, 1976). As a result, these settings have commonly been seen as noxious for men and antagonistic to men's emotional well-being. Of late, however, there seems to be a trend toward new types of organizational structures and corporate leaders who are more self-aware, adaptive, flexible, resilient, and "willing to look inward" (Kruger, 1999, p. 124). Hills, Carlstrom, and Evanow (2005) noted how these characteristics are often alien to those found in traditional male executives: "Looking inward is clearly not something most men readily choose" (p. 55).

Partially because of the changing environments within the worlds of business, the profession of executive coaching has experienced explosive growth over the past 2 decades. There are many variants and many types of practitioners of executive coaching, but all have more or less the same objectives. As described by Kilburg (2007), it is "a helping relationship . . . to help the client achieve a mutually identified set of goals to improve his or her professional performance and personal satisfaction . . . within a formally defined coaching agreement" (p. 28).

Because business and corporate communities have moved away from reverence for authoritarian leadership to greater emphasis on leaders with more interpersonal skills, these settings have become more challenging for many men. However, the demand for broader behavioral repertoires in these men has opened avenues for change agents (coaches) to reach men and aid in their psychological growth. In this regard, Hills et al. (2005) contended that the "inner-journey" emphasis of executive coaching is highly similar to the emphases of counseling and therapy: "If a man becomes more interpersonally effective, he will probably become a better leader and a better friend, father, and partner" (p. 55).

Sports and Athletic Settings

Much as the executive coach has unique access to a group of men not prone to seeking psychotherapy, the sports psychologist also has access to a therapy-aversive male population (and typically a population more represented by men of color). Sport psychology is a recently appearing area of study and has been described as "the scientific study of the psychological factors that are associated with participation and performance in sport, exercise, and other types of physical activity" (American Psychological Association Division of Exercise and Sport Psychology, 2008). As would be expected, sport psychologists employ a variety of psychological principles to help athletes function at a higher level. However, the focus on performance enhancement is only one aspect of this work, as these mental health professionals report interest in also improving the mental health of athletes and "understanding how participation in sport, exercise, and physical activity affects an individual's psychological development, health, and well-being throughout the life span" (APA Division 47, Exercise and Sport Psychology Web site, http://www.apa.org/about/division/div47.html). In fact, Petitpas, Giges, and Danish (1999) argued that sport psychology and counseling psychology are highly similar because of their preference for developmental help over remedial help and their mutual emphasis on improving existing psychological skills or teaching new skills to enhance an individual's performance.

Robertson and Newton (2001) made a powerful case that mental health professionals wishing to work with men would do well to be familiar with sports and their influence on their male treatment populations: "In North American culture, masculinity and sports are virtually inseparable experiences. . . . The masculinity issues that sports raise for men may vary over the life span and among cultures, but the need to address these issues continues throughout life" (p. 92).

In terms of intervention modality, Robertson and Newton (2001) described the utility of both individual counseling and workshop/class formats. In the former, athletes are typically referred for issues with their performance, with content issues likely to involve coping with injuries, substance abuse, eating disorders, performance-inhibiting anxiety, attention or learning problems, and motivation conflicts. Although a performance focus makes it somewhat easier for male athletes to consider traditional individual counseling, the psychoeducational formats of workshops and classes are nevertheless much preferred (Robertson & Newton, 2005). Representative of this workshop model are the Performance Enhancement Training program (Robertson & Newton, 2001) and the Leadership Training program (Newton, Rathbun, & Arck, 1999). The Life Skills Program includes an emphasis on personal development and emotional well-being. Each program focuses primarily on factors impeding athletic performance, yet consciousness raising is inevitable because the programs cannot avoid addressing and discussing themes inherent in male socialization. Further, Robertson and Newton indicate that participation in such a class "breaks down the inhibitions many of the students have in seeking counseling for performance or personal concerns. . . . A large portion of these students (well over half) return in one way or another to seek advice, counsel, or referral information" (p. 117).

Churches and Religious Settings

There can be no doubt that most American men identify a religion and a church as important in their lives. More than 90% of North Americans have reported a religious affiliation (Barrett & Johnson, 1998), and 65% have noted that religion is an important part of their daily lives (Gallup Organization, 2009). Reporting a religious affiliation is not the same, of course, as being an active practitioner of a religious faith or a regular church attendee; in fact, many more women than men attend church services (Maples & Roberston, 2005). Nevertheless, a man is far more likely to spend time in a church than in a psychotherapist's office. Also, the far greater popularity of the Promise Keepers movement in relation to any other men's movement activity attests to the greater tendency of religiously affiliated men to participate collectively with other men (in nonsports activities). Those interested in enhancing men's lives and encouraging troubled men to consider therapy would do well to establish connections with churches and religious communities. It is unfortunate that, for many complex reasons, this has not been the case, as religion and the mental health professions have often been mutually alienated (Richards & Bergin, 2000).

As noted in chapter 2 of this volume, there are enormous differences in the philosophies of the various segments of the men's movement. Profeminist men in particular have been highly critical of the Promise Keepers organization for its conservative stance on women's roles, homosexuality, and male leadership in the family (Consason, Ross, & Cokorinos, 1996; Silverstein & Auerbach, 1999). This negative sentiment may combine with historical tensions between mental health practitioners and religion to produce a broad aversion on the part of mental health practitioners toward religiously affiliated men. Nevertheless, there is far greater variability among religious men than is commonly recognized, and many of these men are struggling to incorporate cultural changes of the past half-century into meaningful new identities. Richards and Bergin (2000) and Stanford (2008) have noted that religiously affiliated persons generally fail to use mental health services, and these authors urged mental health professionals to improve this situation by developing competency in religious diversity.

Men's groups within churches have a long history. To date, most of these church-based men's groups have had conservative agendas and have, naturally, focused on issues of a spiritual nature (as illustrated by Promise Keepers and the National Fellowship of Catholic Men). However, not all church-based men's groups share a conservative agenda. For example, the Unitarian Universalist Men's Network (UUMeN) is far more embracing of new ideas about manhood and intergender relations, describing itself as "male-positive, pro-feminist/womanist, gay-affirming, culturally and racially inclusive and diverse" (http://www.uumen.org). The efforts of the many members of lesbian, gay, bisexual, and transgender communities to function within established religions or establish their own churches illustrate the potential of maintaining ties with religiously affiliated persons and integrating spirituality with other psychological growth movements (Davidson, 2000).

Certainly, there is great variability among religious settings regarding the changing culture and its impact on traditional male and female roles. Although many religious organizations are skeptical of the implications of changing roles and are quite conservative in their reaction to them, most all recognize the immediacy and scope of this phenomenon. Because many churches have begun to organize new men's groups (Fitzhugh-Craig, 1996), there are now substantial opportunities for proactive interventions with religious men, particularly when there is understanding and respect for the religious framework of these men's lives. In fact, when one considers the central role of the Protestant, Catholic, and Islamic faiths in the lives of so many ethnic minority men, it becomes clear that neglect of men in these settings risks continued ethnocentrism within the men's movement.

Military and VA Settings

In the opening portion of this chapter, I differentiated between proactive outreach activities directed at settings without a formal mental health emphasis (medical settings, corporations, sports settings, and churches) and those that have had a mental health presence but have generally been blind to the role of gender role strain in the lives of their male clients (that is, they do not recognize the *maleness* of their clients' problems). Historically, treatment services offered to soldiers and military veterans have been highly representative of this pattern of gender blindness. For example, as I have previously noted, "because the VA treatment population has been predominantly male, most practitioners were able to ignore masculinity as a relevant aspect of their clients' lives. Much as fish are unaware of the existence of water, the VA has been . . . inattentive to how men's socialization into masculinity has affected their lives" (Brooks, 2005, p. 104).

With the dramatic rise in the number of women entering the military over the past 2 decades, the VA responded by establishing a Women's Veterans Program Office in 1994. The VA national medical director then called for programs targeting the needs of special populations, of which women veterans were one principal group (Kizer, 1996). Despite the implicit recognition that veterans' experiences vary by gender, the VA has remained slow in addressing the intersection of masculinity and military service. Recently, however, some psychologists within the VA system have initiated pilot projects to treat posttraumatic stress disorder that take into account men's gender role stress, alexithymia, and lack of social support (Jakupcak, Osborne, & Scott, 2006). Mental health practitioners who understand the wide-ranging implications of the "warrior" male role (Doyle, 1994) will be far better prepared to provide therapeutic interventions with men who have been shaped by the hypermasculine world of the military.

Rehabilitation Settings

Although both genders are well represented in a variety of settings offering rehabilitation services, men outnumber women in two very common ones. Men are more likely than women to appear for services in settings focusing on rehabilitation for traumatic injuries and those aiding recovery from alcohol abuse. Marini (2005) observed that men are more likely to sustain incapacitating trauma from spinal cord injury, myocardial infarction, or stroke, yet "there is scant focus on the particular disability-related issues of what males endure" (p. 88). Because any loss of physical capability has both common and unique challenges for members of each gender, Marini recommended that therapists working with men in these settings become fully aware of the impact of disability on a man's masculine identity and develop interventions to circumvent the dysfunctional aspects of men's common coping styles.

Because men have more alcohol-related problems and tend to have poorer outcomes than women following alcohol rehabilitation treatment, there has been recent recognition that men's issues need to be better incorporated in intervention programs. Numerous authors have commented on the close association of manhood and alcohol use. Isenhart (2005) stated that "alcohol use has been inextricably integrated into the masculine role for many years" (p. 137). Lemle and Mishkind (1989) observed that "alcohol is the only drug which is part of the male sex role, the only mood altering drug which society promotes as manly" (p. 217). Much like Marini's recommendations for work with men in physical disability settings, Brooks and Willoughby (2004) and Isenhart (2005) have urged alcohol treatment programs to include components specifically addressing the relationship between masculinity and alcohol abuse.

Prisons and Forensic Settings

A tragic and alarming trend over the 1980s and 1990s was the quadrupling of the U.S. prison population. Given that more than 90% of this population is male (Kupers, 1999; 2001), it seems quite apparent that this would be a setting with extraordinary access to troubled men. Furthermore, the data are astounding regarding the disproportionate representation of ethnic minority men. More than 70% of prison populations are made up of African American, Latino, and Native American men, and one third of young African American men are involved at some level with the criminal justice system (Mauer & Hurling, 1995). Given these statistics, two facts seem obvious: First, any prison mental health program must incorporate a focus on men's issues. Second, far greater effort needs to be extended on behalf of these men who will battle not only racism but also the additional burden of their ex-felon status. Kupers (1999, 2001) has described the prison setting as one of the most extreme settings for the exacerbation of *toxic masculinity*, which he considers to be the "constellation of traits in men that serve to foster domination, the devaluation of women, homophobia, and wanton violence" (p. 171). To counter this toxic masculinity, Kupers calls for far greater attention to the mental health needs of imprisoned men, as well as more programs targeted specifically at "exaggerated bravado, male posturing, rape, and domestic violence" (p. 171).

Of course, referring to these venues and activities as out-of-office implies that there are some complementary in-office activities—that is, one venue begs the other. The important thing to remember is that in both cases, the implicit modifier is *therapeutic*. These out-of-office activities may assuage the therapeutic community's concern about preventive mental health, in that entire populations of sufferers find some sort of collective early treatment that is designed to maintain extant states of health and to ward off environmental factors that aggravate the individual's specific problem. But the therapist must first get the male sufferer aware of the problem's extent, accepting of the notion that psychotherapy is the best way to resolve these ineffable impasses he's come to, and, eventually, engaged in the therapeutic process.

That's a tall order indeed, but the skilled therapist who specializes in men's problems—ranging from substance abuse and hyperaggression to the more profound mid-life crisis—knows that flexibility is the key. Out-of-office activities provide such therapeutic flexibility; they allow troubled men to explore and gain insight into their specific gender-related psychic malady. In terms of therapeutic outcomes, though, out-of-office activities are just a beginning—and a cursory one at that. To gain a deeper and more meaningful appreciation of the problem requires the client and therapist to work closely together to figure out what the client needs to change and how to go about it. In the transition from out-of-office activities to the therapist's office, the therapist, of course, plays a crucial role: He must make the client's passage from the group setting to the couch or chair a comforting and trustful transition, especially for precontemplative men.

These men must be engaged somehow in the therapeutic process, and out-of-office activities are just one way—but a major way—of getting troubled men to begin to realize that to relieve their pain and end their self-destructive habits they have no better course than therapy.

4

ON THE DOORSTEP—ENGAGING MEN IN PSYCHOTHERAPY

Woodrow was clearly uncomfortable throughout our initial session. An African American staff sergeant in the U.S. Army and part-time night watchman, he had been pressured into counseling by his superior officers. Apparently, his work performance had declined after a marital separation, and there was suspicion that he had been abusing marijuana to manage his distress. The first appointment had been scheduled by his oldest daughter, who had voiced additional concern about his withdrawal from all four of his children and from his usually high level of participation in their Baptist church. Throughout the session, Woodrow made minimal eye contact and appeared highly restless as he continually clenched and unclenched his fists.

Woodrow: Sorry, I just don't know what to tell you. Maybe you just need to ask questions or something.

Therapist: It appears to me that this appointment wasn't exactly your idea. Maybe you'd actually rather be somewhere else right now.

Woodrow: (lifting his eyes to make the first eye contact with the therapist): Yeah, I guess there's some truth in that.

Therapist:	In fact, I'm getting the impression that just about everybody has been jumping your case lately. Maybe things are coming at you from all directions.
Woodrow:	Got that right!
Therapist:	It's pretty damn frustrating when you bust your hump to make rank, provide a decent living for your family, and generally be a stand-up guy. All you get in return is hassles and lack of appreciation.
Woodrow:	Can't argue with that.
Therapist:	And then, to make things worse, you end up being forced to see a shrink—just what you need: another thing on your plate.
Woodrow:	(nodding): I know that's right.
Therapist:	Tell you what: As long as you're here anyway, let's see if we can figure out what's happening in your life. How things got to this point. Most of all though, how do we get folks off your back and some satisfaction into your life?
Woodrow:	You know, you are making a whole lot of sense.

At the close of the session, the therapist comments:

Therapist:	By the way, you might be interested in knowing about a group of men I consult with who have been meeting monthly at a local Christian church. They call themselves "New Christian Men" and talk about how to incorporate their beliefs into this crazy, changing world. Here's a brochure. Give it some thought.

Woodrow is the most common type of client to be seen by male-oriented therapists, but there are also many who seek psychotherapy independently and engage actively in the therapeutic process. In fact, there appears to be a modest national trend toward increased therapy use among men (Olufson, Marcus, Druss, & Pincus, 2002). However, these data can be highly misleading because many men appear at the door of a therapist's office with great initial reluctance, as did Woodrow. Many men come to a therapist's office through coercion or because they have no practical options. Unfortunately, many of these men will participate half-heartedly or drop out quickly. This is not surprising, in part because the drop rate for both genders across all therapies has been found to be about 50% (Wierzbicki & Pekarik, 1993). Furthermore, the largest percentages of persons who drop out of therapy do so after one session (Odell & Quinn, 1998), and those who return after the initial session tend to stay until completion (Tryon, 1986).

Because of these disconcerting realities, it becomes quite clear that the initial engagement process with an ambivalent male client is the sine qua non before substantive therapeutic change can take place. No matter how skillful the therapist or how creative the therapeutic techniques, nothing will happen unless the antitherapy barriers of traditional men have been managed. Umbarger (1983) used the metaphor of knocking on the door to characterize the earliest phase of joining between therapists and clients. Wonderfully illustrative of these critical moments is a scene from the film *Ordinary People* when the traumatized and postsuicidal Conrad Jarrett (Timothy Hutton) rides the elevator to his first therapy appointment. Long before knocking on the wrong door to the office, he has been shown muttering and repeatedly rehearsing his planned presentation— "I'm fine. . . . Things are going well. . . . I'm really quite fine."

An argument has previously been presented that most men are highly disinterested in psychotherapy and, at some level, ashamed of themselves for needing outside help. As a result, rapid engagement into a therapeutic relationship is quite critical, and it is therefore important to spend time considering methods to facilitate that process. This first encounter phase of therapeutic engagement with male clients can considered as composed of diagnostic assessment, motivational/contextual assessment, and relationship building.

MALE-SPECIFIC DIAGNOSTIC ASSESSMENT

There is nothing unique or unusual about a therapist making an initial assessment of a client's presenting symptoms and/or evaluating for extreme psychopathology that would make therapy difficult or impossible. Some therapists require a formal battery of tests whereas others incorporate assessment into early sessions. Whether the client is male or female, it is important to recognize the presence of prohibitively high levels of anxiety, depression, or the interpersonal distortions of severe character disorder. Aside from the usual diagnostic assessment, however, there has been far too little attention paid to the considerable benefit accruing from evaluating the role of gender-role socialization upon the client. More than 20 years ago, Laura Brown (1986) presented the case for "gender role analysis" as a "neglected component" in the psychological assessment process, stating that "gender roles remain rich depositories of information for young humans . . . it is surprising that such an important and universal variable seems to be so poorly addressed by standard and traditional approaches to psychodiagnosis" (p. 243).

This plea for greater attention to gender roles is quite relevant for assessment of male clients, whereby care must be exercised to recognize when a man's presenting problems might be a manifestation of unrecognized emotional turmoil rather than simply bad behavior. Since many men externalize distress though action, distraction, or compulsive acting out (Nolen-Hoeksema, 1990; Rabinowitz & Cochran, 2002), men's underlying anxiety and depression may be neglected and the more obvious behavioral issues (e.g., violence, substance abuse, sexual compulsivity) may receive exclusive therapeutic attention.

On the other hand, even when common male behavioral excesses are not obvious, care must be taken to be certain that they are not present in a disguised form. Unfortunately, by not drinking, not fighting, and not becoming sexually preoccupied, a man violates central aspects of the traditional male code. Therefore, therapists need to be continually alert to complications that may result from these faulty coping strategies.

Aside from the standard screening for overt pathology, early-therapy assessment with males should include a gender-role strain assessment. As noted earlier, the gender-role strain model assumes that all males have had to struggle with conflicts inherent in trying to meet the conflicting demands of the male role. Therefore, no male client can be completely issue-free. For example, because boys and men have been taught to be competitive with other males, they may have become overly developed in this area and lost touch with capacities for empathy, compassion, and cooperation. Because they have been encouraged to focus on their work, they have a great likelihood of becoming isolated from others and disconnected from their children. Because they have been taught to suppress their emotions, they may have become affectively deadened or prone to emotional overreactions. Because they have been expected to deny vulnerabilities, they may have neglected self-care and jeopardized their health. Because they have been encouraged to sexualize their intimacy needs, they may have become engrossed in pornography or questionable relationships.

This male-specific initial assessment can be accomplished in a number of ways, as governed by the situation. First, a separate diagnostic session could be used whereby a male client could take any of the masculinity inventories (e.g., Gender Role Conflict Scale, Male Role Norms Inventory, Conformity to Male Role Norms Inventory; O'Neil, Helms, Gable, David, & Wrightman, 1986; Levant & Fischer, 1998; Mahalik et al., 2003). Alternatively, the male client could be asked to respond to specific provocative questions about his views of manhood (see Exhibit 4.1, which includes a set of provocative questions tailored for adolescent males). In these cases, the generated information would not only inform therapy but it would also stimulate a male client to reflect on material he may have never before considered relevant.

In another way, the "ideas on being a man (a guy)" questions could be incorporated into the early phase of therapy, a particularly useful strategy when a male client is highly guarded or intimidated or when there is a need to move slowly in approaching sensitive issues. At times, when there is no

EXHIBIT 4.1
Ten Provocative Thought Questions

For Adult Male Clients
 1. What has been the role of your work in your life?
 2. What sort of relationship have you had (did you have) with your father?
 3. How have you treated your body (and how has it treated you)?
 4. How important have male friends been in your life?
 5. Who have been the most important women in your life? Why?
 6. How much do you think about or focus on the emotions you experience from day to day?
 7. How frustrated are you?
 8. Who is in (has been in) your "male chorus"?
 9. What has fatherhood meant to you? (Or what has it meant to *not* be a father?)
10. Are you now where you expected to be in your life?

For Boy Clients
 1. At this time do you have an idea of what you want to do for life work?
 2. How do you get along with your father? Do you have a relationship with a father-type guy?
 3. Are you happy with the way your body is growing?
 4. Do you have some good buddies?
 5. At this point, what are you thinking about girls (young women)?
 6. What do you do when something (somebody) really ticks you off?
 7. Have any bigger (older) guys ever given you any crap?
 8. What guys do you look up to or admire?
 9. If you have ever had anyone or anything you've been responsible to look after, what was that like?
10. Are you disappointed or frustrated about anything?

pressing agenda, these questions could be used to initiate a therapy session, or they could be introduced when a relevant theme emerges.

MOTIVATIONAL ASSESSMENT OF MALE CLIENTS

Most therapists learn quickly that it is a major error to assume that all clients, especially male clients, are ideal in terms of their objectives for the therapy encounter. Most male clients have far more complicated motivations than straightforwardly seeking therapy when approaching the therapist's office. Of the matter of mixed motivations, Fisch, Weakland, and Segal (1982) long ago noted, "the principal error that therapists make in this situation is to embark on treatment as if the patient is ready to get down to business but is simply having trouble doing so" (p. 40). In their view, this "window shopper" is not the true customer of therapy, and time is wasted if the therapist acts as if the situation were otherwise. In brief, these authors caution that it is vital to determine whether the impetus for change is coming from the client or from forces in his social environment.

Differentiating Motivational Pressures

In the Prochaska and Norcross stages of change model, each client is conceptualized as having some distinct level of motivation to seek (or avoid) psychotherapy. Like the window shopper, the precontemplator is not really motivated to participate in the change processes of therapy. This stage of change conceptualization has been exceptionally helpful in understanding therapy efforts that go awry, and it seems especially useful in appreciating problems with male clients. Many male clients likely to be window shoppers or precontemplators, but their social contexts will differ. That is, some will be reinforced by family and associates in their avoidance of anything like psychotherapy, while others will be encouraged or pressured to seek help. Therefore, the matter is more complicated than simply assessing the male client's stage of change. The therapist's approach needs to be informed by awareness of both the client's motivation and the degree of situational pressure to change (see Figure 4.1).

To illustrate, let us envision male clients at two different stages of change (precontemplation and action) who are also in two separate social contexts. In one situation the male client is heavily pressured to participate actively in therapy (or actively supported in doing so). In the other, he is under no pressure (or is discouraged from participation). Therefore, there are four possible situations: (a) precontemplative man under heavy coercive pressure; (b) action stage man under heavy coercive pressure; (c) action stage man under no pressure; and (d) precontemplative man under no coercive pressure. Each of these situations poses a vastly different challenge and calls for a different approach by the therapist.

The easiest situation for the therapist, of course, would be the action-stage man/change-supporting environment. The man wants to change and has considerable external pressure or support for that course of action. In this situation, the therapist and client can immediately get to work while spending less time dealing with motivational impediments.

The most difficult situation would be the precontemplative-man/non-change-supporting environment situation, in which the male client is disinterested in therapeutic change and is really under no consistent duress to make changes. Usually, no therapist contact would take place in this situation, but such contact might occur if the male client vacillates in his motivational level or if he is occasionally pressured to change. A therapist would have minimal opportunity to operate under these circumstances, unless there was some means to elevate the degree of pressure for therapy participation. In some cases, the therapist can work collaboratively with outsiders (e.g., partners, court systems, bosses) to reinforce their pro-therapy position.

A less common, but occasional situation, is the action-stage-man/non-change-supporting-environment—the circumstance when the greatest

<table>
<tr><td colspan="3">← low ————— client's external pressure to change ————— high →</td></tr>
<tr>
<td rowspan="2" style="writing-mode: vertical">high →</td>
<td>least common</td>
<td>most congruent</td>
</tr>
<tr>
<td>

Action-stage man/low pressure to change

Goals: Pursue client goals beyond first-order (symptom-only) to second-order change (transformative change in masculinity definition); validate motivation for change and build resilience to counter regressive cultural forces.

Tasks: Assist client to build change-enhancing support system outside of therapist s office; build change-enhancing support system within therapy (men's group and collaborative therapy relationship).

Bond: Therapist is supportive facilitator.

</td>
<td>

Action-stage man/high pressure to change

Goals: Encourage and reinforce motivation for change; pursue client goals beyond first-order to second-order change.

Tasks: Pursue more collegial/collaborative therapy process.

Bond: Therapist is empathetic facilitator, acts as change process consultant.

</td>
</tr>
<tr>
<td>most challenging</td>
<td>most common</td>
</tr>
<tr>
<td>

Precontemplative man/low pressure to change

Goals: Increase awareness of masculinity crisis and of contribution of gender-role strain to men's hidden pain; demonstrate connection between men's pain and crisis of masculinity; enhance awareness of new/redefined roles and multiple benefits of role flexibility.

Tasks: Expand definition of therapeutic activities to include primary prevention/proactive outreach, consciousness raising, and psychoeducation.

Bond: Therapist viewed as agent of change and fellow traveler in male gender-role journey; advocate for men (and their loved ones).

</td>
<td>

Precontemplative man/high pressure to change

Goals: Reduce defensiveness and shame through positive psychology's emphasis on client's strengths and assets; maintain therapeutic leverage by reinforcing pressure to change; utilize strategic position as mediator between client and change-demanding forces; develop "win-win" reconciliation through introduction of second-order change and broader male role possibilities.

Tasks: Conduct separate sessions with change-pressuring agents and provide support to client; empathize with male client's stress and frustration, acknowledge his reasons for resistance; introduce motivational, consciousness-raising activities; soft sell/hard sell or confrontational style; offer realistic and more gratifying path out of life impasses.

Bond: Therapist viewed as empathetic, concerned agent of change; supportive; realistic provider of life alternatives.

</td>
</tr>
</table>

Figure 4.1. Therapeutic alliance with the four types of male therapy-seekers.

impetus for change is coming from the male client in an environment that is indifferent or opposed to his changes. In this situation, the therapist would need to direct energies to helping the male client integrate his personal growth with those persons in his life who will be affected. At times, he will need to make changes more slowly, at times he might be connected with a new change-enhancing support group, and at times he might be encouraged to consider a change in his life circumstances.

Finally, as all the literature has noted, the most common situation over the years in work with men has been the precontemplative-man/pressure-to-change-environment. That is, most men in therapy are there because of some degree of coercive pressure. How, then, should the therapist proceed?

Although there once had been a school of thought that resistance should be confronted and challenged, recent evidence has demonstrated that a confrontational style commonly produces premature therapy termination (Miller & Rollnick, 2002). Therefore, a more nuanced approach is now recognized as more likely to succeed. For example, Prochaska and Norcross (2003b) recommended that the therapist adopt a role "like that of a *nurturing parent* joining with the resistant and defensive youngster who is both drawn to and repelled by the prospects of becoming independent" (p. 308). In my own writing (Brooks, 1998), I have recommended a soft-sell approach that recognizes the coercive aspects of the man's situation and acknowledges the reasons for his resistance. When that resistance can be openly discussed and any initial conflict defused, the resulting environment is far more harmonious, and this approach usually allows for the consciousness-raising and motivational enhancement activities—the out-of-office activities detailed in the previous chapter—that may enhance a man's interest in pursuing therapy.

In the Prochaska and Norcross (2003b) stages of change conceptualization, *consciousness raising* refers somewhat narrowly to "increasing information about self and problem" (p. 305). In my own thinking, this stage is much broader and consistent with the ideas of feminist therapists who place emphasis on "institutional structures and social norms as legitimate frames of analysis" (Worell & Johnson, 2001, p. 319). At this stage of a man's therapy journey, consciousness raising involves helping him see how his behavior and his stresses are related to the sometimes unforgiving demands of the traditional male role. His resistance to help seeking is validated as consistent with his ideas about masculinity, yet shown to be ultimately destructive to the well-being of his loved ones and his own welfare.

Recognizing and Surmounting Motivational Hurdles

Given the go-it-alone and self-reliant components in the social construction of masculinity, it is well established that most men resist help seeking and approach therapy with a defensive mind-set (Addis & Mahalik, 2003). Therefore, a primary skill for therapists working with most men would be facility with transforming this defensiveness into a more therapy-embracing attitude. Fortunately, because many men's therapy resistance is somewhat of a superficial posture and their gender-role strain and emotional distress run deep, this transformation can frequently take place.

The first step in this process is for the therapist to recognize the cultural roots of men's resistance, to avoid taking this resistance as a personal affront, and to not automatically classify it as psychic pathology. Men's resistance to "mind shrinking" or "psychobabble" must be honored for what it is in a man's frame of reference—a refusal to give in to "weakness" and a determination to cope in spite of pain. As such, a reticent man can be openly acknowledged for his skepticism and attitude of self-reliance. This posture is consistent with Miller and Rollnick's (2002) motivational interviewing, with its emphasis on "expressing empathy, developing discrepancies between values and current behavior, rolling with resistance, and supporting self-efficacy."

Once the therapist demonstrates contextual understanding of a male client's defensiveness and recognizes the positive features of his overall behavior, the client can then be encouraged to explore any discrepancies between his professed values (being a good man) and his current behavior (self-destruction through going it alone). Rather than arguing for a new attitude, the therapist can roll with the resistance by expressing understanding for the value of not changing. The inherent inconsistencies and self-defeating features of male role prescriptions are identified, and change is acknowledged as unsettling, yet the client is reinforced for his potential to consider alternative life paths. In the common situations in which the male client is experiencing external pressure to participate in therapy, his distaste for that pressure can be acknowledged and validated. Through this process, resistant male clients will often feel validated and understood as well as deprived of an additional stimulus for resistance.

At times, however, it may be helpful to consider an alternative approach, one that could be called a "benevolent confrontation" or, as I have previously referred to it, the "hard sell" (Brooks, 1998). In this approach, the therapist would acknowledge a resistant man for his competence and his capabilities but would then confess authentic sadness about the likely negative outcome of his overly rigid antitherapy stance and his self-destructive lifestyle. When the therapist is genuine in his or her concern, and the connection is convincingly made between the client's behavior and eventual problems, some men recognize the compassion of the therapist and reconsider their resistant position.

Because many men enter therapy expecting the worst, it is commonly helpful to short-circuit negative expectations by validating those parts of their behavior that have been valuable (while placing the more negative parts in gender context). In some ways, this recommendation is quite harmonious with the positive psychology perspective espoused by Kiselica, Englar-Carlson, Horne, and Fischer (2008). In this regard, it is worthwhile to note the Adlerian concept of encouragement as an essential component of early phases of treatment. As described by Sweeny (1998), Adler attempted to empower discouraged clients by focusing on effort rather than outcome, that is, focusing on what was intended rather than what may have gone wrong. To the extent that therapists are skillful in pointing out the best intentions of a male client, a positive therapy alliance is more likely to occur.

Regardless of the forces initially propelling him into therapy, a man is more likely to return if he leaves his first therapy appointment feeling valued. It should be noted, however, that the effort to accentuate the positive does not mean that the therapist should ignore or excuse the negative. Men need to be held accountable for their actions. Also, accentuating the positive does not mean that therapists should limit their therapy goals to validation, since most men have the capacity to rise above their pretherapy level of functioning and transcend previous role limitations.

One additional therapist activity is deserving of mention at this therapy juncture. Although the intention at this stage has been to shift the male client from a therapy skeptic to a therapy proponent, it is wise to remember that external motivation often remains a significant motivational variable. In the common situation in which a male client has been more or less coerced into therapy, a therapist is prudent to maximize the strategic benefits of a *triangulated position* (i.e., the therapist may be the go-between in a struggle between the male client and a therapy-pressuring person or agency). Much like the good cop/bad cop cliché, there is a great deal to be gained from offering empathic support to the troubled client while simultaneously using the leverage accorded from the external pressure. For example, useful questions might be as follows: "What is it that your wife (boss, doctor, judge) is so worked up about?" "What do we need to do to get them off your back?" From this position, the therapist can mediate benevolently between the troubled factions without losing credibility with either. Because this strategic position can be maintained only when the external parties are resolute in their pressure, it is sometimes useful for the therapist to reinforce them in their insistence for change. Also, the advantages of this position will be lost if the therapist is seen as too closely allied with others and is considered to be just another person who does not understand the male client's distress.

These suggestions can be quite helpful in overcoming the motivational hurdles of work with male clients. However, before the actual therapeutic work involved in getting the reluctant male client to make some basic changes in his life begins, the client must first become engaged in the therapeutic process. That is a challenging first step for both the client and the therapist because both are trying to negotiate the boundaries of a foundational working bond, one that instills in the client a sense of trust, professional care, and empathetic concern from the therapist. This is where the therapeutic alliance becomes crucial.

FOSTERING THE THERAPEUTIC ALLIANCE

Recent trends within the psychotherapy and counseling fields bear heavily on the task of engaging men in therapy. One of these trends has been the movement to establish the scientific basis of psychotherapy through outcome research. For many years, psychotherapy outcome research emulated medical model research, with efforts to match discrete types of interventions with specific pathological conditions (Lambert & Barley, 2002). The best representation of this approach may well be the efforts of clinical psychologists within the American Psychological Association (APA) to develop empirically supported treatments (ESTs) for various diagnostic categories, with the ultimate purpose of setting standards of practice (APA Division 12 Task Force on Promotion and Dissemination of Psychological Procedures, 1995). Although this approach has been successful in advocating a number of recommended and, to some extent empirically validated, treatments (http://www.apa.org/divisions/div12/cppi.html; Chambless & Hollon, 1998), it also has generated significant negative reactions to its methods and conclusions.

Primarily, the objection to the EST line of research has been that its efforts toward scientific empiricism have introduced a grossly oversimplified view of the psychotherapy process and neglected the most relevant variables. Lambert and Barley (2002) noted that the developed standards poorly applied the long history of therapy outcome research, which had demonstrated that specific techniques account for only a small portion of the variance in therapy outcome. It is here that we encounter a second significant trend: the emphasis on discovering the basic curative factors inherent in all psychotherapies that cut across various therapeutic approaches. Beginning with the work of Jerome Frank's classic *Persuasion and Healing* (1961) and extending through the common factors theorizing of Sol Garfield (1973, 1994), theorists have made extensive efforts to distill the overwhelming array of therapy schools and orientations into formats comprehensible for therapists who are not exclusively wedded to a single therapeutic modality. Some researchers (Lambert & Ogles, 2004; Norcross, 2005) have conducted extensive reviews of the relevant research and have posited that specific therapy approaches and techniques are far less important in therapy outcome than are a group of factors that cut across all psychotherapies and are related to the therapeutic relationship.

What, then, are these relationship factors, and what do they have to tell us about creatively engaging with reluctant male clients? Perhaps the most central of these relationship factors is that referred to as the *working alliance* (Bordin, 1994) or the *therapeutic alliance* (Lambert & Barley, 2002) or simply *the alliance* (Horvath & Bedi, 2002). Bordin considered this working alliance to consist of three components: agreement on the therapeutic *goals*; consensus about the *tasks*, behaviors, and activities within the therapy sessions; and the *relational bond* between client and therapist. Additional issues related to the maintenance of successful therapeutic relationships are empathy, resistance, congruence, positive regard, and repair of alliance ruptures, self-disclosure, and countertransference. Several of these are briefly reviewed in relation to the special case of working with men who are on the cusp of therapy involvement.

Goals

Finding agreement in therapeutic goals between client and therapist may seem to be a formidable task since so many men view therapy as designed to make them into something they have no desire to be. As noted in chapter 2, the demands of the client role, at least superficially, seem to conflict with the primary tenets of the traditional male role—to be in control, to suppress emotions, to be self-reliant, and to prefer action over introspection. However, when therapists are attuned to this issue, they can correct misconceptions about the goals of therapy and its desired outcomes. Reluctant males can be shown that therapy intends to help them replace false control over their lives with more meaningful, genuine control. Help seeking, therefore, can be framed as a temporary step that is not intended to foster dependency but rather is designed to create greater self-sufficiency in the long term. It also can be shown that improved awareness of one's emotional states does not produce unbridled emotional lability but actually liberates a man from domination by his anger, bitterness, and frustration. Finally, the embarrassment and shame that a man so commonly associates with the vulnerability of help seeking can be tempered by recognition of the normativeness of his distress. That is, as noted by Addis and Mahalik (2003), many men avoid help seeking from the mistaken idea that their problems are unique and help seeking is something no other man does.

Tasks

Bordin's (1994) second component of the therapeutic alliance—agreement on the tasks and procedures of therapy—can also be a substantial obstacle if the therapist is unaware or hostile to male interpersonal styles. In chapter 2, I described the problems that result when therapists are overly demanding of male clients to interact in ways more comfortable for women, and efforts are not made to develop more user-friendly therapy for these male clients. Therefore, to accomplish this component of the therapeutic alliance, therapists must make it clear to male clients that therapy (at least initially) will not require them to interact in ways alien to their interpersonal style and masculine habits. For example, when they first enter the office they will not be expected to "spill their guts," "get in touch with their feelings," reveal deep inner pain, or reexperience childhood trauma. If they are quiet, tentative, or unclear about how to proceed, they will not be labeled as resistant and forcefully challenged to become more cooperative with therapy. This matter is discussed more fully in the subsequent discussion of in-session styles, but for now it is sufficient to emphasize that a therapeutic alliance with a male client is enhanced when his early therapy contacts disconfirm his fear that the therapy tasks are outside his comfort range.

Bond

The third and seemingly broadest and most encompassing component of the therapeutic alliance is that of the relational bond between the therapist and the client. This component focuses most on the quality of the affective relationship, which would include "mutual trust, liking, respect, and caring" (Horvath & Bedi, 2002, p. 41). Among the various components of the therapeutic alliance, the relational bond is perhaps the most crucial for precontemplators, for the therapist is seen in these cases as the *agent of change*. At the same time, the therapist must also appear to be flexible and open to new methods of making the male client aware of the need to make some basic changes in his life. Of all the elements that touch upon initial development of the therapeutic alliance, two are especially critical in this early stage of a male's therapy journey: (a) empathy and positive regard and (b) countertransference.

Empathy and positive regard, central components of Rogerian client-centered therapy, have long been cited as critical to the establishment of successful therapy relationships. Although there has been considerable scientific questioning of the early claims about this concept, Bohart, Elliott, Greenberg, and Watson (2002) noted that "the time is ripe for reexamination and rehabilitation of therapist empathy as a key change process in psychotherapy" (p. 89). Of course, empathy is a critical component in therapy with both genders, but it may have special importance when working with some men. Because many men enter therapy only after a period of resistance, when they finally relent, they do so expecting to be poorly understood and to be criticized for their failings. As a result, a therapist who transmits positive regard will provide welcome relief from the male client's pretherapy anxieties and will allow a male client to feel valued. The therapist who appreciates his client's worldview will have a major advantage in establishing the empathic connection necessary for an effective therapeutic alliance.

Countertransference has long been a central concept in psychotherapy. As originally conceived by Freud, the term was pejorative, implying unrecognized and unhelpful feelings that clients generated in therapists. More recently, however, views of countertransference have shifted from considering it a flaw in the therapist to an inevitable outcome of therapeutic encounters. In reviewing the evolution of this concept, Gelso and Hayes (2002) described the view inherent in interpersonal, relational, and object relations therapy approaches that countertransference is a complement to the patient's style of relating. "According to the complementary conception, the patient exhibits certain 'pulls' on the therapist. . . . The good therapist . . . seeks to understand what the patient is doing to stir up these reactions" (Gelso & Hayes, 2002, p. 269).

In the MASTERY model (Brooks, 2003), I contended that "monitoring of one's emotional reactivity to men" is an essential aspect of successful therapy with them. Regardless of whether one thinks of this process as emotional reactivity or countertransference, there are two significant reasons that it is an especially critical issue in work with male populations. First, a highly controversial claim has emanated from many observers who believe that the past few decades have been characterized by a popular cultural trend of "male bashing." Warren Farrell, a leading proponent of this view, argued that male bashing is "the new sexism" (Farrell, 1986, p. 191). Glicken (2005), concurring with other observers who have noted that male bashing is common not only in the women's movement but also in popular culture from television programs to humorous greeting cards, described this phenomena as "one of those serious problems in America we tend not to take very seriously" (p. 52).

It is not surprising the notion of male bashing is a highly complex one that has generated intense reactions and stormy debates. Whether or not we are witnessing a cultural trend toward reverse sexism, it is clear that the women's movement has generated an atmosphere of enormous impatience with patriarchy and male privilege. There is no reason to believe that this impatience with men as a group would necessarily spill over into hostility toward any individual male client, yet it certainly could contribute to negative emotional reactivity in some cases. Oddly enough, an opposite reactivity could also occur. Given the historical pressure on women to emotionally overfunction and protect the men in their lives (Bepko & Krestan, 1990), some female therapists might experience too much positive reactivity toward a male client.

A second reason for paying special attention to countertransference toward male clients is related to men's therapy avoidance. Because of their extreme aversion to help seeking, many men cope with distress with a variety of dysfunctional behaviors. Louise Silverstein and I have referred to this pattern as "the dark side of masculinity" (Brooks & Silverstein, 1995). Rather than seeking help, many men seek to ease their psychic pain with substance abuse, violence, sexual preoccupation, and flight or emotional withdrawal. As a result, many men enter treatment only after displaying behaviors that make them likely to provoke some degree of distaste in therapists.

Before these types of issues can be addressed in a therapeutic relationship, such a relationship must exist. That is, the male-oriented therapist must be adept at engaging a typically reluctant male client in the therapeutic process. The therapist must convey a genuine empathetic concern over the prospective client's plight and present him- or herself as the much-needed agent of change in their first encounters. With precontemplators, the choice of an engagement strategy can make all the difference in a successful course of therapy, and the therapist can employ a few key strategies, based on the initial assessment of the client.

In the case of Woodrow, presented at the beginning of this chapter, a soft-sell strategy of engagement seemed the best course. The hard sell—exemplified in the dialogue excerpt below—seemed appropriate in the case of Andrew, given this prospective client's rigid position against therapy and his reluctance to admit that he was facing any problems in his life, which so far had witnessed many professional accomplishments.

All indications were that therapy work with Andrew would be difficult at best, and perhaps impossible at worst. His wife, Vivian, had arranged for his first two appointments, each of which he had his assistant cancel because of "pressing issues" at work. A mid-50s vice-president at the largest local bank, Andrew had been pressured by Vivian to either get help for his increasingly frequent outbursts of rage and increased drinking or face divorce proceedings. When he finally appeared for his first appointment, Andrew was obviously less than enthusiastic. After a brief introduction, the following exchange took place.

> *Andrew:* (gazing at my diplomas on the wall): So, just what type of training is it that you have, Doc? I mean, I'm sure they teach some important things in psychology school, but do those things apply everywhere? With all due respect, do you know anything at all about banking? I mean, let's cut to the chase here: I'm all for that Oprah-type chitchatting to help a person get something off his chest, but is that feel-good stuff really going to make any difference in the real world out there?

> *Therapist:* Good question. Have a seat and let's consider the situation.

Over the next 40 minutes, matters improved little, with each inquiry receiving a terse response layered with not-so-subtle contempt for the entire therapeutic enterprise. Near the conclusion of the initial hour, this exchange occurred in response to a question about future therapy plans.

Andrew: Beats me. I can endure this as long as necessary. . . . What's your professional synopsis of the situation? Am I about to go ballistic and start shooting up some shopping mall?

Therapist: (smiling) No, I actually think you are in pretty good control of many parts of your life and can probably continue along the same path for a while. But, in all honesty, I owe you an observation based on my experience with a number of men in a wide range of life situations—from blue collar guys to very successful guys like yourself. Many of the guys I've encountered look pretty good on the surface, but they're much more messed up underneath. Many are unsatisfied with careers, lonely for close relationships, or frustrated about many parts of their lives. Most have a strong need to hide their discomfort and are just as negative as you are about letting anybody behind their wall. Some hold it together for quite a while, but eventually they screw things up, get sick, or even fall over dead. I greatly respect your good sense—you've certainly done very well in many ways. I have no interest in wasting our mutual time in something you have minimal interest in, but I do worry that you are heading down a road with lots of potential problems. I'd hate to see you be one of those fatalities.

Andrew: (silent for several moments) Okay, I appreciate your honesty. Let me think about what you've said.

Despite the apparent trend for increased acceptance of psychotherapy among many men, many more men at some level will be uncomfortable, ambivalent, and defensive when entering a psychotherapy office. As a result, therapists will need to do all they can within that first contact to maximize the potential for therapeutic engagement. This process is facilitated by a male-specific assessment process and through efforts to evaluate and enhance the male client's motivation. Even more crucial, though, is that the first session must generate a deep empathic connection and therapeutic alliance. Those therapists who can monitor any personal reactivity, can recognize the most positive aspects of a male client's behavior, and can convey compassion and sensitivity to his struggles will be those most likely to establish this therapeutic alliance.

When that is accomplished, the therapist and client will be able to more easily negotiate a transition to intensive psychotherapeutic work—specifically, on effective therapeutic outcomes—by focusing on the goals and tasks of therapy now that they share a trustful and empathic bond as fellow travelers in the male-role journey.

5

MALE-FRIENDLY PSYCHOTHERAPY FOR BOYS AND MEN

In the previous chapter, considerable attention was given to therapist stances, behaviors, and strategic processes that are likely to help an ambivalent male client commit himself to the psychotherapy endeavor. The development of a therapeutic alliance was described as a key factor in whether the male client crosses the threshold of the therapist's office and settles assuredly (and expectantly) into the client's chair. Once this occurs, the ball moves into the therapist's court—the question now is, what therapeutic models and techniques are at the therapist's disposal to allow the *action stage* client to perpetuate therapeutic engagement with therapeutic change? This chapter addresses that question with an array of user-friendly therapies for boys and men.

ADAPTING ESTABLISHED THERAPY APPROACHES

Men's low rate of therapy utilization is not a function of a lack of psychotherapy alternatives. Whereas the early years of this profession were dominated by psychoanalytic and psychodynamic approaches, the past several decades have witnessed a proliferation of therapies. In fact, Prochaska and Norcross (2003a) noted that there now are more than 400 therapy systems and contended that this "hyperinflation of brand-name therapies has produced narcissistic fatigue" (p. 482). Naturally, no effort can be made here to examine each of the therapies, and it is only realistic to focus on the therapy orientations that surveys have found to be the most commonly adopted: psychodynamic, cognitive, interpersonal, and behavioral (Bechtoldt, Norcross, Wyckoff, Pokrywa, & Campbell, 2001). In particular, this section first focuses on recent efforts to adapt each of these approaches to male client populations. Next, attention is given to the orientation that has become the most popular— eclectic/integrative—and to how this orientation would be manifested in work with boys and men.

Male-Friendly Psychodynamic and Object Relations Approaches

As a gay man, Chris had periodically been in some form of psychotherapy since his early teen years. The only child of wealthy parents, Chris had struggled with issues of his sexual orientation and difficulties coping with parental rejection. He had eventually established a somewhat uneasy rapprochement with them, although they continued to threaten him with disinheritance whenever they were unhappy with one of his relationship partners.

In therapy, Chris had an outspoken aversion to exploring his childhood experiences and anything that "smacked of analytic mind f—ing." Having previously spent 4 years with an analyst who considered homosexuality a sexual perversion, Chris considered any type of "depth therapy" to be dangerous to his health. He insisted on dealing with current life issues and pursuing only gay-affirmative therapy. Because his current therapist was a major referral source within the lesbian, gay, bisexual, and transgender (LGBT) community, this trepidation was appreciated and respected.

In the 4th month of therapy, however, the therapeutic situation changed dramatically. Chris suddenly plummeted into a deep depression and fantasized about various methods to end his life. In therapy, Chris and the therapist identified possible precipitants to this crisis as a seemingly innocuous relationship breakup and a random mention of a call-up of the therapist into military active duty. In spite of his reluctance, Chris recognized that it made no sense to continue to avoid exploring childhood roots to his extreme reaction to recent life events. Over the next several months, Chris described several childhood traumas, most vividly illustrated by a time at age 4 when his father opted to euthanize Daisy, the family cocker spaniel. When discovering the event for which he had been completely unprepared, Chris became hysterically tearful and inconsolable. After an hour of scolding for his "sissy girl" reaction, Chris was sent to his room to stay until he could "start acting like a young man." In describing this event, Chris became tearful and slid into a painful description of a series of "brutal" interactions with his father and the complete obliviousness of his "total narcissistic bitch" mother. He spent the next several sessions describing his successful efforts to erect a completely impervious wall against any emotional vulnerabilities and dangers of ever again being harmed by the rejection of his needs.

For several reasons, the psychoanalytic or psychodynamic therapies would seem to be least likely to appeal to most men. First, the negative media portrayals of psychotherapy typically rely on stereotypical Freudian therapists who are presented as overly intellectual, aloof, and judgmental. Also, the previously noted mismatch between male socialization and the demands of psychotherapy seems to be more problematic in this form of therapy that is generally considered to demand the most from clients. In fact, some men's studies writers (Levant, 2001b; Shay, 1996) have argued that most men have so much difficulty with emotional expressiveness, introspection, and relatively passive therapists that alternative formats (e.g., psychoeducational) be substituted. Third, there has been some perception that the psychoanalytic developmental viewpoint clashes with the gender-role strain perspective of many men's studies advocates. Rabinowitz and Cochran (2002) spoke to this matter, noting the apparent conflict between a view that focuses mainly on early childhood development and intrapsychic matters and one that emphasizes the here-and-now of everyday life. They contended, however, that "merging of these two traditions offers the optimal means by which to more fully understand men's lives" (p. 34).

In their writings, Rabinowitz and Cochran reviewed the history of psychoanalytic and object relation formulations with particular reference to views of young boys' psychic development. They noted the work of Chodorow (1978), who argued that young boys face the gender-specific developmental challenge of disidentification with mothers to seek substitutive connection with a marginally available father. Rabinowitz and Cochran (2002) found a necessary "common ground" to integrate psychoanalytic and object relations perspectives with gender-role strain formulations of masculinity. In their research on this common ground, they found several significant convergences that can be briefly described.

First, both developmental and gender-role strain perspectives recognize that very early in their lives, boys are expected to repress their longing for emotional comforting and disavow their basic human needs for love and nurturance. As a result, a process is set in motion, and later reinforced, for males to have lifelong conflicts over connection and intimacy. Second, both perspectives agree that male development is characterized by prohibitions against experiencing the grief and sadness necessary to cope with life's losses: "When this normal process of grieving is truncated and thrown off course, anger, shame, and control-oriented defenses arise as a means of self-protection. . . . Many men develop powerful and ultimately problematic defenses around the complete and healthy resolution of what is in fact a normative human experience: the experience of loss and sadness that arises from the making and breaking of human bonds" (Rabinowitz & Cochran, 2002, p. 47).

Rabinowitz and Cochran (2002) also contended that both psychoanalytic and gender-role strain perspectives are consistent with the idea that developmental and cultural pressures contribute to the development of "problematic masculine-specific self-structures" (p. 48). They find that over the course of their lives, males are compelled to develop a façade of invulnerability and emotional imperturbability that grossly interferes with their capacity to engage with others, cope with negative emotions, and acknowledge sadness or depression.

Rabinowitz and Cochran (2002) concluded that male development and cultural pressures intersect in terms of a balance between *being* and *doing*. "Cultural values, as imparted through the early caretaking environment, tend to differentiate these two human capacities into masculine and feminine elements and to value one over the other in boys (doing) and girls (being)" (Rabinowitz & Cochran, 2002, p. 49). Consistent with the observations of many others about men's tendencies toward externalizing ego defenses (Levit, 1991; Nolen-Hoeksema, 1990), this doing emphasis contributes to many of the problematic dark-side behaviors (e.g., substance abuse, violence, sexual compulsivity, risk-taking) many men engage in to escape painful emotional states.

In terms of integrating psychoanalytic perspectives with men's studies, no one has contributed more than William Pollack (1990, 1995, 1998, 2005). Pollack acknowledged the contributions of Chodorow (1978) and Greenson (1968), who posited that young boys must hurdle an additional developmental stage characterized by separation or disidentification. However, rather than viewing this extra stage as part of a process of healthy development, Pollack considered it to be far more negative and deeply wounding of young men's character development and emotional growth. He noted that "this premature push for separation in boys is not a healthy form of self-differentiation but, rather, a traumatic disruption of their early holding environment. . . . We are seeing a developmental basis for a normative male-gender-linked trauma (or impingement)— a lifecycle loss in boys that may show itself later in adulthood in symptomatic behavior and characterological disturbance" (Pollack, 2005, p. 205).

In essence, Pollack (2005) viewed this process as causing males to develop an external presentation of exaggerated self-sufficiency and emotional mastery that he considers to be "a mask of masculinity" or "defensive autonomy" (p. 205). As a result of their emotional abandonment, males are likely to have highly disrupted relationship capacities and commonly seek "transitional object" or "self-object" (p. 205) relationships with women who are expected to function as mother substitutes.

As yet, the theoretical formulations of Chodorow and Pollack about young men's development have not received strong empirical support, and, in fact, some (Kiselica & O'Brien, 2001; Nichols & Good, 2004) believe this theorizing contributes to an unfair characterization of young men as developmentally deficient. However, until this matter is empirically resolved, it seems reasonable to give some weight to these issues as quite relevant for work with many male clients. As such, the work of Rabinowitz and Cochran and that of Pollack has contributed important theoretical underpinnings for masculinity-based psychodynamic therapies. What, then, are the practical therapeutic implications for those wishing to adapt their therapeutic approach?

First, and most obviously, it is apparent that some men's studies writers believe that psychoanalytic and psychodynamic therapies are both possible and desirable for many men. Although no one seems to argue that analytic therapies are always the treatment of choice for men, Rabinowitz and Cochran (2002) stated that "we make the assumption that all men have psychological depth, but for many this terrain has been obscured by years of neglect and active avoidance inspired by our culture" (p. 4).

In terms of therapeutic modifications, suggestions have been made in terms of conceptualizations of the issues and practices of the therapist. On the conceptualizing level, all of the aforementioned authors encourage therapists to pay special attention to certain unique psychic damages experienced by boys during their normative developmental processes. Pollack's (2005) description of the shattering of the boy's holding environment is similar to the description Rabinowitz and Cochran (2002) provided for the wounding experiences common to men's lives. Because these early-life traumatic experiences are considered to produce defensive coping postures and to set the stage for lifelong issues with trust and intimate relationships, their roots must be uncovered for true therapeutic progress. Recognition of this level of developmental disruption inspired Pollack to emphasize the need for symbolic recreation of that early holding environment. Rabinowitz and Cochran (2002) conceptualized the key issue in deepening of psychotherapy as that of the *portal*, which they described as "the constellation of images, words, thematic elements, emotional associations, and bodily sensations" (p. 26) that reflects a man's inner psychic life.

In this type of therapeutic work with men, special prominence is given to the issues of loss and grief. Consonant with Robert Bly's belief that "grief is the pathway to a man's soul" (Bly, 1990), Rabinowtiz and Cochran (2002) called for special attention to the damage that results from prohibitions against men truly mourning losses and fully experiencing grief. Pollack (2005) noted that when therapists listen empathically to men, they will discover that "unearthed beneath layers of repression and anger, a deep sadness often comes forward, a delayed mourning for a tragic loss" (p. 204). Silverberg (1986) noted that a man's loss of emotional connection with his mother and loss of close relationship with his father are quite significant, yet equally devastating is "the loss of what is probably the most precious, dynamic component of his personality, the feminine soul with all its affective richness forever buried with the premature separation from his mother" (p. 61).

In addition to their ideas for incorporating male-specific conceptualizations into theorizing about client issues, Pollack and Rabinowitz and Cochran have suggested subtle shifts in the manner therapy is conducted. First, when therapists recognize the wounding and trauma inherent in male development, empathy is more easily transmitted and problematic countertransference reactions are lessened. What previously may have been seen as narcissism or resistance can now be recognized as an understandable fear of vulnerability, a sense of shame, or a manifestation of "defensive autonomy." A particular source of countertransference is that of the way in which a male client's issues may awaken similar issues in the life of the therapist. "A therapist must be willing to revisit his or her own developmental crises[:] . . . separation from one's mother, the relationship with one's father, creation of a false self, counterphobic risk-taking, rejection" (Rabinowitz & Cochran, 2002, p. 101).

Also, therapists can alter their initial expectations of male clients and alter their own allegiance to therapeutic inactivity and neutrality. In my own writing (Brooks, 1998), I have suggested that it is unrealistic to expect unsophisticated or guarded male clients to take charge of the first therapy sessions and insightfully lay out their fears and conflicts. As a result, therapists may need to take a more active part in the initial therapy sessions to avoid increasing a man's discomfort and solidifying his defenses. This breaking from a therapeutic stance of passivity and neutrality is consistent with observations of others. For example, Rabinowitz and Cochran commented, "In the early sessions, the therapist must act in way that lets the male client know he is welcomed and appreciated" (p. 99). Pollack (2005) noted that "therapists must reach out to the men in their care and without forcing them to admit their frailties" (p. 214).

Finally, there appears to be a solid consensus that therapists should anticipate depth therapy with men to be an erratic and somewhat discontinuous process. Winnicott (1974) wrote about the need to go slowly and avoid disrupting a client's motivation by prematurely forcing recognition of external pressures. Pollack has referenced Winnicott's ideas, cited Modell's concept of "the illusion of self-sufficiency" (Modell, 1976) and contended that therapists should not prematurely push male clients to give up their denial and belief that "both the therapy and the therapist are unimportant to him" (Pollack, 2005, p. 210).

Many observers have echoed the theme that any form of therapy reliant upon intensely intimate relationships between a male client and a therapist will inevitably stir anxieties rooted in early attachment and abandonment conflicts, frequently producing emotional or actual flight reactions (Brooks,

1998; Cochran & Rabinowitz, 2002; Osherson & Krugman, 1990; Scher, 1990). Hence, therapists must be exceptionally patient with this fits-and-starts type of therapy, realizing that even when therapy starts positively, it will not always result in the preferred smooth and linear unfolding of a long-term therapeutic journey. Sometimes, these predictable disruptions can be anticipated and processed; at other times, however, they come unexpectedly. In many of these cases, therapists will do well to recognize the process as, at least partially, a product of men's deep-seated relational conflicts and faulty coping strategies. With this perspective in mind, a therapist can better understand a male client's retreat from therapeutic connection and can avoid reactivity. In cases of actual termination, the man's withdrawal can be framed in a positive light, and an invitation can be offered to return at a future time.

Male-Friendly Cognitive Therapy and Cognitive Behavior Therapy

Clint was a 17-year-old high school junior referred to the therapy office by his family physician. An A student and all-district basketball player, he had begun complaining of migraine headaches and inability to sleep more than a few hours per night. When seen, he acknowledged a high degree of stress following his parents' divorce the previous year. Clint had always received the bulk of his father's attention, while a younger sister had been largely ignored. The physician father attended all of Clint's games and expected him to make the all-state team yet maintain perfect grades to make it possible to enter a top-tier medical school.

> Clint: This has probably been the worst week of all. I blew a lay-up in the last game, then got an 84 on my biology mid-term. If I drop to a B+ in biology, my life is totally screwed!

> Therapist: Could you help me understand how your thinking goes on this?

> Clint: Simple—No basketball scholarship, no free ride on tuition. That won't even matter if I don't ace biology. It's pretty obvious.

> Therapist: I think I see your point. I'm not sure I follow the whole sequence, though. Do you mean that your whole life will be ruined if you don't make a top med school? Can we look at what type of basic beliefs about life you're working with here?

> Clint: It's plain as day to me: A guy who has hopes to amount to anything or have anything had better find some way to stand out—to say nothing about not being a complete loser in the dating department: Hot girls really want to be with zeros, right?

Over the next several sessions the therapist and Clint examine his unrealistic cognitive schema regarding competition, success, and self-worth. In this process, he begins to consider how his over-incorporation of some traditional ideas of masculinity and exaggerated beliefs about achievement are tied to his fears and anxieties.

If psychoanalysis seems to be the least likely therapy approach to be embraced by men, then the cognitive approaches may be those most likely to appeal to men. Even the very earliest writers on difficulties of men in therapy noted that therapies that focused too much on affect and discussion of feelings would be resisted (Skovholt, 1978; Toomer, 1978). In the early years of searching for male-friendly therapy approaches, the focus was commonly placed on psychoeducation and consciousness raising about masculinity and male roles, but little attention was given to the benefits of specific therapy orientations. Davis and Padesky (1989) began to look at differential applicability of cognitive therapy for women, but suggestions of specific applications for men did not appear until Mooney (1998) and (2005a). As we review this earlier work and consider what we know about masculinity, it seems that this application is both beneficial and long overdue.

There are multiple reasons that the match between male clients and cognitive therapy would be especially productive. First, cognitive therapy works well with a wide variety of populations, as it is consistently listed among the most validated of all the empirically supported treatments (Chambless & Hollon, 1998). Aside from its broad utility, however, this approach has many advantages for work with men. Perhaps the most basic advantages of cognitive therapy for men are rooted in what it is not about (or does not seem to be about at an overt level). That is, it is not about immediate exploration of intense feeling states. It is not about searching for repressed childhood traumas. It is not about pursuing seemingly ambiguous or amorphous or long-term goals. Although many men would be quite comfortable in therapies with those features, those men would have to be among the relative minority of men who have surmounted the restrictive tenets of the traditional male role and male socialization.

In describing the benefits of the cognitive approach, Mahalik (2005a) stated that "although emotions are a central part of the work that goes on in cognitive therapy, its focus on the importance of thoughts is likely to feel more congruent for men who conform to traditional gender roles regarding emotional expression" (p. 217). Mahalik's assertion is backed by the research of Wisch, Mahalik, Hayes, and Nutt (1995), which found that highly traditional men preferred a cognition-focused counseling approach.

Mooney (1998) characterized cognitive therapy as a "nonblaming" approach, suggesting that it would be welcomed by male clients experiencing shame regarding their need for therapy. Levant (1997) indicated that many of his male clients greatly valued an "action" orientation to therapy—that is, one conducive to concrete tasks and homework assignments.

One major advantage of the cognitive approach is illustrated in this book's opening vignette, when the members of a men's group were asked to identify their ideas about what manhood is about (i.e., "What does it mean to be a man?"). When male clients are asked to think about cultural pressures on men, the focus shifts off them individually and onto broader, culture-wide issues. This shift in problem attribution is especially beneficial for men who have taken on too much responsibility for their difficulties—if such difficulties do not manifest themselves as any of the Big Three psychopathologies (see Introduction, this volume) common among men—and this often leads to enthusiastic discussion of issues previously unrecognized. Once cultural mandates are brought into the open, it is an easy step to explore how each male client has integrated cultural shoulds and musts into his own cognitive schema and masculinity-based self-talk.

Another advantage of cognitive therapy is the "rapidity-of-effect" feature noted by Seligman (2006): "Changing thoughts can be relatively rapid. Experiencing positive gains early in treatment increases people's motivation and optimism" (p. 274). Because many male clients expect fairly rapid and tangible results from therapy, this aspect of cognitive therapy is additionally valuable.

Several men's studies writers have expressed concern that many men avoid therapy because it is too shaming of men and that efforts are needed to develop a "positive psychology perspective" for this work (Kiselica, Englar-Carlson, Horne, & Fisher, 2008). An approach that objectively calls for evocation of masculinity role mandates and then critically examines their utility is one that is inherently nonpejorative. For example, the common injunction that "real men are tough" can be explored in terms of times and locations when that expectation is useful and socially sanctioned as well as times when it is harmful and vilified (as well as times when both expectations coexist). The corollary self-talk—"I must always be seen as tough by others"—can be similarly critiqued.

It should be noted that although the exploration of gender-based role mandates can be done in a nonblaming and positive fashion (i.e., acknowledging that many aspects of the traditional male role have always had some beneficial aspects), most of the rigidly adopted beliefs have had negative consequences for men. An abundance of research on gender-role conflict (O'Neil, 2008) and gender-role stress (Eisler, 1995) has discovered an extensive range of negative interpersonal consequences from strict adherence to these role mandates. Thus, a major advantage of the cognitive approach is that exploration of a male's masculinity-based cognitive schema will highlight the negative outcomes as well as the inherent contradictions among the mandates (as noted by Pleck's [1995] description of the gender-role strain model).

How, then, does one proceed to conduct gender-informed cognitive therapy with males? It is not surprising that the first step would be to work with the client to discover his basic cognitive schema and the self-talk that it produces. In adapting this approach to males, the objective would be to uncover masculinity-related cognitive distortions—that is, harmful distortions rooted in traditional masculine ideology and men's gender-role strain. In this regard, Mahalik (2005a) identified "nine injunctions of traditional masculinity" and the gender-related cognitive distortions they produce: winning, emotional control, risk taking, violence, playboy-ism, self-reliance, primacy of work, disdain of homosexuals, and physical toughness. Familiarity with the male gender role (as described in chapter 1 of this volume) enables a therapist to see how these distortions can be generated. For example, the "winning" injunction is likely to generate distorted self-talk such as "I must be the best at everything"; "Whenever I screw up I feel like a complete sissified weenie"; "Only the most successful guys get the best babes." (Obviously, many of these have considerable overlap.)

In terms of therapeutic process, Mahalik (2005a) suggested the following sequence: (a) disconfirming of clients' cognitive distortions by exploring past experiences; (b) pointing out inconsistent and illogical aspects of current cognitive distortions; and (c) creating personal experiments to test the accuracy of cognitive distortions. Mooney (1998) recommended a similar process of first increasing awareness of "awfulizing" and "catastrophizing" internal sentences and then engaging in behaviors that disconfirm those beliefs. Similar to Mahalik's ideas about personal experiments is Moony's recommending the "shame-attacking exercises" described by Ellis (1988).

Male-Friendly Behavioral Therapy

The first few minutes of the appointment with Andre had been strained and awkward. Encouraged by his boss to seek help with his declining work performance, Andre had agreed to try counseling but was not particularly enthusiastic. The therapist noted a resistance to talking too extensively about his background and a need to come up some practical intervention. He proposed that two to three sessions be spent in a behavioral analysis of the sequences involved in Andre's work habits and work avoidance. In this process, it quickly became apparent that whenever he encountered unpleasant work tasks, Andre would leave the project and log on to the Internet for extended periods before belatedly returning to his work responsibilities. The therapist suggested a few simple alterations, including a contract whereby Andre would never log on to the Internet until he had completed a given unit of work (at which time he would log on for a carefully monitored 10-minute period).

The simple operant principle of shifting behavior and reinforcement was remarkably effective and inspired Andre to question the therapist about broader issues in his life. Several weeks later, Andre confessed that much of his Internet browsing had been on pornography sites. Realizing the need to overcome what appeared to be a growing compulsion, Andre welcomed the therapist's help with other behavioral techniques, such as behavior monitoring and stimulus control interventions.

Much like cognitive therapy, behavior therapy can be easily seen as an ideal therapy format for men. Oddly enough, however, in spite of the enormous body of literature regarding behavioral methods, most all writing is inattentive to gender differences, and there has yet to be a thorough analysis of the general advantages of this therapy variant with male populations. For example, even the most recent handbooks of behavior therapy (Ammerman & Hersen, 1993; Watson & Gresham, 1998) are completely devoid of any chapters discussing differential application or benefits of interventions for males and females.

In spite of this lack of attention to gender-specificity, there seem to be at least three compelling reasons for consideration of behavioral approaches with men: harmony with men's help-seeking preferences and interpersonal style, demonstrated utility of behavioral interventions for problems common in men, and the ease of integration of behavioral methods into an eclectic treatment plan.

Stylistic Issues

First, behavior therapy is the single approach least likely to tap men's aversions to psychotherapy and the most likely to suit most men's problem-solving style. As many writers have noted (Brooks, 1998; Mahalik, 2005a; Scher, 1990), many men dislike the basic idea of therapy because of the belief that they must maintain control of their environments and the concomitant fear that therapy would involve ceding control to another. Behavior therapies, with their collaborative goal-setting emphasis, are the least likely to stir those fears. Obviously, techniques referred to as *behavioral self-control* and *contingency management* would be attractive to men seeking mastery over their environments.

Also, behavior therapies are practical and problem focused, clearly putting the male client's self-identified issues at the forefront of treatment. That is, the skill enhancement and performance issues most likely to be presented by men can be addressed immediately with a range of distinct behavioral techniques. No male client needs to leave an initial therapy session dissatisfied that his presenting problem was ignored or considered to be only a surface representation of a repressed deeper conflict.

To the extent that a man had dreaded his therapy appointment and viewed it as shameful and representative of a stigmatized mental illness, he will be relieved by the primary emphasis this approach places on specific behaviors and skills building. This emphasis parallels the oft-noted recommendations given to nascent group therapists regarding effective feedback (Leszcz, 1992). Individuals are far more receptive to input from others when the focus is placed on the person's behavior and not on character or personal worth (i.e., "It is not you I am criticizing; it is this specific behavior."). With this orientation, a defensive male client can see quickly that the therapist has no interest in attacking or demeaning him. This can be especially true when another recommendation regarding effective feedback is followed—that is, packaging a critical comment with a positive one—and problematic behavior is considered in context of the male client's coexisting positive behaviors.

Because behavior therapies are primarily not talk therapies, they place much less demand on the emotional awareness and verbal expressiveness of the client. This characteristic makes them more congruent with male clients and alexithymia issues noted by Levant (2003) or the concrete communication styles noted by Tannen (1990). Only a portion of male clients have ready access to their inner lives, but all are able to identify the areas where their behaviors are too extreme or too deficient.

Behavior therapy, unlike most all other orientations, can be as hands-on, instrumental, and technically focused as necessary for any man who criticizes psychotherapy as too nebulous, abstract, or mystical. Definitive goals can be developed and progress can be readily demonstrated. Clients can be assigned specific tasks, can be asked to keep precise records, and can be shown objective evidence of their progress. At times, instrumentation can be incorporated through a variety of biofeedback or interactive technologies. The well-documented preference of most men for action over rumination (Cochran & Rabinowitz, 2000; Nolen-Hoeksema, 1990) is well served in this therapeutic orientation.

Applicability to Male Problems

Behavior therapy has been shown to be effective with a wide range of problems presented by women, men, children, and couples, with the majority of all therapy outcome studies having behavioral elements (Kazdin, 1994; Orlinsky, Ronnestad, & Willutzki, 2004). In fact, the literature is so vast that it could not possibly be reviewed in this section. However, it is possible to highlight the established utility of many behavioral methods with a variety of problems common to men. These interventions can be categorized in four interrelated areas: management of harmful behaviors, management of harmful emotions, improving men's physical functioning, and building or enhancing of interpersonal skills.

First, behavioral methods have always been integral components of programs targeting men's violence/anger management, substance abuse, and sexual compulsivity (Laws & Marshall, 2003; McCrady & Morgenstern, 1993; Novaco, 1995). Although these programs typically broaden into cognitive–behavioral techniques, basic behavior therapy methods are the bedrock of the programs. Aversive conditioning and covert sensitization have a long, if somewhat controversial, history for treatment of these impulse control problems (Koocher, 1976). Aside from this "punishment" paradigm, desensitization/relaxation interventions are common to interrupt dysfunctional buildup of destructive emotions that might, for example, lead to temper problems, substance abuse episodes, or sexual acting out (Borkovec, Crnic, & Costello, 1993). Self-control and contingency management strategies can also be used to help male clients limit exposure to situations likely to overcome their coping abilities (Thorpe & Olson, 1997). Finally, behavioral activation therapy, an intervention using activity scheduling and operant reinforcement, has been demonstrated to be highly effective with both depression (Dimidjian, Martell, & Addis, 2008) and posttraumatic stress disorder in men (Jakupcak et al., 2006).

Behavior therapy has a clearly established role in improving many aspects of men's physical functioning. Sports psychologists help males improve athletic performance through a variety of methods, including progressive relaxation, desensitization, guided imagery, biofeedback, and self-regulation (Niednagel, 1997; Robertson & Newton, 2001). Similar interventions have been used in health psychology to help ameliorate a variety of psychophysiological disorders (Brannon & Feist, 2000). Among the oldest applications of behavioral interventions for men have been in the area of sex therapy (Kaplan, 1974: Masters & Johnson, 1970) in which sensate focus and counterconditioning of anxiety exercises are among the many processes designed to help men relieve performance pressures in their approach to sexual activity.

Modeling and operant reinforcement techniques, typically used in programs designed to build interpersonal skill repertoires, can be especially useful for skill deficiencies inherent in male socialization. For example, Levant (2003) described an emotional skills program for treatment of normative male alexithymia. Because many men (especially men with a history of problems from temper dyscontrol) attempt to cope with their anger through repression or avoidance, assertiveness training can provide surprisingly useful skills to teach men more effective methods to manage interpersonal dissatisfactions. Related to this, John Gottman's well-validated interventions for marital couples (Gottman, 1994; Gottman, Ryan, Carrere, & Erly, 2002) include special behavioral methods to combat men's higher levels of "diffuse physiological arousal" through "softened start-up" and "soothing" activities (Gottman, 1994, p. 432).

Integration With Other Approaches

Although behavior therapy first appeared as a maverick approach challenging the theoretical assumptions and practices of most other therapy orientations, it has more recently become one of most likely to be integrated with others (Norcross & Goldfried, 2005). Prochaska and Norcross (2003a) observed that "certainly there is no unifying theory behind what is called behavior therapy . . . there are merely a series of techniques and a unifying commitment to determine which approaches work best with which types of problems" (p. 326). Although many behaviorists would contest the claim that behavior therapy is relatively atheoretical, it is obvious that many of its proven techniques can be used by therapists of many orientations. This adaptability characteristic can be particularly appealing for therapy with men, because it allows for incorporation of one or more behavioral techniques into the initial phase of an overall treatment plan. When this intervention produces improvement in presenting symptoms, the therapeutic enterprise will often be more fully embraced by a formerly reluctant male client.

Before leaving this section, an important caveat should be mentioned regarding application of behavioral techniques with men experiencing situational distress. When a male client's distress is considered within the context of the gender-role strain paradigm, his presenting symptom can be seen as part of a larger complex of attitudes, values, and behaviors that ought to receive attention. That is, emotional pain can be reduced and performance can be enhanced, but the question remains: To what end? Kantrowitz and Ballou (1992) raised this concern as a feminist issue when behavioral methods are applied to subjugate women to the normative standards of the dominant social group. In a related way, the argument is made that the presenting symptom of a male client also needs to be seen within the larger context of the restrictive male code that itself needs to be examined. Symptom relief may be an initial step for therapeutic engagement, but the next step usually needs to be consciousness raising regarding gender-role strain in the male client's life.

Male-Friendly Interpersonal Psychotherapy

As a dean in the economics department of a large state university, Louis had encountered mixed success in his ability to manage his staff and faculty. Insistent and demanding, he believed that clear expectations and firm discipline were required for departmental leadership. After repeated faculty defections and a marginal annual performance review, however, he became concerned enough to seek a therapy referral from a friend in the psychology department.

In therapy, Louis displayed the aggressive and somewhat domineering style typical of all of his interactions. At the beginning of his third session, he presented the therapist with a list of "My Unresolved Issues" and the clear expectation that the therapist provide him with a timeline for their resolution. Expecting a battle royal over this challenge, Louis was stunned by the therapist's calm and compassionate response. Instead of reacting defensively or apologetically, the therapist acknowledged the justification for Louis's impatience but also suggested an exploration of the advantages and disadvantages of his approach to the matter. With this interaction as a springboard, Louis and his therapist spent the next several months reviewing Louis's relationship history and experimenting with alternative relationship patterns and styles.

As noted in the opening of this chapter, many schools of psychotherapy have emerged over the past several decades, with many interrelated and only partially distinct from one another. Interpersonal therapy is being given special attention here because of the apparent upsurge in its popularity (Bechtoldt et al., 2001) and because of its special benefits in addressing relationship disruptions in males (Mahalik, 2005b).

Developed in the 1970s and 1980s by Klerman and colleagues (Klerman, Weissman, Rounsaville, & Chevron, 1984), interpersonal psychotherapy (IPT) has been an outgrowth of the interpersonal psychiatry of Harry Stack Sullivan (1953) and Adolph Meyer (1957). The IPT approach combines the concepts of attachment theory (Bowlby, 1969) and the object relations approach noted earlier with a cognitive–behavioral emphasis on reinforcing interpersonal patterns in the here-and-now. As described by Halgin and Whitbourne (1993), the current life relational problem has roots in childhood failures to acquire sufficient emotional nurturance and the associated behavioral skills, thereby producing poor-quality relationships and resulting in despair, loneliness, and depression. Once this state of deprivation has been established, it is compounded by a generalized lack of adequate social skills and generalized overreactions to emotional rejection. In essence, a vicious circle is created, whereby the individual's emotional distress and isolation are both the cause and the result of poor interpersonal strategies.

This description of IPT is grossly oversimplified, of course, yet it is obvious how the model coincides with the previously articulated developmental trajectory so common for young boys. As noted earlier, Pollack (2005) spoke of the disruption of the holding environment for young boys, and Gilbert and Scher (1999) commented on how boys, as opposed to girls, are coerced to emotionally disconnect from others to project an image of exaggerated self-sufficiency. The damage from this process is more than merely theoretical, as a large body of empirical evidence has demonstrated that men, in general, are reported to be more hostile, detached, cold, distant, mistrusting, and aloof than women (Tracey & Schneider, 1995). This complex of interpersonal stances has been shown by Mahalik (2000) to be related to masculine gender-role conflict.

That is, men who adopt a more traditional male role are more likely to have relationships characterized by those qualities and to emphasize dominance and control over cooperation and mutuality.

The primary theory of therapeutic processes in IPT seems quite adaptable to the special challenges of work with therapy-reticent males. The approach does not demand that the client engage in a lengthy and demanding effort to uncover long-buried childhood experiences and overcome deeply ingrained defenses to slowly achieve emotional insight. Instead, the IPT approach is "a short-term, present-oriented psychotherapy focused mainly on the patient's current interpersonal relations and life situations" (Prochaska & Norcross, 2007).

IPT, originally developed to treat depression, is organized around efforts to resolve interpersonal difficulties that result from four types of problems: loss and grief, role disputes, role transitions, and interpersonal deficits (Klerman et al., 1984). None of these problems are exclusive to men, but they have enormous saliency for men today. Loss and grief problems have been described as highly relevant problems for men as a product of their harsh early-life socialization (Bergman, 1995; Cochran, 2001) and disconnection with fathers (Osherson, 1986). Problems from role disputes and role transitions are integral parts of the literature of the new psychology of men (Levant & Pollack, 1995). Interpersonal deficits, as theorized in this model, refer to lifelong difficulties in establishing and maintaining relationships characterized by both collaboration and intimacy. As has been thoroughly discussed already, this issue is especially relevant for most men whose relational lives are characterized more by surface-level collaboration than by intimacy.

To date, the clearest description of the application of interpersonal therapy to men has been provided by Mahalik (2001, 2005b). In his explication of the unique benefits of IPT for men, Mahalik focused primarily on the interpersonal deficits created by rigid socialization into the traditional male role. He noted that interpersonal theorists (Kieser, 1983; Leary, 1957) have considered maladjusted behavior to be a reflection of recurrent interpersonal behaviors that are both inflexible and self-defeating. The core of IPT is the conceptualization of the "interpersonal circle," which conceptualizes human motivation as organized around two axes: the need for control (power and dominance) and the need for affiliation (love and friendliness). To grossly simplify, each person's interpersonal style can be charted on this interpersonal circle—that is, characterized by the preference for a particular combination of the two variables and a relative position in terms of intensity of that commitment (see Keiser, 1983, p. 189, for a graphic illustration of the interpersonal circle).

A thorough description of the interpersonal circle is not possible here, but the implications for therapy with men are fairly straightforward. Mahalik

(2005b) observed that masculine socialization radically restricts men's flexibility in interpersonal relationships and predisposes them to interact far more frequently in dominant and hostile ways (as opposed to submissive and friendly ways). Further, "one is likely to observe the male client withdrawing from connection to others and neglecting or repressing his emotional self" (Mahalik, 2005b, p. 239).

A critical aspect of the interpersonal framework is the idea of relationship reciprocity. That is, extreme behaviors on the interpersonal circle induce or "pull" certain behaviors from the other person in a relationship. In his summary of Keiser's ideas, Mahalik (2005b) noted, "Interactional complementarity takes place when interpersonal behavior is reciprocal along the control dimension (that is, dominance "pulls" submission, submission "pulls" dominance) and corresponding along the affiliation dimension (that is hostility pulls hostility, friendliness pulls friendliness)" (p. 237).

On the basis of this theory of interactional complementarity, Keiser (1983) considered interpersonal therapy to be about interrupting and altering the "vicious cycle of self-defeating action" (p. 22). The tasks of the therapist, as summarized by Mahalik (2005b), are considered to be fivefold. First, the effort is to reduce the client's interpersonal extremeness and increase the interpersonal repertoire. Next, the therapist needs to anticipate "being hooked" into complementary responses, but he or she must then identify what the client is pulling for and disengage from that automatic response. In this manner the therapist will create "beneficial uncertainty" in the client, allowing for the final therapeutic process of experimenting with alternative and more flexible behaviors within the therapeutic relationship.

In describing his convictions about the benefits of IPT for male clients, Mahalik (2005b) contended that this approach is especially useful in helping men unlearn some of the more basic messages taught to men about relating with others. He stated, "Whereas the masculine socialization process encourages developing a sense of self through renouncing 'femininity,' interpersonal psychotherapists can help traditionally socialized men integrate parts of themselves that have been underdeveloped . . . [and] move toward relationships with others and integrate an emotional life" (p. 245).

Male-Friendly Humanistic, Existential, and Experiential Therapies

> Therapy with Donald had been primarily symptom focused, with complaints of sleep problems, increased alcohol use, and generalized apathy about all aspects of his life. In his late 50s, he had established an extremely comfortable lifestyle through shrewd real estate investments and a fanatical work pace. Over the years, his marriage had become routinized, and he had lost contact with most all of his former friends and both of his children. His primary emotional attachments were occasional

erotic massage workers who would provide sexual gratification and fleeting emotional attachment. Although Donald's therapy participation had been somewhat listless, he entered his fourth session in an odd and detached mood. As the session progressed, he traced the onset of his latest discomfort to his watching a morose foreign film that had stimulated a nightmare about his own death. With that opportunity, the therapist encouraged Donald to engage in an imagery exercise to picture his funeral, its attendees, the eulogy, and any messages he wanted to convey to survivors. Donald seemed only partially engaged in the exercise and left the office in a distant and remote mood.

Three days before his next session, he called to plead for an urgent appointment. In session, he described an overwhelming sense of sadness following the last session and a desperate feeling that his life had been wasted. As he began to describe his loneliness and sense of emotional isolation, he became choked up with his feelings of futility. He stated that he had felt boxed in by his life and had always felt on a path he had never really chosen. Realizing he was approaching his 60s, he could see that his life options were vanishing with no hope of recovery. Using that image, the therapist encouraged him to visualize a rheostat that would allow him to reverse the dimming of one image while causing the others to disappear. The remainder of the session was emotionally intense as Donald struggled with the pain of killing off some of his dreams, yet committing to others. Over the next several sessions Donald admitted that he had been on an emotional roller coaster, but he felt more direction and energy than at any time since his youth.

Although an extremely small number of psychotherapists identify themselves exclusively as Rogerian, gestalt, or humanistic/existential in their theoretical orientation (Bechtoldt et al., 2001), the combined impact of their relatively similar perspectives has been substantial. There are differences among the orientations, but many more commonalities. Seligman (2006) summed up the commonalities in her description of gestalt therapy:

> Gestalt therapy encompasses many of the concepts of both existential and person-centered counseling. It emphasizes the importance of the therapeutic alliance and is phenomenological, experiential, humanistic, and optimistic. Promoting awareness and responsibility are important in Gestalt therapy. The present receives more attention than the past, and exploring and experiencing emotions and sensations are integral to treatment (p. 214).

At their core, these approaches are concerned with heightening clients' awareness of their here-and-now existence, their life choices, and factors that impinge upon their freedom and maximal fulfillment. Rogerian therapy focuses upon overcoming socially imposed conditions of personal worth, while Gestalt therapy emphasizes remediation of emotional cut-offs from vital aspects of oneself. Existential therapy calls for work with clients regarding the core life issues of isolation, meaninglessness, freedom and responsibility, and the inevitability of death. Each of these approaches has focused upon unavoidable problems in the human condition; none has placed much emphasis on differences between women and men. Nevertheless, there have been efforts within men's studies to integrate existential/humanist perspectives into understanding men's problems and guiding therapy interventions.

Kilmartin (2007) applied the Rogerian concept of *conditional worth* to male development, noting that the gender-role strain paradigm illustrates how traditional male socialization requires rejection of essential parts of oneself and makes authentic living impossible. He also noted the conflict between the existential need to make difficult life choices based upon full recognition of freedom and responsibility with typical male socialization. "If the vigorous experience of the self provides the data upon which to base existential decisions, then many men are basing their decisions on limited information. The socialization of boys to avoid emotion leaves a large gap in their experience of the self" (Kilmartin, 2007, p. 141).

The most elaborated incorporation of humanistic and existential perspectives into therapy work with men has been provided by Rabinowitz and Cochran (2002). In their *Deepening Psychotherapy With Men*, the authors challenged the proposal made by some (e.g., Shay, 1996) that therapy needs to be modified (i.e., watered down) to fit a more masculine framework. They contended that men benefit greatly from therapy that breaks from a more passive mode and is able to achieve greater meaning and depth through an active and more structured format. To accomplish this, they noted, "We have found that experiential interventions that allow a man active expression of his feelings and behavior enhance the therapy process and work well in combination with traditional psychotherapeutic strategies" (p. 4).

From an existential perspective, Rabinowitz and Cochran (2002) suggested techniques such as "confronting internal discrepancies" and "asking existential questions" to force the male client to "move beyond his empty storytelling and intellectualizing and toward more authentic engagement with his psychological dilemmas" (p. 66). They also suggested activities for "demystifying life's false promises," "acknowledging death and mortality," "confronting freedom of choice," and "facing aloneness" (Rabinowitz & Cochran, 2002, pp. 66–67). Through these techniques, the authors sought to help a client see below the surface of their therapy concerns and face the basic complexities of a man's life.

Because of the commonly reported disconnections of most men from all emotions except anger (Levant, 2001a; Long, 1987), experiential activities to heighten emotional intensity and awareness may have particular utility for some men. In this regard, Rabinowitz and Cochran (2002) suggested a wide array of activities drawn from gestalt therapy, Reichian body work (Reich, 1973), Lowen's bioengetics (1975), and Jungian imagery exercises. The use of these techniques is not new, of course, but the unique benefit here is to offer them as a counter to those who argue that we must settle for psychoeducational and more cerebral approaches to men. "These classic and depth-oriented interventions, combined with the theoretical and clinical understanding of the new psychology of men, create a therapy process that is both expansive and eclectic" (Rabinowitz & Cochran, 2002, p. 88).

Male-Friendly Feminist Therapy

For some persons, the notion of feminist therapy for men seems to be an oxymoron. That is, many people think of feminist therapy as exclusively concerned with altering therapy practices toward women that have resulted from dominant male biases throughout the history of psychology. That impression is accurate, much as it is also accurate to think of women's studies to be about greater understanding of the lives of women. However, as women's studies scholarship encompassed the cultural factors impinging on women's lives, it became clear that gender has been a critical organizing variable in the lives of men as well as women. As noted extensively in chapter 1 of this volume, the manifestations of gender in women and men's lives have been dramatically different, with patriarchy granting many privileges to men as a group. Among the distinctive features of feminist therapy as described by Worell and Johnson (2001) are four primary characteristics.

First, feminist therapy pays great attention to the negative impact of economic and political disadvantages of women. Viewing women's problems in political and gender contexts makes empowerment a major objective of therapy. Second, feminist therapy is particularly intentional in avoiding replication of therapy formats that have historically oppressed women. Therefore, feminist therapy emphasizes egalitarian therapy relationships characterized by "self-disclosure, collaborative goal setting, honoring clients' experience, and affirming clients' strengths" (Worrell & Johnson, 2001, p. 323). Third, feminist therapy is inclusive of the experiences of all women, including women of color, varied sexual orientations, and differing physical abilities. Fourth, feminist therapy pays particular attention to providing interventions for special populations of victimized women, as represented by the development of rape crisis centers and domestic violence shelters.

In some ways, the feminist model is less relevant to men, who, as a group, have not experienced the victimization and oppression of women.

However, the appearance of the women's movement brought gender into critical focus and paved the way for the development of the men's movement. The subsequent development of feminist therapy made it clear that psychotherapy and counseling must be conducted with awareness of the gender context of both female and male clients' problems. Feminist therapy, by illuminating the gender-role strain in clients' lives, provides an important pathway to the development of an integrated male-friendly model of therapy for men.

Male-Friendly Group Therapy: The Special Utility of Male Groups

Group therapy has long been recognized as a psychotherapy format with unique and powerful advantages. It has been well-established within the history of psychotherapy (Yalom, 2005) and, in an era of demands for empirical validation of effectiveness, it has fared very well (Fuhriman & Burlingame, 2001; Smith, Glass, & Miller, 1980). Although the literature has demonstrated that group psychotherapy is typically as effective as individual therapy for most types of client problems, many group therapists see this format as especially helpful with problems at the interpersonal level. Yalom's definition of *universality* as one of the major therapeutic factors in groups explains why group formats are common among those facing similar struggles, such as divorce, bereavement, substance abuse, and posttrauma recovery. With the appearance of new literature on psychotherapy for men, all-male groups have become identified as particularly useful to help men cope with the demands of the male gender role and gender-role strain (Andronico, 1996; Sternbach, 1992). Note that Jolliff (1994) introduced a special issue of the *Journal for Specialists in Group Work* with a personal account of why men benefit from all-male groups. Also, Horne, Jolliff, and Roth (1996) described how these groups are uniquely suited as venues for facilitating men's communicating frankly about topics they might otherwise avoid.

In this section I review this work and report my own observations on the special role of the all-male group in a male-friendly model of psychotherapy. (Those seeking a full discussion of specific technique issues might consult Andronico, 1996; Brooks, 1998; and Rabinowitz, 2005.)

Early engagement of reluctant men into therapy requires a carefully developed therapeutic alliance and attention to the therapy processes most effective for clients at the precontemplation stage of change. For many reasons, the all-male group is an ideal format to maximize this engagement process. In earlier works (Brooks, 1996, 1998), I noted several distinctive qualities that men's groups might provide.

First, all-male groups help individual men overcome the shame they experience in being in a situation of needing help. Rather than seeing themselves as "losers," they can experience the relief that comes from recognizing the universality of problems that all men face. Because a man has probably bought into the façade of imperturbability propagated by other men, it comes as dramatic relief to realize that he is not alone is his struggles.

Second, the male group promotes easier communication because of its side-by-side nature. Face-to-face communication is atypical and difficult for most men. The all male group seems like more of a natural environment for those who are accustomed to interacting with other men through hobbies and similar activities: sports, playing poker, working on cars, or eating and drinking coffee through the "good ol' boy sociability group" (Farr, 1986).

Another benefit of the group format is the opportunity it provides for participative self-disclosure. That is, when a therapist is able to create a group climate of trust and support, one group member may reveal a small part of his private self. When that revelation is not met with the typical teasing or demeaning from other men, the stage is set for another group member to venture even further into this atypical territory. This experience provides both consciousness raising and emotional catharsis so critical in the early stages of change.

Because a group is generally recognized as a social microcosm, it allows for firsthand experiences of improved interpersonal relationship skills. For example, Farrell (1987) described men as likely to practice "self-listening," whereby a man "listens to a conversation, not to take in or genuinely appreciate what a person is saying, but only to be able to jump in and discuss his own experiences" (p. 143). Also, Tannen (1990) described men's tendency to rely on "report talk" over "rapport talk"—that is, having difficulty with language acknowledging intimacy and connection. In a group environment, over-reliance on either self-listening or report talk can be recognized and more facilitative patterns can be modeled and reinforced.

Men's groups also provide a learning opportunity that is not possible in any other therapy format. Simply put, men can learn that it is not necessary to depend exclusively on women for emotional intimacy and caring. When a healing environment is created, men will learn that men can support, soothe, and nurture each other without exclusively relying on a woman to carry the customary emotional burdens. It is equally important that they recognize the many ways that rampant homophobia has prevented them from developing closer relationships with other men.

Finally, an all-male group can be an unparalleled source of inspiration for men who are struggling with their personal gender-role journeys. Consistent with the "instillation of hope" factor identified by Yalom (2005), men can encounter other men who have faced and overcome similar challenges implicit in new roles for men. Rather than resorting to withdrawal or backlash, they can be reassured about realistic fears and empowered to make needed changes in their lives.

Male-Friendly Marital Therapy and Family Therapy

Modern marital and family therapies have distinguished themselves from the more established individual therapies by advocating a shift from an exclusive intrapsychic focus to a broader focus on systems dynamics—that is, viewing a client's presenting problems in the context of the family interactive system. In describing this orientation, Goldenberg and Goldenberg (2004) wrote, "A family is far more than a collection of individuals sharing a specific physical and psychological space. . . . [It's] a natural social system . . . [with] powerful, durable, and reciprocal emotional attachments and loyalties" (p. 3). Although marital therapy has a somewhat longer history than family therapy, it has a shared interest in interpersonal variables over intrapsychic variables. The major advantage of these approaches has been the opening of wider conceptual vistas with attendant intervention options. Unfortunately, the earlier family systems models were not broad enough in their conceptual focus, particularly in the area of recognizing the role of gender in organizing family experiences. However, as noted by Silverstein (2003), many feminist critics challenged the androcentric domination of family systems and changed gender from its invisible status. This feminist corrective to heighten attention to women's experiences in marital and family life ultimately has made it possible to begin conceptualizing marital and family interventions that are harmonious with men's experiences. A thorough analysis of family and marital therapy is beyond the scope of this section, yet it warrants mention here in terms of its special benefits and possible pitfalls in its application to boys and men. Also, I must recognize that, as noted by Clark and Serovich (1997) and Ossana (2000), gay and bisexual men have similar issues in couple relationships, yet they also have multiple unique challenges not common to heterosexual couples. Because of my far greater familiarity and experience with heterosexual couples, I write more directly about this population. However, I strongly encourage readers to avoid heterosexist assumptions and learn as much as possible about alternative couple and family therapeutic forms (e.g., Malley & McCann, 2002; Bieschke, Perez, & DeBord, 2007).

Marital Therapy for Heterosexual Men

Marital therapy with heterosexual men needs to be informed by an awareness of the psychosocial context in which men enter couple relationships, men's views and expectations of women, the construction of marriage as social institution, and the political dimensions of traditional marriage.

Several components of normative male socialization affect the way men enter relationships with women. As noted in chapter 1, boys have been encouraged to make sharp breaks from their mothers and from anything considered to be feminine. They are raised in environments where they are taught to seek women for sexual gratification, yet they are distrustful of women's apparent superiority in social and emotional skills. Despite their many cultural advantages, men often come to feel one-down and overly dependent upon women. This situation creates anxiety that is sometimes exacerbated by misogynistic elements in the broader culture.

Compounding the problems inherent in male emotional socialization and ambivalence toward women are issues resulting from the traditional views of marriage as a cultural institution. From an early age men are taught that marriage is something good for women and suffocating for men. Despite the evidence that men actually accrue emotional, logistical, and physical health benefits from marriage (Bernard, 1981; Brooks & Gilbert, 1995; Gove, 1972), the mythology persists. In spite of public portrayals, most married men are more satisfied than women with their marital relationships (Barnett & Baruch, 1987; Hochschild, 1989; Maracek, 2001) and actually have greater difficulty coping with divorce or becoming widowed (Cooper, 2001).

This trend toward differential satisfaction levels in traditional marriage compounds the problems inherent in men's reluctance to engage in relationship maintenance and their generalized resistance to seeking psychotherapy. As a result, women are more typically the initiators of couple's therapy, sometimes buttressing their therapy insistence with threats of separation or divorce. As a result, many men enter couples therapy under coercion and in a defensive posture. Further complicating matters for those men (male partners), the empowerment benefits of the women's movement have allowed women to reflect upon their changing status and their previously unrealized emotional needs and life opportunities. By and large, most men have done comparatively very little by way of consciousness raising and see no obvious benefit in changing their marital relationship. In fact, some men will engage in a variety of superficially positive (e.g., currying favor, promising change) and negative (e.g., threatening, manipulating) strategies to circumvent their partner's push for relationship change (Brooks, 1998).

Because of the likelihood of differing agendas and readiness for therapy, I believe that couples therapy is frequently premature. Many men are simply not as prepared as their female partners to engage in relationship negotiations, because of both their lower levels of relational skills and their general distrust of therapy and therapists. Thus, prior to holding conjoint meetings, a therapist should give serious consideration to separate meetings with each partner, primarily to allow for consciousness raising and more time for development of a therapeutic alliance with the more defensive man.

In terms of therapy processes, several gender-informed practices have been recommended. In his comprehensive and empirically validated model of marital therapy, John Gottman pays considerable attention to the tendency of men in a couple relationship to become overwhelmed by emotional intensity and cope with the emotional onslaught through *stonewalling*—that is, becoming defensive or shutting down emotionally (Carstensen, Gottman, & Levenson, 1995; Gottman, 2000; Gottman et al., 2002). To manage this problem, Gottman recommended that the therapist push for "softened start-up," whereby a woman partner is able to soothe her distraught male partner enough for him to participate less defensively.

Lusterman (1989) offered the "empathic interview" technique, during which each marital partner interviews the other regarding differing gender perspectives. In this process, the therapist coaches the partners to listen empathically and refrain from interrupting or defending. Philpot, Brooks, Lusterman, and Nutt (1997) also offered the techniques of *the gender inquiry* (a psychoeducational exercise) and *intergender translating and reframing* (a communication-facilitating activity).

Family Therapy for Males

Feminist perspectives on family therapy have become exceptionally well developed over the past 3 decades. A number of major publications have voiced criticisms of patriarchal practices in family therapy and have articulated feminist alternative models (Goldner, 1985; Luepnitz, 1988; Silverstein & Goodrich, 2003; Walters, Carter, Papp, & Silverstein, 1988). As yet, far less has been written about family therapy with particular emphasis on enhancing interventions with men. Previously, I have offered several suggestions for enhancing family therapy with men (Brooks, 1998). These suggestions include making concerted efforts to include a reluctant male family member, helping males articulate their perspectives, helping families overcome preoccupation with career goals and neglect of relational goals for males, encouraging males to recognize vulnerabilities and prioritize self-care, empowering male family members in nurturing and caretaking, promoting emotional intimacy among male family members, encouraging role latitude for sons, encouraging new fatherhood roles, and conducting family of origin work to explore masculine family heritage.

Interventions for Boys and Adolescent Males

> The first thing one had to notice about Roberto was his physical size. Although nearly 11, he was barely 5 feet tall and exceptionally thin. His clothing was inexpensive but clean, and his grooming was fairly good. A middle child from a working-class Mexican American family of eight, he had been referred because of cutting classes and fights with other students.

Therapist:	Hey, Roberto. How are things going?
Roberto:	Not much to say to you about that—didn't like the last guy and don't care for this much either.
Therapist:	Last guy?
Roberto:	Yeah, some dude who asked a bunch of stupid questions and got all intense and shit.
Therapist:	Okay, I get it. You're not much into talking about what's going on. That's very fine. How about we walk down to the Coke machine for starters?
Roberto:	Don't like Coke. They got any Mountain Dew?

Upon the slow return from the walk down the hall, the therapist offers a suggestion.

Therapist:	Say, how about this: You don't feel much like talking and I got a pile of crap to do to get ready for my next session, so would you mind keeping me company while I copy forms, sharpen pencils, get out test materials, and stuff?
Roberto:	Whatever. It's your office.

Over the next 30 minutes, Roberto observes preparations, then volunteers to help with pencil sharpening and copying forms. As time passes, and he is praised for his dexterity, he describes other times when he has helped his uncles work on their cars.

Therapist:	Wow, look what time it is. I'd better let you get back.
Roberto:	Let me just finish this one last thing. Or should I finish with it next time?

To this point, I have described adaptations and applications of established therapy models to make them maximally suitable for therapeutic work with men. Most of what has been presented is also quite applicable to work with boys and adolescents, but the special challenges of this population warrant additional comment. The material here is drawn from the recent groundbreaking work of Mark Kiselica and his colleagues, who have provided crucial new perspectives for therapy with male youth (Horne & Kiselica, 1999; Kiselica, 1995; Kiselica, Englar-Carlson, & Horne, 2008). Most notably, Kiselica and his colleagues have admonished the psychotherapy establishment for its delay in recognizing the crises in young men's lives and its failure to modify therapy to make it more conducive to their needs. Appropriately, this section is less about any specific therapy orientation and more about a generalized therapeutic approach to young men.

Because the work of Kiselica and his colleagues is firmly grounded within the new psychology of men, it is not surprising that its perspectives and recommendations are highly congruent with previous work on therapy with men (Brooks, 1998; Good & Brooks, 2005; Rabinowitz & Cochran, 2002). The principal thesis of these authors is that there is a mismatch between the standard therapy environment and the relational style of young men. Kiselica and Englar-Carlson referenced the work of Bruch (1978) in noting that traditional counseling environments are geared toward persons with social personality types and less compatible with persons having the conventional and realistic personality types more common among boys and men. Also, they cited Gurian (1997), who attributed many mismatch problems to boys' slower brain development in reading and language skills (as compared to girls), and Levant (2001a), who attributed problems to boys' socialization into an emotionally-suppressive interaction style. Finally, they made reference to the abundant literature demonstrating boys' preference for developing friendships through "instrumental activities with other boys, such as enjoying rough-and-tumble games, participating in sports, playing video and computer games, going fishing, hanging out, and working on projects that involve manual labor" (Kiselica & Englar-Carlson, 2008, p. 50).

In chapter 2, I noted that one reason for men's aversion to psychotherapy is the poor fit between men's interpersonal style and the conventionally expected demands of the therapy world. This point is taken up by Kiselica and his colleagues, who castigated traditional therapists who not only fail to accommodate to a boy's relational style, but also sometimes "misinterpret the boy's behavior as a sign of resistance" (Kiselica & Englar-Carlson, 2008, p. 51). As a remedy for this problem, Kiselica and Englar-Carlson (2008) stated that "the rigid adherence to traditional notions of counseling and psychotherapy is a recipe for failure. . . . Male-friendly adjustments must be made" (p. 51).

To their immense credit, Kiselica and his colleagues go considerably further than simply lobbing broadsides at traditional counseling practices. Their publications (Horne & Kiselica, 1999; Kiselica, Englar-Carlson, & Horne, 2008) are rich with creative recommendations for altering therapy environments and dramatically altering customary therapist behaviors. A sampling of their suggestions is warranted.

First, Kiselica and Carlson urge that counselors deliver services in informal settings, thereby overcoming the alien quality of the formal office and allowing for more easing into relevant conversation. Possible alternative arrangements might include shooting baskets, eating together, taking walks, or playing a game together. Flexibility can also be adaptive in terms of appointment scheduling and session lengths. Brief initial sessions, sessions interspersed with psychoeducational activities, extended sessions during propitious times, and allowance for drop-ins are all worthy of consideration.

As much as possible, counselors should be leery of invoking negative reactions to the stereotypical head-shrinking activities, such as pressuring for too much emotion-laden material, interpreting unconscious motives, or maintaining a distant and silent posture. Good natured humor can defuse tension and frame problems in a manner more palatable for discussion. Appropriate self-disclosure can be helpful as a modeling behavior and also a strategy to lessen the toxicity of the expert or authority role. Self-disclosure in the form of storytelling has been recognized as a useful aspect of culturally sensitive therapy for African American (Hines & Boyd-Franklin, 2005) and Hispanic clients (Hernandez, 2002).

Kiselica and Englar-Carlson also urge therapists to be knowledgeable about the culture of the young men they see and to pay particular attention to creating a "welcoming space." Familiarity with a young man's experiential world, particularly if the young man is from an ethnic or cultural background different from that of the therapist, is essential for allowing tension-reducing conversation. Also, the décor of the office and the cordiality of office staff will send an important message to a young male about the terrain he is entering. Although it would be unreasonable to expect the counselor's office to mimic a fraternity or dorm room, it would also be unwise for it to resemble something from a natural history museum.

In terms of therapy formats and modalities, several authors have cited the advantages of all-male groups for young men. Hedges-Goett and Tannenbaum (2001) noted the advantages of the format for improving social skills, and Kiselica and Englar-Carlson (2008) described success with group models that weave together therapy components and recreational activities. Individual therapy modalities such as cognitive behavior therapies and interpersonal therapies have been suggested for depressed and suicidal young males (Fleming & Englar-Carlson, 2008), whereas behavioral methods have been recommended for boys with attention deficit hyperactivity disorder (Kapalka, 2008).

In reviewing the breadth of suggestions for work with boys and male adolescents, it is impressive to realize the synchronicity of therapy experiences and recommendations of professionals working in very different settings. In calling for creative approaches for boys and adolescents, Kiselica and his colleagues provide suggestions very similar to those offered earlier in this book for work with adult men. It is not surprising that young men who miss out on the benefits of psychotherapy early in their lives seem to carry their therapy aversion into adulthood.

6

THE CHALLENGE OF DIVERSE MASCULINITIES

The first appointment with Lee was precipitated by a severe marital dispute that erupted when his wife of 10 years discovered he had been visiting online pornography sites. Lee was a 32-year-old, second-generation Chinese American man who had worked from his home as a software designer while his wife worked in a domestic violence shelter. When his wife confronted him, Lee explained that he had been "doing research." Pressed to explain further, he eventually admitted with great reticence that his younger brother, William, who lived in a nearby city, had announced to their elderly parents that he was gay and would soon end his childless marriage. Lee explained that his parents, who were devout Christians, had been devastated and had begged Lee to find out what could be done to "correct" William's "sickness." Lee claimed that in researching gay issues and conversion therapies, he had also come across gay Web sites. He then asked the therapist to help him with his marriage and also to find a therapist to help William.

The therapist recognized the multiple and complex layers of Lee's presenting issues but felt completely competent with only some of them. Primarily, she was concerned that the client seemed to be requesting "reparative therapy" (Nicolosi, 1997; Socarides, 1995), a procedure based on the assumption that a gay sexual orientation is a function of pathological development and as such can (and should) be corrected. The therapist responded with respect for his request by noting where such services might be obtained. However, she was quite explicit in informing Lee that these interventions had no scientific support and were viewed by most of the professional community as potentially quite harmful (Haldeman, 1994, 1999; Greene, 2006). After providing Lee with appropriate background material, she suggested that they begin exploring Lee's issues with his wife and parents.

Over the remainder of the first session and through the succeeding session, it became clear to the therapist that one of Lee's issues was a struggle over loyalty and autonomy with his family of origin. Relatively inexperienced in work with Asian American families, she consulted a colleague with greater multicultural expertise. In that consultation, she realized she not only needed to be attuned to Asian American family issues but also to the intersection of Christian religious beliefs and gay-affirmative psychotherapy. After lengthy conversations with her consultant, she recognized that therapy would need to include attention to Lee's cultural conflicts regarding his role in his family of origin. Also, there was a clear need to be knowledgeable of "coming out" issues for helping William. In addition, Lee's online activity suggested the possibility of another issue with his own sexual identity and a need to prioritize that issue. Challenged yet energized, she set up an open consultation arrangement with her multicultural consultant and additional consultation with an expert in lesbian, gay, bisexual, and transgender issues.

Not all men and boys are exactly the same—that is, males define their masculinity in multiple and diverse ways. This fairly obvious reality has never really been acknowledged, certainly not in American society at large, creating the impression that there is a single universal masculine experience. Because this is clearly not the case, some explanation needs to be given for how that impression came about and how it has endured.

Not so long ago, personality theories and psychological interventions were (and, to an extent, still are) dominated by some rather formidable androcentric biases, and feminist critics of the mental health establishment charged that the profession did not fully comprehend the female experience. To correct for these decidedly male-dominated constructs in the mental health profession, the cultural variable of gender was highlighted as a critical organizing dimension in the lives of persons encountering mental health professionals. At the time of this reconceptualization, or shortly thereafter, feminists recognized that this new gender variable was an expedient "solution" and would eventually require explication of the many other cultural variables affecting and disadvantaging women. Over the past several decades, feminist scholars have identified the crucial roles of race, ethnicity, social class, sexual orientation, and physical ability status as additional relevant variables in women's lives.

As men's studies scholars have extended the work of feminists to recognize the male aspect of gender studies, a similar expediency has taken place. The men's studies literature of the 1970s and 1980s was largely devoted to finding the commonalities among men with far less attention given to cultural variations in masculinity. To some extent, this intellectual shortcut has been justified by the notion of *hegemonic masculinity* (Connell, 1995), which recognizes that despite the actual differences in the conduct of men's lives, white, middle-class, heterosexual masculinity has been the dominant template for men: Although most people recognized that Rambo, John Wayne's or Clint Eastwood's various movie roles, James Bond, and John "Die Hard" McClane were merely characters (and stereotypical ones at that), many men were still subject to feelings of inadequacy in failing to live up to these iconic standards.

Despite the utility of identifying the primary features of traditional masculinity, an equal amount of attention should be devoted to the many variations of male experience. For example, it would be foolish and insulting to think of male power, dominance, privilege, and entitlement when considering gay men or men of color as one might think of the same issues with heterosexual, middle-class, white men. In terms of social oppression, some marginalized men share more with the historical status of women than with the status of their more privileged counterparts.

This chapter attempts to highlight the various components that constitute different constructs of masculinity per ethnocultural background, sexual orientation, and physical ability status. The analytical challenge in this survey, then, is to discover the common factors within and among these diverse groups that contribute to peculiarly male problems stemming from male gender-role strain.

MEN OF COLOR—COMMON ISSUES

The cultural backgrounds, experiences, and values of African American, Hispanic, Native American, and Asian American men vary in important ways. In spite of their differences, however, these men share some common values and have had certain essential experiences that will affect their entry in any therapy relationship. First and foremost, males in all of these groups have for centuries been subject to the pernicious effects of racism and multiple forms of oppression. Sue and Sue (2003) noted that "a study of U.S. history must include a study of racism and racist practices directed at people of color. The oppression of the indigenous people of this country (Native Americans), enslavement of African Americans, widespread segregation of Hispanic Americans, passage of exclusionary laws against the Chinese, and the forced internment of Japanese Americans are social realities" (p. 74).

The extent of the damage to males in these groups is impossible to fully convey, yet some realization is gained by consideration of the sobering data in the areas of employment, life expectancy, educational levels, substance abuse, and incarceration. Although many men of color have made significant gains in spite of racism and oppression, African American men have higher rates of mental disorders, suicides, unemployment, limited educational attainment, substance abuse, and health impairments (Majors & Billison, 1992; McKinnon, 2003; Sue & Sue, 2008; White & Cones, 1999). Among the alarming statistics are those that reveal that one third of African American men in their 20s are in jail, on probation, or on parole, and that the life expectancy of this group is 5 to 7 years shorter than that of White Americans (Sue & Sue, 2003).

The powerfully negative effects of racism have also been well-documented among other men of color. Casas, Turner, and Ruiz De Esparza (2005) described how lower levels of economic status have affected Hispanic males' gender roles and have led to further social and psychological problems, such as depression, low self-esteem, and high-risk behaviors. Sue and Sue (2008) reviewed similarly gloomy data among Native American men regarding poverty, educational levels, unemployment, and physical and emotional health.

The effects of racism on Asian American men have been largely reflected in negative stereotypes of Asian masculinity. For example, Niiya (1996) observed, "Asian men have not been given a fair shake . . . stereotypes of being poor at sports, good in mathematics, and villains in mass media contribute to feelings of inferiority" (p. 7). This theme, that Asian men are commonly viewed as inadequate and lacking manly attributes, is echoed by Sue (2005): "Asian American men frequently are not seen to possess the traditional masculine characteristics (physical appearance and behavioral qualities) valued in U.S. society" (p. 357).

The intention here is not to compound injury to men of color by perpetuating negative stereotypes or ignoring the extensive progress made by many men of color despite overwhelming social hardships. Rather, the intent is to reflect the predominant advice of all experts on work with persons of color that the first step for therapists is to recognize the history and substantial effects of racism and oppression. As stated most succinctly by Sue and Sue (2003), "Mental health practitioners must recognize that racial/ethnic minorities . . . in our society live under an umbrella of individual, institutional, and cultural forces that often demean them, disadvantage them, and deny them equal access to opportunity" (p. 68).

Closely related to the common experiences of racism and oppression, men of color also are likely to share a broad distrust of most mental health professionals. Whether this distrust is characterized as "healthy cultural paranoia" (Paniagua, 1998, p. 23) or as a generalized minority distrust of the majority society (Ridley, 1995), any therapy relationship between a White therapist and a male client of color will be affected by the history of racism. "The overall result of the experiences of minorities in the United States has been to increase vigilance and sensitivity to the thoughts and behaviors of Whites in society. . . . White people are perceived as potential enemies unless proven otherwise" (Sue & Sue, 2003, p. 76).

The degree of distrust and possible tension between a White therapist and a man of color will not always be identical, as it is impacted by another important variable—the client's stage of racial/cultural identity. This racial/cultural identity development model (R/CID), as an outgrowth of work by Cross (1995) and Helms (1995), posits that minority persons go through five stages of development "as they struggle to understand themselves in term of their own culture, the dominant culture, and the oppressive relationship between the two" (Sue & Sue, 2008, p. 242). The five stages—conformity, dissonance, resistance and immersion, introspection, and integrative awareness—portray movement from a general lack of awareness (and demeaning) of one's racial/cultural background, through rejection of the dominant culture and immersion in one's own culture, into an ultimate integration of both cultures and a bicultural identity. The most immediate implication for this discussion of therapeutic work with men of color is that the client's stage on the R/CID will have major implications for his willingness to work with a White therapist or his possible insistence on working with therapist from his own racial and cultural group.

Before addressing the special issues of work with specific groups of ethnic minority men, some recognition must be given to the problems created by the value biases within the mental health establishment. As American culture has become more diverse, it has become apparent that its educational and mental health systems have not kept pace with such diversity, developing new approaches for and catering to a principally Euro-American clientele (Highlen, 1994)—a bias has been described variously as *cultural encapsulation* (Wrenn, 1962) and *ethnocentric monoculturalism* (Sue & Sue, 2008). As such, these systems and the fundamental principles they rely on have been poorly understood by many other ethnocultural groups. This limitation in understanding is especially damaging because it is typically unrecognized by those who hold it, and because it also contains a fundamental belief in the superiority of mainstream Euro-American cultural values and tends to pathologize other value systems (Sue & Sue, 2003).

This concept of ethnocentric monoculturalism has been described thoroughly by Sue and Sue (2003) and has been labeled as *White culture* by Katz (1985). To grossly oversimplify, White culture frequently differs from the values and beliefs of ethnic minority culture in terms of its emphasis on independence and individuality, internal locus of control, competition, mastery over nature, emotional control, rigid adherence to time schedules, living in the future, disconnection from extended family, and valuing private owner-ship of goods and property (Katz, 1985). Many men of color, of course, will have bought into this White culture value system, and there will no problems from conflicting values. However, this is not always the case, and therapists must be alert for conflicts in worldviews to avoid imposition of their own cultural values on their ethnic minority male clients.

THERAPEUTIC INTERVENTIONS WITH AFRICAN AMERICAN MEN, ADOLESCENTS, AND BOYS

There has been a welcome flourishing of literature on therapy with African American clients, including representative works of therapy with African American women, men, young women, young men, and families (Boyd-Franklin, 2003; Boyd-Franklin, Franklin, & Toussaint, 2001; Hall, 1998; Jackson & Greene, 2000; Lee, 1992; Parham, 2002). Given this abundance, it is impossi-ble to provide anything other than an overview of some major points on ther-apy with African American males. This brevity is unfair to the complexity of the issues, but omission of this topic would be even more inappropriate.

All writers on therapy with African American males concur that any therapist wishing to establish a therapeutic alliance must first have a deep appreciation of this group's experiences of racism and oppression (Caldwell & White, 2005; Lee, 1992, 1999; Sue & Sue, 2008). Also, therapists must engage in what Caldwell and White (2005) referred to as *self-interrogation* and *self-confrontation* to assess their own internalized racism and acceptance of stereotypes about black males. Further, therapists should honestly assess their preparedness to work with African American clients in terms of knowledge of African American culture and history, intersection of one's own culture with African American culture, and familiarity with Afrocentric counseling theory and skills (Parham, 1999).

Another early-therapy issue for work with an African American male is discussion of his comfort level in working with a member of a different ethnic group (Caldwell & White, 2005; Paniagua, 1998; Boyd-Franklin, 2003). This matter would be less critical with males at an early level of racial and cultural identity but essential with a male who is at the resistance/immersion stage. Nat-urally, when the male client expresses discomfort with the cross-ethnicity pair-ing (and no alternatives are available), efforts are needed to assure the client of the therapist's interest in respecting the differences and learning from the client.

In assessing presenting problems and developing treatment plans, con-sideration must be given to cultural patterns and value issues more common among African American groups. In the area of fathering and family roles, attention needs to given to more flexible definition of family and family roles in African American culture (Boyd-Franklin, 2003). Therapists should be cognizant of the historical role of the Black church as well as the central importance of religion and spirituality in many African American men's lives. Also, the therapist needs to be attuned to paradoxical relationship of African American men with the *educational orientation* described by Sue and Sue (2008): Although African American families have generally placed great emphasis on educational attainment, males have become increasingly dissociated from this value orientation (Osbourne, 1997).

Given the cultural history of negative images of African American males, therapists must make special efforts to adopt a strength-based approach over a deficit model (Paniagua, 1998; Parham, 2002). When the African American male client presents with problematic behaviors previously described as manifestations of the *dark side of masculinity* (i.e., violence, substance abuse, antisocial behavior), a special effort must be expended to integrate understanding of those behaviors not only within the code of masculinity but also with understanding of opportunities denied to men of color. In that regard, Franklin (2004) defined an *invisibility syndrome* whereby African American men are denied recognition and respect and are thereby subject to highly adverse personal consequences. Majors and Billson (1992) described the "Cool Pose" as a survival mechanism often adopted by Black males to cope with assaults on their self-esteem and masculinity. Within the context of racial oppression, the worst-case scenarios of cool-pose behaviors can lead to the self-defeating behaviors such as violence or substance abuse and incarceration. However, in the best-cases scenarios, Black males provide creative models of adaptation amidst extreme adversity.

Several recommendations for psychotherapeutic interventions tailored specially to African American men have appeared over the past 2 decades. Within the psychoeducational realm, White and Cones (1999) proposed fatherhood training, rites of passage programs, and cultural history education as helpful interventions that Caldwell and White (2005) asserted will "assist black males in the redefinition and formulation of an authentic black masculine identity" (p. 330). In this vein, Paniagua (1998) advocated problem-solving, skills training, and family therapy. An especially promising trend in this area is the appearance of Afrocentric therapy approaches. Phillips (1990) developed NTU psychotherapy, an approach described by Caldwell and White (2005) as "spiritually-based and uses the . . . seven principles of the Kwanzaa . . . as guidelines for harmonious living" (p. 329).

Thomas Parham (2002) has been especially outspoken in his convictions that multicultural counselors need to push harder to "raise the bar of competence" for work with the African American population. He called for therapeutic approaches that incorporate the Afrocentric philosophical framework and its core beliefs. Such approaches should explain the basic African nature, the effects of European cultural oppression and White supremacy, and it should have explicit liberation implications. Many of the groundbreaking features of this African-centered therapy would be unfamiliar to most therapists, including its spiritual emphasis, view of the divine nature of African American people, and role of therapists as "healers through which spiritual energy flows" (Parham, 2002, p. xvi).

In earlier chapters, attention was given to the advantages of using community-based therapeutic interventions outside the traditional therapy office. For a number of reasons related to the communal orientation of African American culture, this outreach model has been described as especially valuable for at-risk African American male youth. Leonard, Lee, and Kiselica (1999) described five Afrocentric group-oriented counseling programs that are based in the community and are administered by African American men to address the relevant needs of African American boys: the Respected Elders training program, the Simba Wachanga program, the Young Lions program, Black Manhood Training, and the MAAT program (a rites of passage program based on the ancient Egyptian word *Ma'at*, which means "an ethical way of life"; Leonard, Lee, & Kiselica, 1999, p. 83). These programs have been developed in separate locations and target different age groups of African American youth, but they share the common goals of raising consciousness about African American heritage and shaping of socially responsible and psychologically healthy African American masculinity.

THERAPEUTIC INTERVENTIONS WITH HISPANIC/LATINO MEN, ADOLESCENTS, AND BOYS

Hispanic/Latino males share with other men of color a history of oppression, marginalization of their value systems, and considerable distrust of White institutions (Cuellar & Paniagua, 2000; Mirande, 1997; Sue & Sue, 2008). In addition, Hispanic men have an extreme aversion to any mental health intervention that implies that they are *los locos* ("the crazy ones"; Casas et al., 2005). A nervous disorder (*enfermedad mental*) would be a more acceptable term and would likely be met through help seeking with family, friends, and healers (Paniagua, 1998). Hispanic men's view of psychotherapy is particularly negative, as it is usually considered an activity for *jotos* or *maricones* (derogatory terms for gay men) or *viejas* (old women; Velasquez, Arellano, & McNeill, 2004).

In writing about psychotherapy approaches for Hispanic men, most experts emphasize two primary foci—understanding the central role of machismo in the lives of Hispanic men and accommodating interventions to a value system that is frequently contrary to the value system of psychotherapy. Support for these recommendations is based in a history of research demonstrating that Hispanics, as a group, have consistently been underrepresented in use of mental health services (Rodriguez, 1987) and have been underserved by mental health systems (Myers, Echemendia, & Trimble, 1991).

Like men in virtually all cultures, Hispanic men are restricted in their views of acceptable male behavior, but the demands of machismo (and the corresponding female concept of *marianismo*) contribute to more extreme and narrow gender-role expectations in Hispanic culture. That is, Hispanic men feel powerful pressures to be strong and in charge, while Hispanic women are expected to be "submissive, obedient, timid, and sexually conservative" (Paniagua, 1998, p. 41). Because machismo demands a sense of *respeto* from others, major emphasis needs to be placed upon conducting psychotherapy in a fashion that does not devalue or threaten the self-esteem or dignity of the Hispanic male. To accommodate this issue, Casas et al. (2005) recommended a number of alterations to typical psychotherapy practices.

First, Casas et al. (2005) urged use of community outreach services and public information activities to counter stigma toward mental health services. They recommended efforts to make services as accessible as possible through expanded hours of service, relocation of service delivery sites, and use of mobile services. Also, regarding the settings themselves, they suggested that "every effort be made to make them user-friendly for Hispanic men" (Casas et al., 2005, p. 348). For example, they recommended that other men be present at the site to avoid a "feminized" environment and to reinforce the impression that mental health is women's business. They noted that the total ambience should be culture-friendly in terms of decorations, reading materials, and bilingual personnel. Efforts should be made to recognize the sensitivity of self-conscious Hispanic men by reducing wait times in large reception areas. As much as possible, initial contact should focus on making the client feel welcomed and comfortable, even if it might necessitate a delay in completing demographic and informational forms.

In addition, Casas et al. (2005) encouraged consideration of nontraditional treatment formats such as classes, small groups, or seminars in workshops. To further minimize possible stigma, these services might be delivered in nonmental health settings, such as schools and churches. Finally, these authors encouraged therapists to become familiar with the three-dimensional model proposed by Atkinson, Thompson, and Grant (1993) for work with ethnic minority clients. This model calls for adjusting the therapist role to a client's level of acculturation and attributional style. For example, rather than automatically functioning as a psychotherapist, the professional would have alternative role possibilities of adviser, advocate, consultant, or facilitator of indigenous support systems or healing systems.

When traditional psychotherapy is conducted with Hispanic men, the process is enhanced by attention to values represented in a Hispanic worldview.

Paniagua (1998) proposed that culture-friendly therapy accounts for the historical importance of religious and folk beliefs, as well as the special values of *personalismo, familismo,* and *fatalismo.* In practice, traditional cultural beliefs might stress the importance of sometimes using a folk healer (*el curandero*). *Familisimo* would be represented by approaches that incorporate input from extended family, often including the godfather (*padrino*) and godmother (*madrina*). After an initial phase of therapy characterized by *formalismo, personalismo* would call for a more informal client–therapist relationship, characterized by higher levels of self-disclosure and possible acceptance of gifts. Finally, *fatalismo,* with its emphasis on external or divine control of life events, must be respected as a sometimes adaptive response to uncontrollable life situations (Neff & Hoppe, 1993).

Clinical work with Hispanic boys and adolescents needs to be attentive to these dominant cultural values, but it also benefits from awareness of special issues inherent in their psychosocial development, their loyalty roles in their families, and their needs to integrate their cultural heritage. In writing about these challenges, Arcaya (1999) cautioned about the need to be attuned to intragroup differences among Hispanic youth, but he acknowledged a number of generally helpful perspectives for this work. Arcaya described the heavy masculinity-role pressures that young Hispanic men are expected to be "true to their word, humble, physically tough, brave, decisive, self-reliant, resourceful, and uncomplaining" (p. 115). These powerful pressures frequently lead to predefined male rituals of drinking and womanizing.

Arcaya also noted the important role of extended family loyalty and the frequent need for these young Hispanic males to sacrifice personal advancement for caretaking or breadwinning for the needy family members. He described how cultural and economic factors frequently pressure these youths to shortcut the delayed adolescence typical of mainstream culture and leave school, take on practical trade positions, marry, and sire children as soon as possible. Arcaya encouraged counselors to be aware of common family patterns that produce close and even idealized images of mothers and somewhat distant relations with harsher fathers. Although he made no specific recommendations regarding therapy format, Arcaya seemed to concur with other observers of Hispanic culture, such as Garcia-Preto (2005), who notes the major importance of intervening with considerable respect for the family system forces.

THERAPEUTIC INTERVENTIONS WITH NATIVE AMERICAN MEN, ADOLESCENTS, AND BOYS

The issues of therapeutic intervention with Native American males overlap greatly with the issues in work with men of other ethnic minority groups, yet they are also unique. Like the other groups, Native American males have been subjected to extreme penalties from racism and oppression, yet no other group has experienced the decimation of their population and deprivation of their formerly established identity and way of life. No other group experienced the extent of organized governmental efforts to "civilize" their culture or isolate them into reservations characterized by poverty and deprivation. Sue and Sue (2003) noted, "the experience of American Indians in America is not comparable to that of any other ethnic group . . . they had land and status that were gradually eroded by imperial, colonial, and then federal and state policies" (p. 309).

As a result of this shameful heritage, therapists wishing to work with Native American males must be exceptionally aware of this history as well as keenly attuned to its effects on both Native American male clients and the potential countertransference effects upon that therapy.

Because of the enormous diversity in those groups characterized as Native American, most authors highlight the dangers of overgeneralizing and losing the uniqueness of the several hundred tribal entities (Sutton & Broken Nose, 2005; Thomason, 1991). Nevertheless, given the tribes' similarities in victimization experience and the enormous divergence of these groups from White European worldviews, many advocates have identified a number of perspectives to reduce the damaging effects of ethnocentric monoculturalism.

Many authors have identified several Native American values that differ markedly from those of mainstream White culture (Garwick & Auger, 2000; Herring, 1999; Sutton & Broken Nose, 2005). First, sharing and giving are esteemed more than the accumulation of wealth and material goods. Related to this, cooperation is valued more highly than competition. A posture of noninterference is central, a value that influences both in-group relationships and dominant parenting styles. Time orientation is more likely to be here-and-now, versus an extreme emphasis placed on planning for the future. Finally, Native American cultures place far higher importance on spirituality, that is, major emphasis on the need for harmony between man and nature. Mind, spirit, and body are seen as deeply interconnected, and sickness is commonly viewed as a product of disharmony between the elements.

The common features of the male gender role, when combined with the values and history of Native American men, would seem to make the therapeutic obstacles nearly insurmountable. Nevertheless, many suggestions have been put forward as potentially ameliorating some of these hurdles with Native American clients (Dillard & Manson, 2000; Herring, 1999; Sue & Sue, 2008; Sutton & Broken Nose, 2005; Thomason, 1991; of these, only Herring's work is male-specific).

The foremost issue in any first encounter with a Native American male would be the recognition of the inevitable discomfort of that client and the consequent expectation that the therapist communicate empathy, compassion, and respect for the client's dignity. The shame imparted from a sense of vulnerability or loss of control, coupled with a generalized suspicion of the world of "mind-shrinkers," is common for all men and likely to be even more problematic for Native American males. As a result, the initial contacts are best designed to be less pointed and problem-oriented and more casual, friendly, and conversational (Attneave, 1982). Therapist self-disclosure and sharing of experiences can be helpful in softening the atmosphere (Everett, Proctor, & Cortmell, 1989).

As therapy progresses, most therapists eschew nondirective and psychodynamic therapies in favor of more directive and problem-solving approaches (Dillard & Manson, 2000; Thomason, 1991). As a means to lessen any uncomfortable intensity in the one-on-one therapy environment, therapy groups can be especially facilitative (Dufrene & Coleman, 1992). Group formats for Native American men also have an advantage in their close resemblance to the talking circles endemic in this culture (Neligh, 1990). Because of the somewhat lowered value placed on individuality, family therapies are also useful in many situations (Trimble, Fleming, Beauvais, & Jumper-Thurman, 1996). Often, interventions outside the office have been recommended as logistically realistic and also as a means to minimize historical aversion to White settings (Schacht, Tafoya, & Mirabla, 1989). In this regard, Schacht et al. (1989) developed a model of home-based therapy and Attneave (1982) pioneered an in-the-field approach called *tribal network therapy*.

In terms of content of therapy with Native American men, several primary issues have been noted to have special importance. Acculturation conflicts are especially common, given the longstanding history of problematic relations between traditional tribal culture and mainstream U.S. culture. Most observers have noted this differential pull and described the stresses emanating from efforts in "honoring both traditions and surviving in the modern world" (Thomason, 1991, p. 323). Related to this is the enormous challenge of integrating the identity crisis experienced by all Native American males (Herring, 1999) with the aforementioned challenges of the modern male gender role. Therapy content must also include attention to the many dark side of masculinity behaviors frequently engaged in by men to cope with emotional distress. Tragically, rates of suicide, domestic violence, and alcohol/substance abuse are dramatically higher among Native American men, necessitating careful screening of clients for indicators of problems in these areas.

Therapeutic interventions specifically targeted to Native American male youth described by Herring (1999) have been conceptualized within a proactive developmental perspective. As conceived by Herring, these interventions are "synergistic with traditional Native community-oriented guidance systems" (p. 128) and focus on modifying the effects of political and socioeconomic forces. In this network therapy approach, traditional Native healing practices are incorporated in established mental health treatment approaches. Two such practices described by Herring are the four circles and the talking circle. Each approach relies upon tapping spiritual healing metaphors and incorporating these into "an environment of total acceptance without time constraints, using sacred objects, the pipe, and prayer" (p. 128). Other variations of these interventions are the vision quest (Heinrich, Corbin, & Thomas, 1990) and the sweat lodge (Garrett & Osborne, 1995).

THERAPEUTIC INTERVENTIONS WITH ASIAN AMERICAN MEN, ADOLESCENTS, AND BOYS

In some ways, the need for therapy to accommodate the special challenges of Asian American males would seem to be relatively lower than for other ethnic minorities. After all, a common stereotype of this male population tends to be that of an engineering student at a prestigious university or a successful entrepreneur of a cohesive family of similarly ambitious members. There is some justification for this image, as the proportions of Asian American students at Harvard, Berkeley, and MIT are higher than in the U.S. population (Sandhu, 1997). Also, the median income of Asian American families is higher than that of other groups in the United States (U.S. Census Bureau, 2004).

Data like these lead to an erroneous idea that Asian Americans represent a "model minority," a notion that is described and challenged by Sue and Sue (2008). Among the many problematic realities hidden by this surface image is the fact of substantial within-group disparities in education and income, with many less recognized ghetto areas of poverty, unemployment, health problems, and juvenile delinquency. Additionally, even those financially successful Asian Americans remain subject to racism and discrimination, with the rate of racially motivated hate crimes on the increase (Mathee, 1997). Finally, Asian Americans tend to avoid mental health services, with many adjustment difficulties hidden because of shame and cultural prohibitions against revealing private family matters (Lee & Mock, 2005; Sue & Sue, 2008).

In describing the knowledge necessary for work with Asian Americans, the primary experts echo the previously identified need for therapists to be aware of diversity within the ethnic group and avoid assuming homogeneity throughout the Asian American population (Lee & Mock, 2005). Despite these differences, however, there are many common experiences and worldviews that therapists should recognize.

One important demographic factor with the Asian American population is related to the relatively recent acceleration in immigration to the United States (Sue & Sue, 2008). Compared with other groups, a disproportionate percentage of the Asian American population is foreign-born, resulting in intergenerational conflicts and major challenges for acculturation. Also, since many Asian American immigrants came to the United States to escape war and political upheaval, many will have been exposed to trauma and its aftermath (Lee & Mock, 2005).

Aside from factors resulting from immigration history, Asian Americans share worldviews and values that are not always compatible with those of most mainstream U.S. therapists. The most commonly recognized value difference is the clash between the dominant individualistic orientation of the United States and the collectivist orientation of Asian American culture. As was noted with Hispanic and Native American cultures, personal achievement is less emphasized than loyalty to one's family. "Rather than an 'I' identity, Asians are taught to embrace a 'we' identity. The individual does not stand alone, but is seen as the product of all the generations of his or her family" (Lee & Mock, 2005, p. 272). As a result, an individual Asian man's actions reflect not only on himself but also on his extended family and on his ancestors (Hong & Ham, 2001).

Critical for understanding the issues of the Asian American male is the hierarchy and status structure within their families (Sue & Sue, 2008). Older family members are traditionally accorded respect and authority, and patriarchal privileges are accorded to male family members. As a result, older sons are granted benefits but also are burdened by their sense of responsibility and need to honor the family tradition. Loyalty to the lineage, as well as expectations to financially assist other family members, contributes markedly to the pressure on Asian men to pursue advanced education and career success (Sue, 1999). As noted by Espiritu (1999), however, not all Asian men have been able to make an accommodation: "The patriarchal authority of Asian immigrant men, particularly those of the working class, has been challenged due to the social and economic losses they have suffered in their transition to the status of men of color in the United States" (p. 628).

Several factors contribute to the special identity issues and relationship problems common to Asian American males. As an outgrowth of pressure to carry on family traditions, males tend to acculturate more slowly (Huang, 1994; Sue, 2005) and are susceptible to being viewed as old-fashioned and less appealing by the more rapidly acculturating Asian females. Obviously, this problem is only compounded in a U.S. culture that has witnessed significant progress in women's relative status with men and that has empowered Asian American women to challenge traditional male entitlements. Further, the traditional Asian sanction on expression of strong emotion creates adjustment issues for Asian American men as relationship partners and as fathers to more acculturated children (Lee & Mock, 2005; Sue, 2005).

Two other factors have been identified as creating adjustment issues for Asian males. First, the culturally imbued reluctance to self-promote has been noted by Sue (1999) as inhibiting their ability to advance in the managerial and corporate world. Second, the prominent media images of attractiveness, primarily rooted in Eurocentric standards, tend to create self-image issues for young Asian males. For example, some researchers (Chen & Yang, 1986; Huang & Ying, 1991) have reported many Asian adolescent males and females to be dissatisfied with their appearance and that of their opposite sex counterparts.

In reviewing the recommendations that have been made for therapeutic intervention with Asian American men (Okazaki, 2000; Sue, 1999; Sue, 2005), there appear to be three primary needs: to be aware of these men's historical antipathy for recognizing and acknowledging emotional problems; to adapt interventions to the level of acculturation; and to utilize interventions congruent with Asian American relational style.

The stigma against reporting psychological problems and preference for expressing emotional distress in somatic language (Okazaki, 2000) create a need for therapists to be flexible in their initial approach to Asian American males. For example, there may be a need for the clinician to initially present with greater emphasis upon professional credentials (e.g., doctor status) as a means of establishing credibility. No expectation should be held for immediate psychological insight or deep revelation of inner emotional turmoil. Sue (2005) recommended modified cognitive therapy for Asian men "whose cultural background supports emotional restraint and practical solutions" (p. 790). Atkinson, Kim, and Caldwell (1998) reported a preference in Asian American therapy formats for a consultation model and a problem-solving approach as well as a general distaste for "personal discussion that might lead to shame" and low ratings for "intrapsychic exploration" (p. 422).

In general, Sue (1999, 2005) offered similar therapy recommendations for the content and conduct of therapy with both adult and adolescent Asian American males. He identified consciousness raising and cognitive appraisal about male role conflicts as especially valuable therapeutic activities. For example, in advocating for the therapist to make culture conflicts a primary therapeutic focus, he emphasized the face-saving qualities for shame-prone individuals. In terms of therapist activity, he proposed that the therapist function actively as *mediator*. This mediator role, similar to the concept of *culture broker* (Owen, 2005), calls for the therapist to assist the client to negotiate an acceptable compromise between himself and his cultural heritage as well as within his own family of origin. "The cognitive approach allows the Asian male to identify acculturation conflicts as the source of family problems and . . . healthy ways of accommodating can be addressed. . . . New ways of defining or reframing successful relationships among family members and peers can be acknowledged" (Sue, 2005, p. 365).

THERAPEUTIC INTERVENTIONS WITH GAY AND BISEXUAL MEN, ADOLESCENTS, AND BOYS

Over the past 4 decades, a monumental shift has taken place within the mental health fields in their view of gays, lesbians, and bisexuals. Once considered sexually deviant and an outgrowth of pathological development, gay, lesbian, and bisexual orientations are now recognized to be one of the many forms of cultural diversity. With the overturning of the pathologizing paradigm, marked most publicly by the removal of homosexuality from the *Diagnostic and Statistical Manual of Mental Disorders, Fourth Edition* (American Psychiatric Association, 1994), and other authoritative lists of mental disorders, professional organizations began calling for a new literature describing affirmative and appropriate services for lesbians and gay men (Garnets, Hancock, Cochran, Goodchilds, & Peplau, 1991). We can be thankful that literature has appeared, most notably in the form of the *Handbook of Counseling and Psychotherapy With Lesbian, Gay, and Bisexual Clients* (Beischke, Perez, & DeBord, 2007; Perez, DeBord, & Bieschke, 2000). The two editions of that handbook and many other important works have greatly enriched therapists' familiarity with the demands and opportunities in work with these populations. Although it would certainly be impossible to capture all that has been written in this area, some critical information will be provided about the context of gay and bisexual men's lives, the barriers to their seeking and receiving treatment, the important content areas needing to be addressed in therapy, process issues of that therapy, and therapist impediments to gay-affirming psychotherapy.

The Context of the Lives of Gay and Bisexual Males

Despite considerable gains in the recent past, gay and bisexual men still live in a country that is highly divergent and deeply divided in attitudes toward them. Hate crimes continue against gay men (Herek, 1991, 1992; Mason, 2001), a high percentage of gay males report victimization from physical or verbal abuse, and psychological safety continues to be an issue for gay men when entering new and unfamiliar environments (Hershberger & D'Augelli, 2000). Greater acceptance of gay lifestyles, gay marriage, and gay adoption is found in many areas of the United States and many segments of the U.S. population, yet many other segments and areas hold highly antagonistic attitudes toward gay men, and each legislative gain is threatened by conservative political and religious efforts for reversal (Stanton & Maier, 2004). Furthermore, the adverse impact of gay men's victimized life experiences are exponentially more problematic for ethnic minority men (Greene, 1994), older men (Berger & Kelly, 1996), and men living in rural areas (D'Augelli & Garnets, 1995). Even many branches of the mental health field continue to hold various pathologizing views of lesbian, gay, bisexual, and transgender issues (Kilgore, Sideman, Amin, Baca, & Bohanske, 2005). Also, a movement to "repair" homosexuality has received considerable attention in some mental health circles (Nicolosi, 1997; Yarhouse, 2005), despite the extensive questions raised about the ethics and scientific basis for these approaches (Haldeman, 1994, 2001a).

Aside from the oppression created by a culture still hostile to anyone not fully heterosexual, many gay and bisexual men must also struggle with internalized self-hatred inherent in childhood trauma. As noted by Haldeman (2005), "Nearly every gay or bisexual man reports, in his developmental years, some scarring experiences directly related to sexual orientation" (p. 369).

Barriers to Treatment

There is a regrettable irony about the relationship of the psychotherapy community to gay and bisexual men. Although a gay or bisexual man is more likely than a heterosexual man to seek psychotherapy (Dworkin, 2000; Haldeman, 2005), the psychotherapist he ultimately sees is much less likely to be adequately prepared to treat him in an informed and competent manner. A considerable body of literature has demonstrated that therapists-in-training feel largely unprepared for work with lesbian, gay, and bisexual (LGB) clients (Phillips & Fischer, 1998; Pilkington & Cantor, 1996). Many students report knowing more about the issues than their instructors or supervisors (Buhrke, 1989) and also report that some of their supervisors retain outdated and inaccurate views of the LGB population.

The poor level of preparedness of therapists for work with LGB clients is compounded by problems in the areas of awareness and level of knowledge about LGB lifestyles and challenges. In the *Guidelines for Psychotherapy with Lesbian, Gay, and Bisexual Clients* (American Psychological Association [APA] Division 44, 2000), problems were identified from therapists' frequent lack of awareness of their internalized heterosexism as well as their underappreciation of the effects of social stigmatization upon this population.

When this lack of awareness critique is applied to the issues of work with a gay or bisexual male, it could be manifested by either a *minimization* of the importance of his sexual orientation or, conversely, by an *exaggeration* of the importance of his sexual orientation. That is, a gay or bisexual man's mental health problems frequently need to be understood less as a product of personal pathology than the result of life in a homophobic and heterosexist culture (Herek, 1991, 1992; Meyer, 1995). On the other hand, when homosexuality or bisexuality are considered to be evidence of a mental illness, that sexual orientation is likely to be viewed as the major source of the client's psychological difficulties even when sexual orientation has not been presented as problematic (Garnets et al., 1991; Liddle, 1996).

Special Therapy Content Areas

There are multiple areas in which therapists' lack of adequate knowledge impedes therapeutic work with gay and bisexual male clients. First, heterosexual therapists frequently lack sufficient knowledge about the norms, lifestyles, and daily issues of gay and bisexual men. In this regard, Haldeman (2005) identified a need for "gay cultural literacy . . . the ability to view the lives of gay and bisexual men through the appropriate lens—a gay-bisexual sensibility, as opposed to a heterocentric one" (p. 374). Among these differing norms may be those related to variety in sexual behavior, emphasis placed on the man's circle of friends and community (sometimes referred to as a "family of choice" or what Scrivner [personal communication, March, 4, 1994] referred to as his "gay family"), and varying levels of situation-dependent disclosure.

A few of the many other areas for increased therapist knowledge can be noted. Therapists wishing to work with gay and bisexual men need to understand the special nature of couple and family relationships (Garnets & Kimmel, 1993). Therapists must comprehend the challenges of parenting and the varieties of family structures (Allen & Burrell, 1996; Haldeman, 2005). There must be understanding of the enormous health and psychological challenges presented by HIV (Kauth, Hartwig, & Kalichman, 2000). Therapists need to consider the complex interweaving of issues of gay and bisexual identity for aging men (Herdt & deVries, 2004), men of color (Fukuyama & Ferguson, 2000), and physically disabled men (Haldeman, 2005; Olkin, 1999).

Of the areas requiring therapist knowledge, none are more critical than knowledge about gay and bisexual identity development and the coming out process (APA, 2000; Haldeman, 2005; Savin-Williams, 2001). Since gay and bisexual clients commonly rely heavily upon therapists to guide them in making the complicated and consequential decisions involved in revealing their sexual orientation, therapists must have deep appreciation of the critical decision variables. In addition, gay and bisexual men who are early in their gay or bisexual identity development will be exceptionally susceptible to the influence of their therapist. For this reason, therapists must be familiar with identity developmental models, able to assist with identity management, competent to address internalized homophobia, and alert to the effects of societal heterosexism (Reynolds & Hanjorgiris, 2000).

An especially problematic issue for therapists working in this area is the vexing problem of males wishing to "cure" their homosexuality and undergo conversion or "reparative" therapy (Nicolosi, 1997). From an ethical and diversity perspective, any therapist will be challenged to balance the sensitivities of a gay or bisexual man who holds strong religious beliefs that any homosexual activity is sinful with the equally necessary respect for the perspectives of the LGB community. In this situation, the therapist must be familiar with the religious perspective of the client but must also be quite aware of the scientific information available about reparative therapies and the ethical responsibilities of informed consent. This issue has been thoroughly reviewed by Haldeman (1994) and Glassgold, Fitzgerald, and Haldeman (2002), who make a compelling case for the lack of credible scientific evidence regarding the effectiveness of reparative therapy.

Psychotherapy Processes

The most fundamental process requirement of therapy with gay and bisexual clients is that it be conducted in a gay-affirming fashion (Brown, 1989; Morrow, 2000; Schwartzberg & Rosenberg, 1998). Gay-affirming therapy is that which provides emotional support, identity validation, and personal empowerment. Of this process, McHenry and Johnson (1993) noted, "If psychotherapy with gays and lesbians is truly successful, the outcome will be numerous individuals who no longer attempt to conform to a heterosexual world, but who will instead creatively seek the enhancement of their own identities" (p. 150).

Amidst the complications of affirmative psychotherapy with gay and bisexual men are several unique advantages for this work vis-à-vis work with heterosexual men. At one level, these men pose the usual challenge of therapy resistance because of indoctrination into the traditional male code of self-sufficiency, avoidance of vulnerability, and suppression of feelings. However, by virtue of gay identity formation, they have commonly surmounted many of the restrictions of the male code. Schwartzberg and Rosenberg (1998) observed, "Gay men grow up both gay and male, and as such face significant obstacles, but also unique opportunities in developing a unique sense of self" (p. 260). On this matter, Brown (1989) suggested that three aspects of contemporary gay life—biculturalism, marginality, and forging of new cultural norms—allow for the creation of an enhanced life perspective. For gay and bisexual men, the potential for integration of both masculine and feminine human qualities allows for a type of role transcendence that would offer broad personal benefits, not the least of which would be greater openness to participation in psychotherapy.

In terms of specific therapeutic modalities and processes for work with gay and bisexual men, most all therapy orientations can be conducted in an affirmative manner (Dworkin, 2000). For example, Fassinger (2000) provided an overview of possible benefits and pitfalls of several therapeutic approaches including humanistic, cognitive–behavioral, psychodynamic, and systems-cultural approaches.

Group therapy has been identified as having special advantages for work with gay and bisexual men because of the opportunities to work on self-esteem, family-of-origin issues, and interpersonal skills related to emotional intimacy (DeBord & Perez, 2000; Holahan & Gibson, 1994). Also, since so many men in this group have been victims of family and societal rejection, therapy groups offer an environment of support, safety, and a place of acceptance in a world that is commonly hostile or threatening. The aforementioned group therapy benefits of universality, modeling, and instillation of hope seem especially beneficial for men struggling to cope with a homophobic society.

Relationship counseling is often recommended for gay men because of the challenges inherent when both partners have been socialized into the male gender role. Although gay men are relatively less conforming to the male code, they have nevertheless been found to be more likely than heterosexual couples to openly struggle with relationship problems rooted in traditional masculinity (Johnson & Keren, 1996). In part, this may be a function of both partners being socialized toward achievement, competitiveness, aggression, and narrow attitudes toward sex (Hawkins, 1992). In general, however, this matter, as described by Ossana (2000), appears to be a product of the complex interplay of male socialization and the intricacies of gay identity formation.

Family therapy for gay and bisexual men is also potentially quite helpful, but this matter requires considerable clarification of how one defines *family*. As noted by Matthews and Lease (2000), the LGB concept of family is far broader and more inclusive than that assumed within heterosexist conceptualizations. For LGB persons the term *family* could be a family of origin, a family of creation, or a family of choice. This matter is addressed by Weston (1994), who described kinship patterns among lesbians and gays as more flexible than in traditional families, with the inclusion of both blood relatives and people purposely chosen because of "symbolic demonstrations of love, shared history, material or emotional assistance, and other signs of enduring solidarity" (p. 527). Among the many issues that might be addressed in this therapy format might be issues related to donor insemination, surrogate mothering, adoption, step-parenting, and relationships with family of origin.

Challenges of Work With Gay and Bisexual Male Adolescents

If a 2006 cover story in *Newsweek*, "The Trouble with Boys," is at all representative of national sentiment, there certainly is great concern about young American men. As has been noted already, all young men are troubled by the need to accommodate their physical and psychological development with the need to create a healthy male role amidst an abundance of negative images. Gay and bisexual youth face all of these challenges as well as the extra formidable challenge of integrating their psychological needs with a newly emerging gay identity. It is not surprising, therefore, that many experts have identified this group of young men as an exceptionally at-risk population worthy of far greater awareness from the mental health community (APA, 2000; Barber & Mobley, 1999; Hershberger & D'Augelli, 2000; Kiselica, Mule et al., 2008). On this situation, Barber and Mobley (1999) noted, "In light of the recent finding . . . that gay youth are 2 to 3 times as likely to attempt suicide as other young people, the time is at hand for helping professionals of good conscience to begin to explore counseling strategies for this population" (p. 161).

There are stresses in abundance for gay and bisexual youth. First, a primary issue is related to the need to strategize the shift from a life of secrecy and hidden feelings into the process of coming out to self and to family. Research indicates that young men become aware of being gay generally around age 12 (Newman & Muzzonigro, 1993), a most vulnerable life stage to face potential familial rejection and hostility. Since therapists will often play a role in this decision-making process, it is incumbent on them to be thoroughly aware of the issues and risks.

Also, schools and religious institutions are rarely supportive and often are punitive toward gay youth (Barber & Mobley, 1999). For example, Sears (1991) observed, "For a gay student high school is often a lonely place . . . a gay high school student is faced with the choice of watching from the sidelines . . . or 'passing' and going through the motions" (p. 326). As a result of this isolation, therapists may be among the only accessible persons supportive of these young men.

In some fortunate circumstances acceptance of gay youth is becoming more common, but gay bashing and victimization continue to be prevalent (D'Augelli, Hershberger, & Pilkington, 1998; Wilchins, 2008). Given the emphasis in the traditional male code on expressing physical aggression, a victimized young male is especially vulnerable to shame and humiliation. Many observers have suggested that the higher incidence of substance abuse among gay youth (Rotheram-Borus, Luna, Marotta, & Kelly, 1994) is related to the need to anesthetize the pain of their victimization as well as a symptom of their emotional isolation, role confusion, and self-hatred (Barber & Mobley, 1999). Needless to say, high-risk behavior and poor awareness of HIV-related issues can create an especially dangerous dilemma for gay and bisexual youth and an educational challenge for therapists.

Clearly, therapeutic expertise for work with gay and bisexual youth is both highly needed and significantly challenging. A newly emerging literature is invaluable in this regard (Bieschke et al., 2007; Firestein, 2007; Kiselica, Mule et al., 2008; Lee, 2007). Also, therapists need to be aware of several national organizations that can provide exceptional resources for this work: Parents and Friends of Lesbians and Gays (PFLAG), http://www.pflag.org; the GLBT National Help Center, http://www.glnh.org/index2.html; National

Advocacy Youth Coalition, http://www.nyacyouth.org; National Black Lesbian and Gay Leadership Forum, (202) 483-6786; and the Hetrick Martin Institute, http://www.hmi.org/Page.aspx?pid=214.

Finally, mention should be made of the "gay affirmative counseling process" described by Kiselica, Mule, and Haldeman (2008). Several highlights of this process are especially noteworthy. First, the authors recommended the establishment of a safe environment through empathy, gay-sensitive language, and gay advocacy. In addition, they encouraged therapists to be familiar with the gay community and develop a support network. They also urged that therapy include the teaching of coping skills specific to the gay experience. They also suggested family therapy interventions as appropriate and timely to help "family members move toward acceptance, stability, and harmony following a son's decision to come out to them" (Kiselica, Mule, & Haldeman, 2008, p. 260).

MEN WITH PHYSICAL DISABILITIES

A once-popular song described a desire for a "hero" who's "gotta be strong, gotta be fast, and gotta be fresh from the fight." Many men with disabilities "fail" on all three counts. Regarding this situation, Murphy (1990) wrote, "Paralytic disability constitutes emasculation of a more direct and total nature . . . the weakening and atrophy of the body threaten all the cultural values of masculinity: strength, activeness, speed, virility, stamina, and fortitude" (p. 94).

The special issues for men with physical disabilities are a product of the negative interaction between two problematic sets of attitudinal systems—the prominent belief systems of mainstream culture about disability and the traditional beliefs about what constitutes "a real man." All men who experience a physical disability join the "disability community" and thereby come to share a common "disability experience" (Olkin, 1999). When this occurs, it becomes incumbent upon them to struggle both with the limitations inherent in their disability as well as the negative stereotypes of physical disability and the reluctance of society at large to provide needed accommodations. In addition, these men will need to determine whether their joining this disability community will be accompanied by a corollary eviction from the community of "real" men.

In this section I review some of the important issues of the disability experience and the efforts of some advocates to counter cultural biases and discrimination against persons with disabilities. I then look at some ideas about how the disability experience differentially affects males. Finally, I look at the implications for this perspective upon therapeutic interventions for males with disabilities.

The Disability Experience

Rhoda Olkin (1999), the foremost psychologist advocating for a bridge between the disability community and the mental health profession, has provided several illuminating facts about persons with disabilities. Based on the definition outlined in the Americans With Disabilities Act (ADA; 1990), persons with disabilities constitute the largest minority group in the United States. Approximately two thirds of persons with disabilities are unemployed, and less than 10% of this population graduates from college. Gender, ethnicity, and disability status are synergistic, with women and ethnic minorities experiencing the most lifestyle restrictions from their disability status.

A central tenet of Olkin's ideas regarding persons with disabilities is that the *minority model* of disability is far more appropriate than the *moral model* (i.e., one that views disability as a form of spiritual test) or the *medical model* (i.e., one that sees medical professionals as the key to benevolent restoration of the problems within the "afflicted" individual). Unlike the other two models, the minority model places the responsibility for improved adaptation upon the larger society and considers full societal access to be a basic right of disabled persons. Olkin (1999) noted, "The minority model . . . posits that disability is a social construction, that the problems lie not within the persons with disabilities but the environment that fails to accommodate" (p. 26).

The minority model of disability has several important implications for psychotherapists working with both male and female disabled persons. Therapists must recognize the degree to which they have consciously or unconsciously bought into prominent stereotypes, how likely they are to erroneously operate from the medical or moral model, how their ignorance of disability etiquette and lifestyles might produce impolite interpersonal actions, and how their own fears of disability might create overreactions to a disabled client. Also, this model of therapy for persons with disabilities, very much like feminist models of therapy for women, posits that appropriate therapy emphasizes personal empowerment over passive adaptation and social action over blaming the victim.

In applying disability perspectives to work with males, several useful suggestions have been offered. Gerschick and Miller (1997) encouraged therapists to be acutely aware of how disabled men are coping with the interacting social dynamics of pressures of being masculine while simultaneously trying to disprove society's perception of them as "weak, pitiful, passive, and dependent" (p. 455). Also, researchers have identified common coping strategies employed by men in reaction to disability status (Charmaz, 1995; Gerschick & Miller, 1997). Some men employ efforts to recapture all aspects of their past selves, while others employ continued reliance on traditional masculine values. In the former case, the strategy ultimately produces depression in the face of reality, while the latter produces overcompensation with hypermasculine risk-taking and potentially self-injurious behavior. Some men, however, are able to reject their previously accepted ideas of acceptable masculine behavior and transcend to an alternative masculine identity, identifying themselves as "persons." This last pattern is most successful when the man is able to join a subculture supportive of his new views (as might be found in a men's support group). To date, this last strategy seems to have shown the best hope for long-term mental health and psychological well-being.

Psychotherapy With Physically Disabled Males

Irmo Marini (2005), who has worked extensively with men in physical rehabilitation settings and has dealt with his own C5 tetraplegia, identified several of the most pressing therapeutic issues and recommended helpful therapeutic strategies. He observed that the primary concern of men with disabilities in rehabilitation settings is the fear of losing sexual prowess. Second, these men fear loss of control of their bodies and of their immediate environment. Third, they are greatly concerned about their finances and future employability. Finally, they have extreme problems coping with the frustration of once again mastering previously acquired skills. He stated, "Having been previously strong and independent, many males may struggle with childlike feelings of dependency and perceive having to ask for assistance to complete the simplest of tasks as embarrassing and shameful" (Marini, 2005, p. 98).

To some extent, the concerns of adolescent males differ somewhat in emphasis from those of midlife males. Simmons and Rosenberg (1975) reported that changes to physical appearance were more troubling in this age group, primarily because of implications for development of intimate relationships. Given the enormous importance of peer relationships during adolescence, it is not surprising that fears of loneliness, rejection, and social isolation are principal concerns for young men.

Therapeutic work with disabled males first revolves around helping clients recognize their cognitive schemata about masculinity and disability, replacing erroneous and unproductive thinking with more adaptive patterns. For example, the common desire of men to have control over their environment can be channeled into an adaptive plan to learn new skills and master assistive technologies. Second, therapists who are familiar with the common concerns of rehabilitating males can find ways to introduce these topics at timely points in the adjustment cycle. Third, therapists need to be prepared to challenge some of the more inappropriate coping patterns, such as substance abuse, high-risk behavior, and social withdrawal. Fourth, therapists who are knowledgeable of disability-specific physiology are able to provide necessary advice to improve physical functioning and avoid common pitfalls.

Finally, therapists may recruit successfully adjusted males to meet with clients earlier in the adjustment process, thereby providing inspirational role models.

Indeed, as this chapter has attempted to illustrate, not all men and boys are exactly the same—particularly when it comes to defining masculinity. And if the therapeutic community is just beginning to come to grips with the *crisis of masculinity* among a typical (yet still-reluctant) clientele with the traditional notion of masculinity, it faces a much more arduous task in trying to understand male gender-role strain in clients with diverse masculinities. Many male-oriented therapists still grapple with their clients' basic problems of trying to adhere to a traditional hegemonic masculine construct that has come under assault over the past few decades. Clients are trying to adhere to a masculinity that is still being socially constructed among men with different ethnocultural heritages and lifestyles as well as physical ability backgrounds. Their presenting problems add a new layer of complexity to the male-oriented therapist's task. Again, many of the psychotherapeutic approaches developed in the United States have neglected masculinity and its attendant problems, let alone masculinities that depart significantly from that of the "typical" male client suffering gender-role strain. How can a therapist focus on problems with the traditional masculine role when more cases present problems with a masculine role that is still being defined or that lacks traditional and more socially pervasive reference points?

The crucial work of multicultural therapy must address a client's problems in situ, as it were, and the male-oriented therapist's task with such a paradigm is to understand how the common factors among men contributing to the core problems of a peculiarly male gender-role strain interact with other environmental risk factors and assets—and how those risks and assets either aggravate or attenuate the symptomatic aspects of male gender-role strain. From the therapist's perspective, multicultural empathy and understanding can seem like a daunting task, especially if he (or especially she) is from a culture, educational level, and socioeconomic background quite different from that of the majority of his (or her) clients. Yet empathy and understanding in the service of positive therapeutic outcomes do not depend on a thorough immersion into the client's cultural milieu and an experiential survey of all of the client's contextual factors; rather, empathy and understanding require a keen therapeutic ability to discern, isolate, and identify the commonalities in troubled men's lives that span cultural and socioeconomic contexts.

A male-friendly therapeutic approach has universal applicability for attracting and, to an extent, engaging many men across different cultural and lifestyle backgrounds. The more challenging task of therapeutic work requires involved interaction between therapist and client to cut through the mostly unfamiliar background narrative of distinct cultural influences and get to the wholly familiar core problems that reside in the tangle of culture, family, community, and lifestyle. In the case of Lee, which opened this chapter, the therapist had to acquire a good understanding of not only the significance of families of origin in Asian culture but also of Christianity's effect on Asian American culture—and of the generational dynamics of those cultural variables. Lee's is a complex case study, but one that is not out of the ordinary in the male-oriented therapist's world.

To be sure, with action-stage men, the therapist must make a role shift from that of a realistic provider of life alternatives to male gender-role strain to that of an active listener and negotiator. The therapist and the client (and, in Lee's case, other therapists) negotiate realistic strategies of tackling the client's core problems within the client's unique environmental/cultural context. The therapist must not only listen, but also acquire a special empathy and understanding for the client's peculiar plight—including the client's particular stage or level of change (precontemplative, contemplative, action-oriented, or maintenance)—and then adopt appropriate goals and tasks for the therapeutic course as negotiated between therapist and client. All the while, the therapist must acknowledge the client's possession of a great deal of relevant contextual knowledge and rely on some sort of eclectic therapeutic template that can integrate such specific knowledge with the technical expertise of innovative therapeutic approaches—and all these therapeutic transactions must be understood and take place within the relevant gender-related paradigm.

This is where an integrative, transtheoretical model of men's therapy can become an extremely valuable therapeutic aid for all men experiencing gender-role strain.

7

A TRANSTHEORETICAL MODEL

The first appointment with Hector was set up following a referral from a counselor with the employee assistance program of his railroad employer. What originally began as a severe back pain complaint was recognized to have emotional stress components. Although initially resistant to "head shrinking," Hector responded well to the counselor, who was a receptive listener regarding the pressures of blue-collar manhood. Also, Hector had been given an informational pamphlet on men and depression that he had found thought provoking. After three sessions, the counselor had recommended further treatment with me, but Hector demurred, citing a much improved mood. It wasn't until several months later that a bitter and near-violent quarrel with his wife prompted Hector to come in.

It was not surprising that Hector was tense and guarded in our initial contact. A 48-year-old Mexican American male, he had been employed for 31 years with the railroad and had never had any contact with a mental health professional. His first marriage, which lasted 20 years, was tumultuous. His second marriage (to Susan) had been stormy from the beginning, with Hector's problematic relationship with his teenage stepdaughters as the focal point of the stress. Hector admitted that he had "nearly lost it" several times in trying to discipline the 13-year-old younger stepdaughter.

In our first session, I chose initially to avoid focusing on Hector's faulty behavior and spent most of our time learning all I could about him—his work, his relationships, and his goals. I was impressed to learn that Hector was a survivor, in that he was the only one of five sons to escape substance abuse and criminal behavior after severe physical abuse from an alcoholic father. Forced to drop out of high school to provide income for his mother and his younger brothers, Hector had found a good employer in the railroad company. Over the previous 3 decades he had frequently worked double shifts to support his new family and his family of origin. Of late, he had become greatly concerned that chronic back pains might force him out of work and into disability retirement.

In my earliest work with Hector I provided validation for his hard work and empathy for his current emotional distress. I exposed him to a variety of consciousness-raising materials and urged him to reflect upon his upbringing and early life lessons about the meanings of manhood. As we became more familiar with each other, he sought feedback about my own ideas regarding the manly duties of the good-provider role and family leadership.

Hector: What about you, Doc? How did you handle all this stuff?

Therapist: You know, many of us guys are pretty similar: We all are trying to figure out how to find a good balance—how much work is enough? What the hell else are we supposed to do?

Hector: You sure are on target there. I get nailed pretty good for being such an insensitive a-hole! I have no clue how to understand any of those women. No matter how much I do, somebody is always climbing my ass.

I opened this chapter with a vignette from Hector's story because it illustrates (and I hope will fully illustrate throughout this chapter) the panoply of issues that constitute a multicultural paradigm in psychotherapy. The fact that Hector is a Mexican American is just one aspect of the multiculturalism that defined the therapeutic relationship: He's also a high school dropout; a blue-collar worker; an ex-substance abuser (and ex-criminal); a stepfather; the son of a physically abusive, alcoholic father; and a provider to not only his immediate family but also to his family of origin and his siblings. Some or all of these roles converged and managed to assail Hector's construct of masculinity; he was obviously experiencing a great deal of strain performing in the roles of a provider to his two families and trying to be a disciplinary head of household with his immediate family.

Hector was also at the contemplative level of change: He wasn't enamored with the idea of therapy, but he also thought he'd run out of options; he knew he was suffering some depression, and his violent temper seemed to be surfacing fairly frequently. He wasn't on the cusp of the action stage, but he had done some exploration regarding his problems and had acquired a degree of insight to motivate him to work on establishing the goals and tasks of therapy—what he wanted from therapy and how should he go about getting it—in our nascent working alliance.

From my perspective as therapist, Hector presented some fairly straightforward symptoms of male gender-role strain. Yet the sources of that conflicted masculinity and the manifest problems they were causing in Hector's life were manifold. The more I empathized and tried to acquire a good understanding of the various multicultural influences that were now driving Hector toward crisis, the more convinced I was that I would have to employ an eclectic mode of therapy to factor in all those various dimensions of his life in order to isolate the core problem in his masculinity construct. Moreover, I would have to rely on Hector to help me discern in his ongoing narrative the salient factors in his culture, his upbringing, his relationship with his wife and stepdaughters, and his relationships with other men (particularly his friends and his coworkers at the railroad) that were causing him so much stress now.

The problem—again, from my perspective as therapist—was that most of the multicultural therapies that seek to integrate all these factors of ethnicity, educational level, socioeconomic status, and basic lifestyle seemed to be missing a crucial component, at least in the case of Hector and other male clients suffering pronounced symptoms of male-gender-role strain: a *masculinity paradigm* by which to assess the relative weight and intensity of the surrounding multicultural influences. The eclectic mode of therapy admitted such variegated social influences in its course, even though it offered up gender as just another independent variable in the mix of factors to be considered in effective therapeutic outcomes. Yet such eclectic (or integrative) modes of therapy didn't account for where clients stood in terms of motivation and external pressures to change self-destructive behaviors.

When questioned about their therapeutic approach, most therapists will now name more than one theoretical orientation; if pressed for specificity, they will describe themselves as "eclectic" or "integrative" (Bechtoldt et al., 2001; Norcross, Karpiak, & Lister, 2005). Although the earliest efforts to integrate psychotherapies can be traced back more than several decades (Arkowitz, 1984; Gold, 1993), the pronounced trend toward this orientation has been primarily within the past 2 decades. In describing the history of psychotherapy integration, Brooks-Harris (2008) attributed the strength of this theoretical movement to two primary factors: the desire of clinicians to choose interventions from a wider array of psychotherapeutic strategies and a cultural shift to postmodern philosophies seeking to explain the multiple constructions of social realities. Regarding this trend toward broader incorporation of therapeutic modalities, Norcross and Goldfried (2005) stated, "Psychotherapy integration has entered young adulthood, no longer an immature or novel approach to clinical work . . . [and] is now well established as the modal orientation of psychotherapists" (p. v).

As the earlier chapters of this book have shown, many therapy approaches have much to offer for work with men (especially when they are adapted to men's special issues and needs). None of these approaches, however, is singularly inclusive enough to capture the benefits of all approaches: An eclectic or integrative approach seems most likely to meet men's needs. Good and Mintz (2005) took a major step in this direction by proposing the first integrative framework for psychotherapy with men. The underlying basis for their approach is the theorizing of Beitman and Yue (1999), which they view as "highly compatible with the clinical and research literature on men's issues . . . to optimally address the concerns of male clients (Good & Mintz, 2005, p. 248).

Consistent with this clear trend toward psychotherapy integration, this chapter provides a brief overview of this movement and takes a further step toward incorporating it with the wealth of information from the *new psychology of men*. Finally, a multitheoretical model is offered that extends the work of Good and Mintz (2005) and offers a gender-informed expansion of the integrative psychotherapy movement. This model is enriched by many of the movement's theoretical strains, including multimodal therapy (MMT; Lazarus, 1976), systematic treatment selection (STS; Beutler & Harwood, 2000), assimilative psychodynamic psychotherapy (Stricker & Gold, 2005), and integrative problem-centered therapy (IPCT; Pinsof, 1995). However, this model is most closely tied to the transtheoretical approach of Prochaska and DiClemente (2005) and the transtheoretical analysis of psychotherapy systems provided by Prochaska and Norcross (2007).

The integration of the transtheoretical approach with the new literature of men's studies represents only the first half of the effort to develop integrative psychotherapy for boys and men. The second half of this effort for a new integrative therapy for males requires that therapists become more knowledgeable regarding the sociocultural contexts in which their clients function, more skillful in adapting therapy interventions to client needs, and more aware of the bias and values they bring into the therapy setting. These requirements have been best elaborated in the landmark work of Derald Wing Sue and David Sue (Sue & Sue, 2003; 2008), who have been the leading proponents for all therapists to develop greater multicultural competence.

INTEGRATIVE MODELS OF PSYCHOTHERAPY

In his review of the historical development of psychotherapy integration, Brooks-Harris (2008) identified the landmark works of Frank (1961), Lazarus (1976), Wachtel (1977), and Prochaska (1979). To provide some organizational structure for the multiple variants of integrative models, Brooks-Harris suggested four general routes along which they could be categorized: common factors; technical eclecticism, assimilative integration, and theoretical integration (or multitheoretical frameworks). Each of these general routes has much to offer in the development of an integrative model of therapy with men, but the multitheoretical framework seems to have the broadest and most direct applicability. Two models within that framework, integrative problem-centered therapy (Pinsof, 1995) and the transtheoretical approach (Prochaska & DiClemente, 2005; Prochaska & Norcross, 2007) seem especially rich in applicability for work with males.

Pinsof (1995) described IPCT as a framework that "provides a set of parameters for interrelating family, individual, and biological treatments" as well as "guidelines for making decisions about what types of interventions to use at which points in therapy with specific types of patients with specific problems" (p. 382). In terms of interventions, Pinsof described six orientations: behavioral, biobehavioral, experiential, family of origin, psychodynamic, and self psychology. These interventions are to be employed at three contextual levels: family/community, couple, and individual. The model calls for sequential movement from the less complex to the more complex levels of problem constraint, based upon two major premises. First, patients are considered to be "healthy until proven sick (incapable of solving their problems without major assistance)" (p. 393). Second, the model presumes that "the problem maintenance structure is superficial and simple until proven otherwise" (p. 384). This model is "failure-driven," in that more involved, elaborate, and expensive interventions of the individual psychodynamic variety are not undertaken until here-and-now behavioral and structural interventions have proven ineffective.

The transtheoretical approach to therapy (Prochaska & DiClemente, 2005) is similar to Pinsof's IPCT in terms of calling for attention to contextual levels of client problems, considering multiple orientations for intervention, and paying special attention to factors that maintain problems and constrain change. However, the transtheoretical model adds major elements to the analysis in terms of explicating critical *processes of change* and recognizing the primary *stages of change*. As a result of this transtheoretical analysis, the fundamental groundwork is laid for the development of an integrative and transtheoretical model of therapy that is uniquely tailored for work with males. This new framework builds upon the work of previous integrative theorists to create a model for male-friendly therapy that incorporates conceptualizations of the fundamental processes involved in producing therapeutic change, the relative readiness of the male client for embracing change, the coordination of therapeutic intervention with his openness to therapy, and the need to target interventions to the most propitious systemic level.

The transtheoretical approach makes an immense contribution to the psychotherapy enterprise. When it is further developed through infusion of the insights of the new psychology of men, it seems possible to take a significant step toward an integrative model of male-friendly psychotherapy that will be described in the later portions of this chapter. First, however, it is necessary to examine some core elements of the transtheoretical model.

Processes of Change

The transtheoretical model of therapy, as articulated by Prochaska and Norcross (2007) and Prochaska and DiClemente (2005), attempts to look beyond the labels and descriptions of individual therapy schools to identify the most salient processes of change that underlie all therapy approaches. As noted previously in chapter 4, this type of analysis was first inspired by the Jerome Frank classic *Persuasion and Healing* (1961) and was later exemplified by the *common factors* approach to therapy of Sol Garfield (1980). Prochaska (1979) was another who sought to further the discovery of the factors common to effective psychotherapy. As noted by Prochaska and Norcross (2007), the earlier research analyzed 24 of the most popular theories of psychotherapy to determine which "overt and covert activities people use to alter emotions, thoughts, behaviors, or relationships related to a particular problem" (Prochaska & Norcross, 2007, p. 11). The outgrowth of this analysis was the production of a middle level of abstraction between global theories (i.e., psychoanalytic, behavioral, and humanistic) and the specific techniques (e.g., dream analysis or desensitization). The initial implication of this analysis was that therapists need to be able to employ different therapy activities to maximize benefits of clients who use differing change processes.

Over the years of this research, 10 processes of change were formulated, and these were presented by Prochaska and Norcross (2007) in the following manner. First, five fundamental process of change were noted: consciousness raising, catharsis, choosing, conditional stimuli, and contingency control. These changes were considered to occur at both the experiential level and the environmental levels, making a total of 10 primary change processes.

Consciousness Raising

Consciousness raising is an integral aspect of most eclectic therapy approaches, as illustrated by the experiential orientation in Pinsof's IPCT (Pinsof, 1995), insight and awareness strategies for internalizing patients in systematic treatment selection (Beutler & Harwood, 2000), and historical and interactional insight sought through assimilative psychodynamic psychotherapy (Stricker & Gold, 2005). In the transtheoretical model, consciousness raising refers to a range of efforts to help clients become more aware of factors influencing their lives. These efforts might include everything from providing greater awareness of the client's personal experience, the therapy process is considered to be feedback. When it is designed to heighten awareness of environmental factors, it is considered to be education.

> Consciousness raising was an integral component of the earliest interventions with Hector. Although his three initial sessions were structured generically as "stress management," the counselor had been able to customize those interventions with special consideration of the unique stresses pressing upon men. Furthermore, an important psychoeducational element had been included through provision of a pamphlet offering thought-provoking ideas about how prevalent conceptions of manhood might contribute to Hector's situational problems. It is not surprising that the subsequent individual therapy sessions continued this consciousness-raising process by helping Hector recognize the problems inherent in his extreme emphasis on work and the good-provider role as the only paths to male self-worth.

Catharsis

Catharsis, of course, refers to the emotional benefits achieved from release of emotions that had previously been repressed. As such, it is a critical change process in the "affective" dimension of MMT (Lazarus, 1976) and in integrative psychodynamic therapy (Stricker & Gold, 2005). In the transtheoretical model, catharsis at the individual level (coming from within the psyche) is considered to be *corrective emotional experience*. At the environmental level (coming from vicarious witnessing of emotional release in the environment) catharsis is thought of as *dramatic relief*.

> Cathartic relief was also a prominent beneficial component in the therapy work with Hector. Previously bewildered by an array of vacillating emotions, he had found a receptive listener who helped him give voice to his frustrations, disappointments, and resentments. As he became more informed by greater recognition of the impossibility of meeting all male role expectations, he became better able to express the more shameful feelings he had been suppressing. Although his problems were certainly not overcome, he was nevertheless greatly relieved to discover that all of his problems were not exclusively the result of his personal failings.

Choosing

This change process relates to emphasis within the humanistic perspective to being aware of possible alternatives and accepting the anxiety inherent in making a responsible choice. For example, in Beutler and Harwood's systematic treatment selection model, this change process would be most applicable in patients with externalizing coping styles that cause them to resist taking responsibility for change. In Prochaska and Norcross's transtheoretical model, choosing takes place on two levels. On the individual or experiential level, this process is considered to be *self-liberation*. That is, deliberately focusing on helping clients create new alternatives for living. At the environmental level, this process is labeled *social liberation* and would involve changes in the environment to make more alternatives available for clients (therapists working as advocates).

> The concept of choosing had been completely foreign to Hector. He had reflexively followed a life path and had adopted core values that he had never questioned and had assumed were immutable. In his unexamined value system, a man was ultimately responsible for leadership of his family and measured solely by his ability to function as a worker and provider. Any failures were unforgivable, whereas weakness and vulnerability were both feared and hidden behind aggressive posturing. Only by examining the unnecessary rigidity of his extreme views was Hector able to recognize that he had greater latitude in his life choices, his self-attributions, and his excessively narrow view of manhood. His male role alternatives broadened as he was helped to consider new ways to contribute through nurturing, caretaking, and providing emotional support for others. With realization that physical strength is only one of many personal assets, he realized greater existential freedom that he had ever thought possible.

Conditional Stimuli

Conditional stimuli are a major focus within the sensory and imagery components of the MMT model of Lazarus (1976). For the transtheoretical model, this change process focuses on issues not accessible to conscious choice and created more by conditioned responses (e.g., trauma reactions) that are not amenable to insight or altered thinking. At an individual level, these responses would be addressed with counterconditioning, perhaps through desensitization and relaxation training. Other issues might be addressed at an environmental level though stimulus control—that is, helping the client engineer his environment by eliminating or avoiding the environmental cues that provoke problem behaviors.

> In the therapy work with Hector, stimulus control interventions were manifested by helping him re-engineer his social context and relational environment. Practical realities necessitated that he continue to function in the same traditional work environment, and he chose to maintain most of his previous friendships. However, he made a determined effort to augment these social influences with ones more congruent with his newly emerging male role definition. He sought out a men's weekend retreat and participated in a follow-up men's support group. He volunteered as a teen mentor through his community's Hispanic support agency and periodically spoke at Al-Anon meetings to help other men manage unresolved issues with alcoholic fathers.

Contingency Control

Contingency control change processes are evident in the behavioral orientation of Pinsof's IPCT and Lazarus's MMT. Within the transtheoretical model, these change processes rely on operant learning models that envision change occurring through contingencies that follow behaviors. Modifying contingencies in the environment is referred to as *contingency management*, whereby clients and therapists contract to provide tangible and intangible rewards for desired behaviors. An alternative proposal for changing outcomes would be to modify a client's responses to consequences of a behavior though a change in one's perspective. This process is referred to as *reevaluation*.

> Behavioral strategies, of both the classical and operant variety were also useful in the overall treatment program with Hector. Relaxation training and new cognitive behavioral skills helped him cope with his emotional reactivity problems, while overt behavioral contracting was implemented during the earlier phases of his experimentation with new interpersonal behaviors. As therapy progressed, therapist praise and support faded in importance as his new behaviors became self-reinforcing through their salutary effects in his life circumstances.

Stages of Change

Many integrative therapy models recognize that clients vary greatly in their readiness to enter therapy and participate fully. In Beutler and Harwood's STS model, for example, considerable attention is given to patient resistance and the "optimizing principle" of "tailoring interventions to redress the level of resistance" (p. 130). A major contribution of the transtheoretical approach is the stages of change concept—recognition that "intentional change is not an all or none phenomenon, but a gradual movement through specific stages" (Prochaska & DiClemente, 2005, p. 149). Although therapists have long recognized that clients differ in their enthusiasm for therapy participation, the issue has previously been addressed in a somewhat elementary fashion with the recalcitrant client labeled as *resistant*. However, the stage of change model has offered a new perspective by recognizing that all clients vary according to their degree of awareness of needed changes as well as their willingness to undertake the necessary tasks to bring change about. After considerable research on various outpatient populations, Prochaska and DiClemente identified five basic stages of change: precontemplation, contemplation, preparation, action, and maintenance.

In brief, the characteristics of each stage are as follows. The *precontemplation* stage is when clients are unaware of the extent of their problems and have no intention to change. In the *contemplation* stage, a client has recognized that a problem exists, but has not yet made a serious commitment to overcoming it. The *preparation* stage is characterized by both intention and behavior. That is, clients have intentions to take actions immediately and introduce small changes in behavior. At the *action* stage, clients actually make modifications in their behavior or their environments to overcome their problems. Finally, the *maintenance* stage is one whereby clients struggle to consolidate gains and prevent relapse.

Integration of Stage of Change With Processes of Change

The integrative flavor of the transtheoretical model becomes apparent with its recognition of the intersection of stages and processes of change. "Twenty-five years of research in behavioral medicine and psychotherapy converge in showing that different processes of change are differentially effective in certain stages of change" (Prochaska & Norcross, 2007, p. 521). The implications of this finding are substantial because they strongly suggest that therapists should adjust their therapeutic emphasis according to their clients' stage of change. Some of the most dramatic implications of this integration of stages and processes can be described.

First, these researchers make a very powerful case for *consciousness raising* as a critical process with clients in the earlier stages of change. Heightening awareness of the unseen causes and consequences of their behavior can be pivotal in moving clients from precontemplation to contemplation. At this early point, *dramatic relief/catharsis* can provide affective fuel for movement to the next stages of change. At the contemplation stage, the change processes within *choosing* become significant. Through bibliotherapy and educational interventions, clients have the opportunity for *self-evaluation* and *environmental reevaluation* to elect whether they wish to continue as usual in their life patterns and role choices. As therapy progresses and clients initiate liberating changes in the action stage, their affective and cognitive gains can be enhanced and reinforced through behavioral processes such as *counterconditioning, contingency management,* and *stimulus control.* In this model, each step is built upon successful accomplishment of earlier steps and consolidation of gains in the maintenance stage is achieved through enhancing earlier gains with behavioral change processes.

Levels of Change

Psychotherapists have long recognized that even when an individual patient presents with a seemingly circumscribed personal problem that problem has implications at many complex and reciprocally related levels of the patient's life. In Pinsof's IPCT this reality is reflected in his description of the *direct* patient system as one in which the therapist has immediate face-to-face contact with the client. The *indirect* patient system, however, includes the larger network of persons affected by and affecting the identified patient. He notes, "historically, systemically sensitive psychotherapists . . . have recognized that they were intervening into systems that were larger than the 'afflicted individual' " (p. 384). IPCT is conceptualized to take place on three contextual levels—individual, couple, and family/community.

The transtheoretical model as described by Prochaska and Norcross (2007) also focuses on the multiple contextual levels by noting that "the content to be changed in a particular therapy system is largely a carryover from that system's theory of personality and psychopathology" (p. 18). Presenting symptoms are rarely accepted as simple and self-contained but usually occur within a complicated social network. To accommodate this reality, they offer a *levels of change* element that they consider to be a "hierarchical organization of five distinct but interrelated levels of psychological problems that can be addressed in psychotherapy" (p. 524). The five levels are symptom/situational problems, maladaptive cognitions, current interpersonal conflicts, family systems conflicts, and intrapersonal conflicts. These levels are considered to vary in terms of their ease of change and accessibility of causal factors. Therefore, Prochaska and Norcross contend that a systematic method for dealing with the levels of problems would be to address situational problems first and not reach the deeper attributions of intrapersonal problems unless necessary to achieve change.

A TRANSTHEORETICAL APPROACH FOR MALE-FRIENDLY PSYCHOTHERAPY

Earlier chapters in this volume described how traditional male socialization and the daily enactment of the male gender role combine to produce strong aversion in males for any consideration of psychotherapy. That train of discussion led to the description of an approach to boys and men that broadens the scope of helpful interventions beyond the standard in-office methods. Additionally, attention was given to the issue of the *therapeutic alliance* as an avenue to enhance the involvement of men who are on the verge of entering (or fleeing) therapy. This analysis led to the description of adaptations that have been made to a number of established individual therapy approaches, making them more accommodating to boys' and men's problematic issues and relational styles. So far, this chapter has reviewed integrative and transtheoretical models of change as a basis for incorporating the previous work on male-friendly psychotherapies, and the remainder of the chapter takes an additional integrative step not yet achieved by any of the previous multitheoretical models: to incorporate the integrative models into the literature on the new psychology of men and multicultural competence among therapists. Most all of the many integrative models identified by Brooks-Harris (2008) and Norcross and Goldfried (2005) seem to invite this type of integration, but the transtheoretical model offered by Prochaska and DiClemente (2005) and Prochaska and Norcross (2007) seems to offer the broadest and richest opportunity for development of a male-friendly integrative model of psychotherapy.

A Male-Friendly Integration of Stages and Processes of Change

As noted earlier, Prochaska and Norcross (2007) are quite clear that they consider the most important finding of their research to be that at each *stage* of change, there will be differential effectiveness of various *processes* of change. Although there can be little disagreement that this discovery has major implications for therapists, it would have even greater benefit if it were to take gender differences into account. That is, when the abundant research findings of the new psychology of men are incorporated into the Prochaska and Norcross transtheoretical model, an even more promising model of male-friendly integrative therapy will result.

Men as Precontemplators

When we look at the description of the therapy precontemplator contained within the transtheoretical model, we cannot help but be struck by his close resemblance to that of a great many males in their first therapy encounter. For example,

> many individuals in the precontemplation stage are unaware or under-aware of their problems. . . . Families, friends, neighbors, or employers, however, are often well aware that the precontemplator has problems. . . . When precontemplators present . . . they often do so because of pressure from others. . . . Once the pressure is off, however, they often return to their old ways. (Prochaska & Norcross, 2007, p. 515)

It would be inaccurate to say that all precontemplators are male, and grossly unfair to characterize all males as therapy resistant; many men are now surmounting the negative aspects of traditional masculinity to seek personal growth. Nevertheless, it would also be unwise to ignore the observations of several decades of clinicians who have found masculinity and psychotherapy to be mutually antagonistic. As a result, it seems prudent for therapists to anticipate that a new male client may very well be a therapy precontemplator. It would also seem to follow that the suggestions for therapy approaches for the precontemplation stage would be applicable to many male first-time clients.

Therapeutic Interventions for Precontemplative Men

The principal psychotherapy change process in the precontemplation stage is consciousness raising. For clients to move from precontemplation to contemplation, they need to become more aware of the roots and consequences of their problems as well as possible alternative coping strategies. In other words, they need to become able to see things they had not seen before. They need to recognize forces driving their behavior that they had not previously appreciated. They need to shift attributions of blame into areas never before considered. In essence, this process is identical to that featured prominently in the feminist model of therapy as well as to many of previously described male-friendly therapies.

The central role of consciousness raising as a planned intervention to facilitate movement from precontemplation to contemplation has been described in therapeutic work with Hector, in which he was helped to recognize the problematic role of *masculinity* in his life problems. A less planned, and actually inadvertent, intervention of this type was the Veterans Administration alcohol treatment group illustrated in the vignette at the beginning of this book. The spontaneous question—What does it mean to be a man?— represented a disjunctive break from the conventional format for treatment of alcoholism. With this question, these *alcoholic men* were asked to focus less on the former aspect of their identity and instead contemplate the latter aspect— that is, their *manhood*. The critical point is this: Although it is fundamentally important to understand all the dynamics and implications of any *DSM–IV* diagnosis, it is also essential that mental health practitioners not overlook the etiological contributions of a man's conflicted gender role that facilitates these psychopathologies. Hyperaggression, substance abuse, and sexual predation need to be understood and treated for what they are, and each man must be ultimately responsible for his behavior. However, gender-informed and male-friendly interventions will result only when all predisposing factors are incorporated into the treatment of a male client.

Chapter 1 described the men's movement as similar to the modern women's movement in terms of heightening awareness of the problematic issues faced by a specific gender. Men's studies scholarship has evolved as an outgrowth of feminist critiques of cultural bias based on gender; popular literature has mushroomed regarding the masculinity crisis affecting boys and men. This emerging national dialogue about the state of contemporary masculinity creates an environment whereby the range of alternative-venue therapeutic interventions (outside- the-office strategies described in chapter 3) will be effective. For men in settings where male populations are dominant (e.g., prisons, substance abuse facilities, sex-offender programs, rehabilitation programs), recommendations have been made to incorporate problems of masculinity into case formulations and treatment plans. Within the psychotherapy office, most all efforts to develop gender-aware therapies have featured substantial psycho-educational components focusing on helping males become more cognizant of gender-role strain and the pressures of the male role. In sum, most all early efforts to intervene therapeutically with men need to place heavy emphasis upon the change process of consciousness raising.

The transtheoretical model also identifies catharsis and dramatic relief as important change processes for clients at the precontemplative stage. In a male-friendly model, this process would be manifested in two ways. First, when a male client is helped to realize that his problems are not unique and not exclusively the products of his personal failures, he will often feel considerable relief from excessive self-blame. In recognizing that he is not alone in his struggles, he may feel fully understood and may experience a surprising sense of validation. Sometimes, men will discover buried memories of childhood abuse, trauma, or emotional abandonment. The enormous affective appeal of the various types of men's retreats, from Bly's wilderness retreats to Promise Keepers rallies, speaks eloquently to the emotional power of men discovering previously hidden emotions.

Catharsis and dramatic relief are also major components of the previously described male-friendly therapy approach of Rabinowitz and Cochran (2002), which illustrates the power of multiple experiential techniques to "deepen" psychotherapy with men and allow for "intensification of emotional of issues and conflicts" (p. 79). It would seem, therefore, that experiential and deepening therapy activities might have an important role in early efforts to enhance therapy progress with precontemplative men.

Therapy for Men in the Contemplation, Preparation, and Action Stages

In the contemplation and preparation stages of change, clients have recognized problems and the need to do something about them: They are "freer to reevaluate themselves both affectively and cognitively" as well as ready to "consider the effects their behaviors have on their environment, especially the people they care about most" (Prochaska & Norcross, 2007, p. 523). At this stage of change, a male client has begun to "get it" in terms of seeing the effects of gender-role strain in his life. He has begun to identify the voices of "the male chorus" (Pittman, 1990) that have judged his behavior, and he has begun to see the need to change both his thinking and his behavior.

> Although my therapist colleague had seemed eager for me to begin family therapy, I felt a need to continue individual work with Hector. Over several sessions we explored the underlying cognitive schema driving his behaviors, including some irrational ideas about proving oneself through work, manly self-sufficiency, and denial of personal needs. We explored how his rigid beliefs created emotional distance and set him up for temper outbursts and eventual flight from meaningful interaction with his

loved ones. From an interpersonal perspective, I provided feedback from our therapy interactions illustrating his vacillations from irritation to passivity and withdrawal. From an existential perspective, we looked at the personal meaning he attached to how his back pain signaled an aging process and his needs to face his physical vulnerabilities. We explored the implications of his life choices and the real freedom to make different choices about how to alter the seemingly predetermined path of his life.

In a male-friendly model, three of the therapy orientations described in chapter 5 seem especially useful for men at this stage of change. First, cognitive therapy would be particularly useful in a male client to see the masculinity-based shoulds and musts that are driving his behavior and underpinning his emotional reactions. He can be aided in challenging unrealistic and contradictory cultural messages; he can be coached to develop alternative self-talk that is more realistic and forgiving. Second, interpersonal therapy can help him recognize flaws in his relational style and help him broaden his behavioral repertoire. Third, existential therapy can be tailored to the special challenges of a man's life cycle. The transtheoretical model considers *self-liberation* to be an essential change process for men at this therapy stage.

In male-friendly therapy, self-liberation would first seem to involve helping a man recognize that he is free to choose a new life path—that is, he is not a prisoner of his biology or of his socialization. Once he sees the ways that he has been regulated by cultural pressures, he becomes freer to choose a new path. He may reject all aspects of the male social role, or, more likely, he may retain those he finds enhancing and create a healthy new masculinity formula. Most important, he can be helped to realize that the freedom coming from his new level of awareness comes with recognition of his mortality and responsibility for his life choices. He can see that the illusive benefits of strict adherence to the male code come at an enormous price in terms of personal development and missed relational opportunities.

Therapy for Men in the Maintenance Stage

In the transtheoretical model, the primary challenges of the maintenance stage are the consolidation of gains and prevention of relapse to previous problematic behaviors. Prochaska and Norcross (2007) proposed that behavioral methods are most effective for this maintenance stage of change. Although behavioral methods were earlier described as a very useful part of a male-friendly approach to men in the early phases of therapy, they certainly have benefits at this later stage as well. Naturally, those males who have struggled with problematic behaviors such as mood regulation, temper dyscontrol, substance abuse, destructive health habits, and dysfunctional sexuality would need an ongoing behavioral plan to avoid returning to their dysfunctional behaviors of the past.

My final therapy contact with Hector came 2 years after the principal therapy sessions. Hector had noticed a tendency to become emotionally overwhelmed and revert to some temper outbursts. In the earlier phases of treatment, relaxation training and cognitive behavioral skills had been helpful with his emotional reactivity problems. On this occasion, before restarting full-blown therapy, we decided to reimplement some behavioral strategies of relaxation and thought management as a type of maintenance strategy. To our satisfaction, Hector reported success with these new techniques and that he felt "back on track." Applauding his use of an apt metaphor, I wished him the best.

In addition to the potential benefits in helping men consolidate their therapeutic gains and prevent relapses, behavioral methods can also have benefits for men with the more general issue of developing a new male lifestyle. For example, men wishing to become more involved as fathers, more compassionate relationship partners, and less homophobic friends to other men with different lifestyles might also benefit from a plan to reinforce their behavioral changes and circumvent factors likely to precipitate a return to old habits. To some extent, there is hope that the previously unrealized benefits of a freer and more flexible lifestyle will provide enough operant reinforcement to begin a cycle of positive changes. Nevertheless, some thought can be given to modeling and stimulus control as useful behavioral interventions for men experimenting with new male role options. Jim O'Neil's concept of "the gender role journey" (O'Neil & Carroll, 1988) is a metaphor for the lengthy process of men's movement from ignorance or hostility toward gender-role changes to a stage of embracing and incorporating those changes into one's life. Implicit in this model and other activities represented by the men's movement is the simple behavioral principle that one's behavioral changes are more likely to be maintained when one alters one's environment to make the new behaviors more likely to occur. This, of course, is the essence of the behavioral method of stimulus control. As applied here, the speculation is that men who are exposed to the company of men who have moved along in this change process will be far more likely to continue their personal gender-role journeys.

Therapeutic Content and Levels of Change for Males

In describing their transtheoretical approach, Prochaska and Norcross (2007) described two concepts that guide therapeutic intervention: therapeutic content and levels of change. These concepts provide recognition that clients' problems and symptoms cannot be conceptualized at a single level and "occur in the context of complex, interrelated levels of human functioning" (Prochaska & Norcross, 2007, p. 524). They identified these levels of change as symptom/situational problems, maladaptive cognitions, current interpersonal conflicts, family systems/conflicts, and intrapersonal conflicts.

In this model *therapeutic content* is determined by the level at which a client's conflict is most troublesome. When the conflict is contained within the client's psyche, it will be manifested by symptoms such as guilt, anxieties, and faulty defenses. When the conflict is considered to be at the interpersonal level, it will be manifested by symptoms such as communication problems, intimacy and sexuality issues, and relational hostility. When the conflict is considered to be at the individuo-social level, it will be manifested by struggles with adjustment and conformity versus transcendence.

A major feature of this levels of change concept is the idea that the levels are hierarchical, varying in terms of complexity, depth, and accessibility to the client's awareness. Situational problems are seen as occupying the most accessible level whereas intrapersonal problems represent the least. As a result, the contention is made that problems at the situational level should be addressed first and therapy discontinued if they are quickly resolved.

A second critical feature of this levels of change concept is the implication for the therapy format. Prochaska and Norcross noted that "a theory's level of personality will dictate the number of people in the therapy room" (2007, p. 20). When the focus is on intrapersonal functioning, the format will be individual therapy. When the focus is on interpersonal functioning, the focus would be on group, couples, or family therapy. When the focus is on individuo-social functioning, the therapist might work with the individual client, but in cases in which the emphasis is on helping the individual overcome social pressures, the work might take place in a group format with clients facing similar challenges.

Levels of Change and Male-Friendly Psychotherapy

> Many months after the initiation of treatment with Hector, individual therapy gave way to marital and family interventions. In couples work, I helped Hector manage his defensiveness with Susan and helped each communicate his or her concerns in a more gender-aware fashion. Of particular concern had been their limited ability to manage conflict, with Susan raising issues and Hector withdrawing. As the issues remained unresolved, both felt emotionally distant, and Hector complained that Susan no longer seemed interested in sexual activity. Over time, Hector learned to manage his anxiety during tense relationship negotiations and even give voice to some of his own fears of divorce and abandonment. Each partner became more aware of the gender-related role demands each had carried into the marriage, and with their increased understanding, a more compassionate mutually appreciating relationship evolved. Ultimately, as they became better able to express their concerns and create a more solid marital bond, they felt ready to expand the therapy to a broader family focus in hope of bridging the emotional distance between Hector and his stepdaughters.

The transtheoretical model holds that a central issue in determining treatment strategy is the agreement between the client and the therapist about which problem level needs to be addressed, and it proposes three corresponding strategies: *shifting levels*, *key levels*, and *maximum impact strategy*. In the first strategy, the treatment would begin at the symptom/situational level and progress along the hierarchy until the problem is resolved. In the second strategy, the focus would be placed upon the level that unambiguously seems to be the primary level of needed intervention. The third strategy would be implemented with the most complex cases, in which variables at every level had been identified as creating or maintaining the client's problems. This third strategy seems similar to Lazarus's (1989) MMT as it is designed to produce "a synergy of change interventions" (Prochaska & Norcross, 2007, p. 527).

This levels of change element, much like the stages of change and the processes of change elements, offers a helpful framework for the development of an integrated model of male-friendly psychotherapy. However, because that framework is inattentive to gender differences, it would benefit from further integration with the insights of the new psychology of men. Two alterations to the Prochaska and Norcross model would be helpful in this regard.

First, there needs to be attention to conceptualizing the critical content of therapy. In the transtheoretical model, individuo-social conflicts are considered as possible targets of therapeutic intervention, perhaps being given consideration alongside intrapsychic and interpersonal conflicts. However, male-friendly therapy, congruent with feminist therapy, alters this model by always placing major emphasis on individuo-social conflicts as an inextricable factor in the development of all intrapersonal and interpersonal conflicts. That is, all client issues are viewed through the lens of gender socialization, the pressures to enact gender scripts, and the gender-role-strain paradigm.

Second, male-friendly psychotherapy, unlike the extant transtheoretical model, views the interaction of the male client with the world of psychotherapy in the larger context of men's traditional aversion to help seeking in general and to psychotherapy in particular. Because of most men's resistance to engaging in psychotherapy, the selection of level of change, and the corollary decision about number of persons in the consulting room, needs to be made with consideration of the best method to maximize the male's therapy participation. This consideration alters the transtheoretical model by emphasizing the critical importance of therapists developing a strong therapeutic alliance with a male client well before conducting therapy at other levels.

The therapeutic alliance, introduced in chapter 4, figures prominently in the male-oriented transtheoretical model. For precontemplative men, the emphasis is on the relational bond between therapist and client, with the therapist attempting to sell the client on the therapeutic option and fulfilling the role of the agent of change who can offer the prospective client some realistic solutions to the ineffable problems he faces stemming from gender-role strain. The therapist's referrals to consciousness-raising groups are meant to solidify the bond with the client as the therapist opens up the precontemplator's experiential and cognitive worlds to other men who share these peculiarly male relational problems.

For male therapy-seekers at later stages of change, however, the emphasis in the therapeutic alliance is on therapeutic content—on the goals and tasks of therapy—as the therapist works with the male client to get to his core problems that lie beneath layers of cultural/environmental context. Sometimes, as with Hector, the other environmental issues relate to the client's immediate family, in which case the therapist must fulfill the role of a facilitator or change-process consultant as he and the client prioritize therapeutic goals and formulate tasks for the client that are aimed at behavioral change at the appropriate or more amenable level (see Figure 4.1).

An earlier work on therapy with traditional male clients (Brooks, 1998) outlined a "sequence of change" that contained the following features. First, efforts are made to postpone a focus on marital or family problems until there has been time develop a solid working alliance with the individual male client. Second, considerable attention is given to consciousness raising about the role of masculinity pressures and gender-role strain in the client's presenting problems. Ideally, this is accomplished by having a male client participate in an all-male therapy group. When this is not feasible, consciousness raising can be accomplished by encouraging the client to participate in a weekend retreat, locate a men's group, watch selected videos, or read and discuss significant literature about the new psychology of men.

Once the male client has become more aware of the ways in which his issues are related to gender-role strain and a positive working alliance has been developed, it would then be possible to move on to explore the emotional and cognitive manifestations of his life problems and, in more extreme cases, the roots of his psychopathology. Eventually, it would be possible to explore the relationship level of therapy with couples or family therapy work. When problems remain refractory to therapy interventions at these levels, more intensive exploration of childhood roots of problems might be considered by some therapists.

> Several weeks after the termination of the marital and family therapy, Hector called again, now describing some inexplicable nightmares where he would see his father lying in a pool of blood and he would be helpless to render aid. We engaged for an additional set of individual sessions that allowed Hector to revisit some unresolved issues emanating from his childhood abuse and the need to resolve issues with his father.

Whether or not a resort to deep psychotherapy is ever needed, the ultimate hope is that the male client might be willing be further his emotional growth and his gender-role journey by seeking more meaningful relationships with the men in his life. At a basic level, this simply might involve closer connections with male friends or involvement with men's collectives. At a more growth-enhancing level, he might actually commit himself to outreach efforts to other troubled men or by engaging in his community's ethnic/cultural organizations to provide outreach to, or to mentor, younger members of the community.

It should be noted that this male-friendly conceptualization of a sequence of change for men is not necessarily incongruent with the transtheoretical model as described by Prochaska and Norcross (2007). In fact, if masculinity and gender-role strain are conceptualized as key levels, the therapy might well unfold quite similarly. However, the primary issue in male-friendly therapy is that problems are always viewed in gender context, and the therapeutic alliance is always attentive to the special issues of male reluctance to enter psychotherapy.

In sum, the dramatic trend toward integrative models of psychotherapy has provided an avenue for the development of a coherent and comprehensive therapeutic approach to male clients. Many of these integrative therapies are innovative, but the transtheoretical model of Prochaska and Norcross (2007) seems most applicable and amenable to incorporation with the new psychology of men. The model's elucidation of the processes of change clarifies the role of consciousness raising in moving therapy-reluctant men from precontemplation to contemplation and action. Its identification of catharsis as a critical process heightens awareness of the important role of emotional relief as a major factor in men's comfort with therapy and stimulus for further change. The model's emphasis on choice offers men alternatives to transcend the paradoxes and dilemmas of gender-role strain. Most important, though, the transtheoretical model proposes that change therapy interventions may be targeted toward many differing contextual levels of a man's life. By incorporating the transtheoretical model with the new psychology of men, an integrative model of male-friendly psychotherapy begins to emerge.

Such a modified integrative model accommodates men's therapy reluctance by incorporating preventive interventions; by focusing on the goals and tasks of therapy as negotiated between therapist and client in a working alliance; and by fostering the client's advance via the working alliance from a symptomatic perspective, in which the therapist is viewed as the agent of change, to a transformative relationship. In a transformative relationship, the male client begins to adopt new, more malleable, and more appropriate contextual definitions of masculinity and thereby acquires more therapeutic agency and responsibility for new, more adaptive behaviors. In a transformative relationship, the client becomes the agent of change.

In the following portions of this chapter, the focus shifts somewhat from attending to the multiple ways that the construction of gender influences the ways that boys and men conduct themselves as psychotherapy participants to the ways that similar sociocultural processes influence the behavior of therapists. Psychotherapy takes place within political and sociocultural contexts, and therapists are not immune to these socializing forces. Thus, considerable attention should be devoted to the manner in which these processes affect therapists' conduct of transtheoretical psychotherapy with boys and men.

MULTICULTURAL COMPETENCE AND PSYCHOTHERAPY FOR BOYS AND MEN

Since the first few sessions with Hector had seemed to go well and we seemed to have developed a fairly solid working alliance, I felt more confident that I could directly challenge what I saw as some of his more extreme macho beliefs. The following interaction took place:

Hector: Hey, I'm sorry, Doc. That's just the way it is—kill or be killed.

Therapist: Oh come on, Hector. That's ridiculous. It's totally fallacious to think that a man needs to act that way. There are lots of better ways of dealing with interpersonal conflict than that.

Hector: (quite upset and standing to leave the office): Oh really, Mister Hot Shit?! Mister Necktie and Fancy-Ass Office! Who the hell are you to tell me what's ridiculous and falamous or whatever the f—k you said! Have you ever had a pistol pointed at your head? Have you ever had to carry a blade to protect your ass? You don't know shit!

Stunned by the intensity of Hector's outburst and completely unclear about the origins of his distress, I felt powerless to keep him from storming out of the office. I called him later, when I thought passions had cooled.

Therapist: Once again, I want to tell you how sorry I am about how I came across to you in the last session. I'm very thankful that you're giving this another chance. Can we go over how we got off track?

Hector: I'm not sure what pissed me off. It just came over me. I kinda felt like a shithead loser the way you were talking.

Therapist: Yeah, I think I know what you mean. Going back over it, I think was acting a bit superior and like a know-it-all. Thanks for not letting me get away with that.

Although therapy with Hector had generally gone very well in our working on the goals and tasks of the therapy, there had been many rocky spots, often because of my lapses in maintaining an empathetic bond. For me, these disconnections had a major implication: Even my best therapeutic insights will be useless unless I am able to bridge the various sociocultural divides between me and my male clients. Therefore, having articulated a transtheoretical framework for psychotherapy with males, it is now possible to shift to the second half of the process of integrating men's studies into latest developments in the psychotherapy literature—the development of multicultural competence for working with boys and men. And in that regard, I draw upon the landmark work of Derald Wing Sue and David Sue (Sue & Sue, 2003, 2008) to apply their model of multicultural counseling and therapy (MCT) to work with this population.

In some ways, it may seem odd to invoke this model for work with males, because a primary thrust of multiculturalism has been to address the inadequacies of a mental health field that has historically been dominated by the perspectives of White men. However, previous chapters have described the paradoxical situation whereby men's economic and political power as embedded in society has produced a generalized lack of power among men in their capacity to use psychotherapy. As a result, there has been a need for greater understanding of men's prevalent distress, their aversion to help seeking, and their alienation from the psychotherapy community. Reflective of this position, Sue and Sue advised, "Realize that MCT (and cultural competence) is inclusive because it includes all groups (including Whites, males, and heterosexuals)" (2008, p. 52). In a similar vein, Pedersen's (1999) call for viewing multiculturalism as a "fourth force" in psychotherapy incorporates a broad definition of culture that includes gender as well as the ethnographic variables of nationality and ethnicity.

There are three principal components of Sue and Sue's (2003) model of MCT and cultural competence. One component is *knowledge*, which calls for the therapist to become as informed as possible about the worldview and life experiences of a client population. A second component is *awareness*, whereby the therapist engages in an active and ongoing process to become aware of values, beliefs, and possible biases that could affect his or her work with a client group. A third component is *skills*, referring to the need to acquire an array of relevant and culturally appropriate intervention strategies.

Multicultural Competence With Male Clients: Knowledge

One of the three major components of Sue and Sue's (2003) conception of multicultural competence is knowledge of a marginalized client group in terms of the history, lifestyles, and cultural values; the experiences of oppression from the dominant culture; the potentially harmful effect of interventions because of the generic characteristics of counseling and therapy; and possible institutional barriers that prevent access to treatment.

It is difficult, and in most ways inappropriate, to think of men as a group "oppressed by the dominant culture." It is true that there are some men's advocates of the men's rights camp (described in chap. 1, this volume) who claim that men are just as oppressed as women by the "New Sexism" (Farrell, 1993). However, given the historically advantaged position of men in patriarchal culture, it seems only realistic to acknowledge that there are few areas in which men, as a gender group, would need to be considered a marginalized group experiencing economic or political oppression or encountering institutional barriers preventing access to treatment. (This would not be as true, of course, for ethnic minority men, disabled men, and gay and bisexual men.)

Also, the commonly accepted view that most all academic scholarship is male-centered seems to suggest that most everyone already has abundant knowledge of men's lives. However, men's studies scholars have consistently pointed out that previous androcentric scholarship was actually inattentive to the private stresses of men's lives; consequently, a new body of scholarship has uncovered the totality of "the male experience" (Doyle, 1994) and "the masculine self" (Kilmartin, 2007). Therapists wishing to work with boys and men now have the opportunity to access a rich new literature about the values, beliefs, and anxieties in the lives of boys and men. Much of this literature has been referenced throughout this book and resources are noted in the Appendix.

Multicultural Competence With Male Clients: Awareness

Without exception, experts in multicultural counseling and therapy identify a fundamentally important step for any therapist hoping to practice in a multiculturally competent manner: To recognize that he or she brings substantial baggage into any therapeutic encounter. All therapists struggle with the inevitable development of ethnocentric monoculturalism, but they vary radically in their success at discovering it within themselves and overcoming its negative effects. For many reasons—not the least of which has been the rise of men's movements and the increase in public discourse about men and masculinity—a therapist's thoughts and feelings about men are a critical topic.

A first major factor universally affecting attitudes toward men, of course, has been the Second Wave of feminism. In its earliest and most radical forms, it identified the offenses of patriarchy in the broader culture and of androcentrism in academic scholarship. From this perspective, men's power is so extensive that therapists need to be keenly attuned to the overt and subtle manifestations of male privilege and not allow their clients or themselves to defer to men. Works such as *Too Good for Her Own Good* (Bepko &

Krestan, 1990) recognized that women customarily denied their own needs to function as emotional protectors and caretakers of the men in their lives. Feminist therapists called attention to common practices within family therapy whereby men were treated with excessive deference and were catered to (Hare-Mustin, 1989; Luepnitz, 1988). An important thesis of feminism has been the need to recognize the ways in which men have been historically been treated *too well* and accorded too much latitude and understanding from society at large, from women in their families, and from therapists themselves.

Over the several decades of this ongoing cultural critique of patriarchy and male privilege, there has been a multifaceted reactionary response to defend men and strike back at the perception of male bashing and antimale discrimination in the national psyche (Ellis, 2005; Faludi, 1999; Farrell, Svoboda, & Sterba, 2007). Men's rights organizations and a number of other men's groups have appeared in response to the perception that men have become the victims of oppressions formerly experienced primarily by women.

Although many who voice these concerns have been highly contentious and antifeminist, there are also some with decidedly profeminist orientations who call for a more nuanced perspective of boys and men. For example, within the Society for the Psychological Study of Men and Masculinity, a self-described profeminist men's organization, sentiments have been expressed that there have been circumstances in which men have been sometimes unfairly characterized and treated. Habben and Petiprin (1997) presented a symposium at an American Psychological Association convention regarding instances of bias against men in psychology graduate programs. In one of the more complex and challenging articulations of this position, Kiselica, Englar-Carlson, Horne, & Fischer (2008) decried what they saw as overemphasis on "the bad things that men and boys do" and little attention to "the many good things that men and boys do" (p. 31). These writers, very much in harmony with profeminist perspectives, called attention to the negative aspects of traditional masculinity, but they also contended that there are positive aspects that should be acknowledged.

Much has been written, and much will continue to be written, on this contentious topic of how to address what McLean (1996) referred to as *the politics of men's pain*—that is, What is the most ethical and socially just manner for a therapist to approach boys and men? It seems imperative that recognition of the historical imbalance of power between the genders, as well as the harm perpetrated by some men upon others, makes it necessary for all therapists to function in a manner that seeks to correct injustices and protect vulnerable parties from harm. Also, on an individual level, the need to see a male client's behavior in the context of his socialization and his role strain does not obviate the need to hold him fully accountable for his actions.

At the same time, however, cultural competence with male clients demands awareness of any values and biases that might harm a male client. Naturally, it would be inappropriate for any therapist to accept without analysis any negative stereotypes of men as a group or to generalize any behavior of some men to suggest inherent unworthiness of all men. Obviously, a therapist must be acutely aware of his or her attitudes and feelings about boys and men, and search for any problematic blind spots. For example, among the most basic factors for a woman therapist to consider would be whether her work with males would be negatively affected by any issues from her history of relationships with the most important males in her life, any experiences of victimization or abuse, or the intensity of her unhappiness with men as a group because of their oppression of women.

For a male therapist, consideration should similarly be given to his history of relationships with men, any unresolved needs for acceptance or approval from other men, any distorting effects from homophobia, and any impairing residuals from bullying or abuse during childhood and adolescence. Also, male therapists would need to be aware of the potential for problematic spillover from any unworkable anger (or defensiveness) toward men as a group because of their victimization of others. Consistent with the principles of MCT, those persons with extremely negative, or even inappropriately positive, feelings and attitudes toward males need to seriously consider whether they should work with this population.

There can be no argument that therapy work progresses best when a therapeutic alliance is established and that such an alliance is far more likely to occur when a therapist values and appreciates the client. In this regard, a "positive psychology perspective" (Kiselica, Englar-Carlson, Horne, & Fischer, 2008) may be needed to counter "conversation [that] is focused on either the bad things that men and boys do or how the male socialization process scars men and boys for life, leaving them chronically flawed and in dire need of fixing" (p. 31). The topic of positive psychology for men is new and has yet to be fully explicated, yet there can be no doubt that most all male clients have many redeeming qualities, and that many of them exemplify the healthy attributes historically displayed by men. As I have noted previously (Brooks, 1998), "almost all traditional men want to do the right thing, even though it is getting harder for them to comprehend just what that is" (p. 241). The gender-role strain perspective is an exceptionally helpful paradigm of most work in this area, because it avoids pathologizing boys and men. Instead, this model focuses on addressing the problems inherent in a *pathologizing culture*— that is, a culture that places rigid and extreme limits on the freedom of boys and men to express their full human potential. From this perspective then, therapy with boys and men can serve as a counterpoint to the dominant social construction of masculinity as well as a positive and highly supportive way for males to find a combination of personal characteristics and behaviors that enhance their lives and the lives of those with whom they interact.

Multicultural Competence With Male Clients: Skills

Earlier chapters of this work provided a range of therapeutic options for approaching boys and men in a variety of situational contexts. This material has been presented to constitute a necessary bridge from standard gender-blind or "one-size-fits-all" psychotherapy to a transtheoretical model of male-friendly psychotherapy. Consistent with the skills aspect of MCT, this model suggests a range of therapeutic techniques inherent in a transtheoretical approach. However, because there has been such emphasis placed on the differences between the dominant phenomenology of male culture and psychotherapy culture, some explication of additional skills seems warranted. Before offering these ideas, however, an important caveat is needed: As has been noted, there are substantial variations among men in nearly all areas—including their receptiveness to psychotherapy. Currently, many therapists report a welcome influx of psychologically sophisticated and intrinsically motivated male clients who are already at the contemplative or action stage at their initial encounters with therapy. The following is therefore intended less for that optimal situation than it is for work with those men who have incorporated the more troublesome antitherapy stances consonant with traditional masculinity. In this more challenging situation, several special intervention skills can be helpful.

Language and Communication Style

Of the most commonly recognized impediments to effective cross-cultural counseling, differences in language and communication style are among the more prominently noted. For many men who are accustomed to communicate in concrete and practical ways, sometimes using colorful or profanity-laced language, the expectations of therapy may be daunting. For example, in the highly popular television program *The Sopranos*, the first exasperated words of Tony Soprano in meeting his therapist were, "It's impossible for me to talk with a shrink!"

Whether the issue is one of discomfort with "shrink talk," fear of violating decorum, or inability to express inner thoughts, many men find therapy environments unwelcoming and alien. As a result, therapists working with some male populations will do well when they can minimize their use of therapeutic jargon and abstract theoretical discourses. Also, initial therapy sessions' emphasis on extended silences and therapist passivity might confuse a new male client and invoke negative therapist stereotypes.

The therapist who is familiar with the slang, language, and idioms of a male subgroup can enhance rapport by accommodating somewhat (when realistic and appropriate) to a male client's more comfortable communication style. For example, the statement, "Looks like you think you really f—ed up" has more punch than, "You seem to be having grave misgivings about your handling of that situation." At a minimum, it is important to dispel any misperceptions that only "proper" language and communication are allowed in therapy.

Therapists deciding to rely less on formal and intellectual communication styles may find metaphors and storytelling to be a useful adjunct to their interventions. Glicken (2005) contended that therapeutic metaphors can be especially useful with men who have difficulty hearing or expressing inner feelings through traditional channels. Metaphors anchored in sports, combat, or technology can sometimes make a point more effectively than any highbrow discourse. Ideas such as "taking one for the team," "they had my back," or "my gears got jammed" may be quite evocative for many less effusive men.

Related to metaphors, storytelling has established a useful place in many male-friendly contexts. The mythopoetic work of Robert Bly (1990) has infused heroic images and storytelling as a powerful way to evoke men's inner emotions. As noted earlier, storytelling has been recognized as an especially culture-sensitive medium for work with African American and Native American men (Parham, 2002; Sutton & Broken Nose, 2005).

Humor, Teasing, and Indirect Expressions of Affection and Acceptance

If a therapist views male clients from a deficit perspective, it is easy to see how many men have enormous problems with direct, straightforward, and assertive interpersonal behavior as well as a general difficulty with metacommunication. From a strength perspective, however, the therapist can easily admire the multiple and nuanced ways that many men can communicate effectively through silence or humor and good-natured teasing. Many men learn to respect the silence of another man and become skillful at allowing exposure of a painful issue to unfold over time. Sometimes, it may be far more helpful for a therapist to avoid an aggressive push for "getting in touch with feelings," and instead offer a telling nod, a shoulder-grasp, or extended eye contact to convey both recognition of a man's distress and respect for his need to guard his rate of disclosure.

In her description of what she labels the "good old boy sociability group," Farr (1986) identified several characteristics of communication among men in certain "naturalistic" men's groups (i.e., taking place in informal settings such as coffee shops and without clear rules or formal structure). A prominent feature she identified is the indirect manner of communicating bonding, acceptance, and affection. Key to this process is the development of teasing and humor of a "testimonial" nature that has no negative edge and conveys connection; in such a way, therapists can convey a therapeutic point in an empathic manner acceptable to even the most guarded male client. For example, a statement such as, "Your interaction with your wife seems consistent with your past pattern" could be replaced (in a well-established relationship) by a more male-friendly teasing comment such as, "I see we haven't lost our expert touch to 'step in it' at the worst possible time," or "Way to go, big guy. Good job in keeping up our image as insensitive jerks."

Male-Friendly Environment

A male client's first entry into a therapist's office may set the stage for a successful initial session or it may heighten his worst anxieties. The first encounter with the therapist may defuse irrational fears of shrinks, or it may reinforce his negative expectations. Multicultural counselors have written extensively about the need to adapt the therapeutic environment to the culture of the client population. This matter is likely to be less problematic for work with most men, but some pitfalls may be avoided. In a previous chapter, I described Kiselica and Englar-Carlson's (2008) ideas about creating a "welcoming space" for boys. Their advice includes ideas ranging from welcoming conduct from support staff to décor familiar to young men. For men, there would be no need to go so far as a stereotypical re-creation of a sports bar or fraternity house, but an extremely "artsy" or feminine environment might discomfit some men. In general, a therapy space that conveys warmth and hominess would seem preferable to one that projects coldness and emotional sterility.

In addition, Sue and Sue's (2003) recommendations regarding *proxemics* (i.e., use of space) and *kinesics* (i.e., bodily movements) deserve mention. For example, some awkwardness could be created by immediately situating a male client in a particularly dark and intimate environment, with chairs overly close and face-to-face. Instead, some anxious men may be more comfortable with an angled seating arrangement, with ample opportunity to adjust spatial distance. Extreme discrepancies in chair sizes and comfort may convey helpful or unhelpful messages. Because many men will be unaware of how to proceed in therapy, more engaged body postures and facial expressions would seem to have an advantage over a stiff posture and stony facial expression. Eye contact would need to be regulated according to cues of the male client. Finally, the distractions afforded by offering coffee, water, or soft drinks may help reduce tensions as well as convey a message of a more relaxed and hospitable situation.

Self-Disclosure and Advice Giving

Self-disclosure is one of the more complex yet potentially beneficial ingredients of successful psychotherapy (Hill & Williams, 2000). In work with men, self-disclosure offers major opportunities for overcoming many men's sense of shame about entering therapy as well as their unrealistic fears of pathological uniqueness. Concern about establishing appropriate therapeutic boundaries can sometimes be so extreme that it eliminates opportunities to humanize the therapist and exaggerates the male client's feeling of inferiority. All therapists recognize the need to provide disclosure of professional credentials, training, and therapeutic orientation, yet many provide little else. Choices about the presence or absence of personal material such as photos and mementos are certainly tied to one's feelings about therapist disclosure. This matter is quite sensitive and needs to factor in the therapist's gender. However, when a therapist provides clues about the person of the therapist, some advantages are afforded in the comfort level of the male client.

At times, the universality benefit of the all-male therapy group can be incorporated into individual therapy when a male therapist acknowledges a similar struggle in his own life. This is a somewhat complicated strategy and one not available to female therapists (working with male clients). However, an alternative strategy of semi-self-disclosure seems quite appropriate and problem free. For example, if a male client were to express some indication of feeling pathologically unique, the therapist might respond, "I understand what you are going through, and based on my observation of many men's lives, this issue is a very common one *to us men*, and one that many men have dealt with successfully."

Another quandary for therapists in this regard is responding to direct questioning about the therapist's opinion on how to manage a problem or life decision. "Pure" therapy, of course, requires that the therapist demur from advice-giving, "punt" the problem back to the client, and perhaps even explore the unconscious motive behind the request. This strategy is usually sound. However, given the prominent practical and instrumental problem-solving orientation of many men, a therapist's staunch refusal to share any of his or her acquired wisdom seems unnecessary. At times, it may be helpful for therapists to at least offer some information based on his or her technical expertise or clinical experience. For example, it would be ethically questionable for a therapist to advise a troubled man to stay in a marriage or abandon it to live with the woman of an affair. However, it would be less problematic for a therapist to share data and insights about the likely outcomes from either course the client chooses.

Utilizing One's Personal Gender Experience

A common question arising during any presentation about psychotherapy with men relates to the issue of the therapist's gender. The commonly asked question is usually phrased as, Can a female therapist work effectively with male clients? This rationale for this question may have some basis in the belief in some early feminist writings that female clients should usually be seen by female therapists. Although there are clear reasons for raising this question, a parallel question should also be raised: Can a female therapist work effectively with male clients?

To address these questions, it is useful to examine the multicultural counseling literature regarding cross-cultural counseling. Two important points then become apparent. First, multicultural competence is far more crucial to effective therapeutic outcomes than any particular characteristic of the therapist (Paniagua, 1998; Sue & Sue, 2008). Second, to large extent almost all counseling is cross-cultural at some level. That is, because the therapist and client will almost never be identical in every possible cultural dimension, there always will be a requirement for a therapist to be empathetic with the client's cultural, socioeconomic, and lifestyle situations.

With this multicultural perspective in mind, more helpful questions might be: What are the advantages of a male client seeing a male therapist? What are the advantages of a male client seeing a female therapist? These are complex questions that have been previously addressed by many writers (Brooks, 1998; Carlson, 1987; Erickson, 1993; Johnson, 2001; Sweet, 2006). Despite the impossibility of thoroughly reviewing all literature in this area, some major points can be noted.

A most useful framework for addressing the issue of same-gender and cross-gender counseling is that of the ethnic validity model provided by Tyler, Sussewell, and Williams-McCoy (1985). Although this model is constructed regarding possible cross-ethnic pairings, its theorizing is directly applicable to the benefits and drawbacks of homogenous and heterogeneous therapist-client gender pairings. In brief, the model identifies the primary potential advantages of homogeneous pairings as the validation of similar worldviews, ease of relationship development, and possibilities of role modeling. The primary potential disadvantages are identified as difficulties in over-development of empathic relationships and possible reinforcement of biases against other ethnic (or gender) groups.

In considering this model and reviewing the literature of this matter, several points seem noteworthy. First, there can be definite advantages in a male client being seen by a male therapist. There are obvious opportunities for the sharing of experiences, empathy development, and role modeling. However, these potential advantages will be realized only when the male therapist is insightful about the new psychology of men and masculinity and is able to see his client's problems in gender context. Also, this advantage is more likely when the male therapist is willing to be somewhat flexible in his expert role, take a one-down position, and occasionally acknowledge some similar struggles with gender-role strain. Also, a male therapist who has made little movement in his own personal gender-role journey can actually hinder the growth of a male client through modeling unhelpful male behavior or by reinforcing reactionary attitudes. In the worst-case scenario of a male client and male therapist, a male client can be helped at one level, yet harmed at another. In the best-case scenario, the client can not only get help with his presenting problems, but he can also progress in his gender-role journey with a positive role model. He can also achieve one objective not possible with a woman therapist: He can learn experientially that a man can be safely intimate with another man.

The situation of a female therapist and male client also seems to have both advantages and challenges. First, there are many reasons to see this situation as highly beneficial. As noted earlier, most men are far more comfortable revealing their inner lives to women and heterosexual men will be less prey to homophobic attitudes with a woman therapist. Also, women traditionally have had greater experience with caretaking, developing empathy, and talking about emotional matters (Brown, 1994). However, consistent with the principles of cross-cultural counseling, the female therapist would need to make efforts to study and learn as much as possible about the male experience. She would need to become aware of possible problematic reactivity in relating with any particular male client. She would also need to be adept at short-circuiting any effort by a male client to de-professionalize her by relating to her as a mother-figure, girlfriend, or daughter (a problem of transference). Finally, a woman therapist has the opportunity to use her "outsider" position to help a male client introspect about his own masculine identity. That is, when appropriate she can adopt a role of researcher about men's lives with questions such as, "I wasn't raised as a man, so would you please help me understand what is was like as a man to encounter that situation?" At other times, however, she can help a man gain insight through a form of self-disclosure: "I was not raised as a man, but I have certainly seen many men in my life experience who have struggled with issues very much like the ones you are describing."

CONCLUSION

Most young girls in the United States will be raised to expect opportunities for themselves never before considered possible or desirable. Many young boys in this same country will be raised in a manner mostly (but not entirely) free of the rigid strictures imposed on previous generations of males. To some extent, girls are now allowed to be competitive as well as cooperative, aggressive as well as deferential, self-focused as well as other-focused. To a lesser extent, though, boys are now allowed to be tender as well as tough, vulnerable as well as heroic, and nurturing as well as stoic. The respective limits in this new flexibility of gender roles are neither prescribed nor entirely explainable. Suffice it to say, though, that the gap between girls' and boys' abilities to adopt—and social tolerance of—such gender-role dualism constitutes for young men the latest manifestation of the crisis of masculinity.

There are indeed many social dimensions of this crisis. First, those men who overfunction in their enactment of traditional masculinity and exhibit the behavioral excesses of the dark side of masculinity are too poorly understood. Rather than being approached with understanding of the contextual roots of their behavior, they are too frequently pathologized and demeaned. Second, the push for such a social transformation of gender roles is not equal, as women generally have been more enthusiastic than most men, and many men have been either skeptical or overtly defensive and resistant. Third, boys and men are rarely able to find anything resembling a model of masculinity that garners broad cultural endorsement or acceptance. Fourth, the mental health fields have not yet become sufficiently attuned to male phenomenology in a manner that would allow for the development of male-friendly models of therapeutic intervention. This crisis of masculinity is indeed quite worrisome, yet there many hopeful trends.

Over the past 4 decades, we have witnessed the appearance of several collectives of men participating in a highly diverse and loosely organized men's movement. Some elements of this movement have entered academia and have created the discipline of men's studies. The appearance of this discipline, with its corollary recognition of the gender-role-strain paradigm, has made it possible to see what was previously obscured by assumptions about men's advantaged position in the culture. It is now possible to see that, despite their relatively privileged position vis-à-vis women in economic and political arenas, boys and men suffer a great deal of psychic pain and major (to some extent self-imposed) impediments in their lives, and they are in far more need of therapeutic interventions than previously realized.

It is sad that the crisis of masculinity and the psychopathology of men's everyday lives—the gender-role strain among contemporary American males—have not been adequately addressed by the fields of counseling and psychotherapy. To a significant extent, men's resistance to all forms of help seeking has contributed to the problem. However, the therapy community has also contributed to the impasse by failing to develop a range of psychotherapies harmonious with the help-seeking styles of males. An important step in this effort could result when therapists and counselors think more creatively about formats and settings for therapeutic interventions with men. The rationale for this position is based in the logic of the prevention movement in mental health and in the reality of men's negative attitudes toward formal mental health care. Preventive activities for boys and men might include participation in organized programs that target the problems common among males, involvement with men's groups, or exposure to psychoeducational pursuits. Therapists themselves might participate, or they might supplement treatment by encouraging client participation in these activities. Finally, therapists in certain special settings can use their consultation skills and familiarity with men's studies to broaden and enrich already existing programs or establish creative new programs designed specifically for men.

Another aspect of this male-friendly engagement process would include a concerted effort to foster a therapeutic alliance by taking the fullest advantage of opportunities presented when a male client is on the threshold of the therapist's office. This process would include a male-specific diagnostic assessment that enriches the therapist's understanding of the client and the client's appreciation of therapeutic relevance. Furthermore, an embrace of the stages of change model provides greater appreciation of men's therapy reluctance and offers additional perspectives to advance men from the precontemplative stage. Most centrally, however, the therapy-reluctant male will be most likely to engage in therapy when there is agreement on the goals and tasks of therapy as well as a strong empathetic bond.

Even when an effective therapeutic alliance is established, psychotherapists still face a challenge to deliver therapeutic interventions congruent with men's unique problem-solving style. Fortunately, the relatively recent and abundant new literature on the new psychology of men incorporates established therapeutic wisdom into the expanding knowledge base of the traditional masculine construct and its new challengers. This new literature identifies male-friendly variants of several individual approaches, the all-male group approach, and marital and family therapy approaches. These therapy variants are not restricted to adult male clients, as there has also been a welcome new body of work offering special adaptations of therapeutic interventions for boys and adolescent males.

Not all men, of course, define *masculine* in the same way or have identical experiences negotiating the male role. Despite the advantages (and distinct challenges) of examining commonalities among all men, there is also a critical need to consider how race, ethnicity, sexual orientation, and physical ability status intersect with the social construction of masculinity in general. Thanks to the greater emphasis on multiculturalism within the mental health fields, it is now possible to further refine interventions for males dependent upon membership in somewhat distinct ethnocultural and lifestyle groups.

Just as the concept of cultural competence is central to working with clients who are members of groups that have been historically marginalized, it can also be relevant to work with *all* male clients. When most all counseling and psychotherapy is recognized at some level to have crosscultural elements, it becomes imperative for mental health professionals to develop cultural competence for working with male populations. In this regard, therapists should be thoroughly knowledgeable about the male experience and facile with therapeutic skills consonant with male help-seeking styles. Less well recognized, but vitally important, is the need for therapists to be supremely familiar with their own history of interactions with males as well as the unique assets and emotional impediments they themselves bring into therapeutic encounters.

Whatever value there may be in offering new ideas for therapeutic interventions with males, the overall benefit is minimized if mental health professionals feel overwhelmed by yet another intervention model amidst the several hundred new therapy possibilities. As a result, it is critical that some effort be made to capture the contemporary trend toward integrative models that provide a coherent and comprehensive approach for male-friendly psychotherapy.

This book represents a step in that direction by integrating a transtheoretical framework into the literature on the new psychology of men.

This model's elucidation of the processes of change clarifies the role of consciousness raising in moving therapy-reluctant men from precontemplation to contemplation and action. Its identification of catharsis as a critical process heightens awareness of the important role of emotional relief as a major factor in men's comfort with therapy and stimulus for further change. The model's emphasis on choice offers men alternatives to transcend the paradoxes and dilemmas of gender-role strain. Most important, this model proposes that change therapy interventions may be targeted toward many differing contextual levels of a man's life.

By incorporating the transtheoretical model with the new psychology of men, an integrative model of male-friendly psychotherapy emerges. This modified model accommodates men's therapy reluctance by proposing preventive interventions, by offering methods to enhance the development of therapeutic alliances, and by identifying male-friendly customizations of traditional therapeutic approaches. The modified model suggests a sequence of therapy intervention levels to maximize a man's capacity to benefit from male-friendly psychotherapy—at both the individual and systemic levels.

APPENDIX: RESOURCES FOR MULTICULTURAL COMPETENCE WITH BOYS AND MEN IN THERAPY

BOOKS

Andronico, M. (Ed.). (1996). *Men in groups: Insights, interventions, and psychoeducational work*. Washington, DC: American Psychological Association.

Boyd-Franklin, N., Franklin, A. J., & Toussaint, P. (2001). *Boys into men: Raising our African American teenage sons*. New York, NY: Plume.

Brooks, G. R. (1995). *The centerfold syndrome*. San Francisco, CA: Jossey Bass.

Brooks, G. R. (1998). *A new psychotherapy for traditional men*. San Francisco, CA: Jossey Bass.

Brooks, G. R., & Good, G. E. (Eds.). (2005). *The new handbook of counseling and psychotherapy with men* [Rev.ed.]. San Francisco, CA: Jossey Bass.

Clatterbaugh, K. (1997). *Contemporary perspectives on masculinity: Men, women, politics in modern society* (2nd ed.). Boulder, CO: Westview Press.

Gilbert, L. A., & Scher, M. (1999). *Gender and sex in counseling and psychotherapy*. Boston, MA: Allyn & Bacon.

Glicken, M. D. (2005). *Working with troubled men: A contemporary practitioner's guide*. Mahwah, NJ: Erlbaum.

Good, G. E., & Brooks, G. R. (Eds.). *A new handbook of counseling and psychotherapy with men*. San Francisco, CA: Jossey Bass.

Horne, A. M., & Kiselica, M. S. (Eds.). (1999). *Handbook of counseling boys and adolescent males*. Thousand Oaks, CA: Sage.

Kiselica, M. S., Englar-Carlson, M., & Horne, A. M. (Eds.), *Counseling troubled boys: A guidebook for professionals*. New York, NY: Routledge.

Kilmartin, C. T. (2007). *The masculine self* (3rd. ed.). Cornwall-on-the-Hudson, NY: Sloan.

Levant, R. F., & Brooks, G. R. (Eds.). *Men and sex: New psychological perspectives*. New York, NY: Wiley.

Levant, R. F., & Kopecky, G. (1995). *Masculinity reconstructed: Changing the rules of manhood—at work, in relationships, and in family life*. New York, NY: Dutton.

Levant, R. F., & Pollack, W. S. (Eds.). (1995). *A new psychology of men*. New York, NY: Basic Books.

Majors, R., & Billson, J. M. (1992). *Cool pose: The dilemmas of black manhood in America*. New York, NY: Lexington.

Norcross, J. C., & Goldfried, M. R. (2005). *Handbook of psychotherapy integration* (2nd ed.). Oxford, England: Oxford University Press.

Olkin, R. (1999). *What psychotherapists should know about disability*. New York, NY: Guilford.

Parham, T. A. (2002). *Counseling persons of African descent: Raising the bar of practitioner competence*. Thousand Oaks, CA: Sage.

Perez, R. M., DeBord, K. A., & Bieschke, K. J. (Eds.). *Handbook of counseling and psychotherapy with lesbian, gay, and bisexual clients*. Washington, DC: American Psychological Association.

Rabinowitz, R. E., & Cochran, S. V. (2002). *Deepening psychotherapy with men*. Washington, DC: American Psychological Association.

Sue, D. W., & Sue, D. (2008). *Counseling the culturally diverse: Theory and practice* (5th ed.). New York, NY: Wiley.

FILM/VIDEO/DVD

National Organization for Men Against Sexism (NOMAS) Video Anthology. (Available at http://www.nomas.org/mmvideos).

Sut Jhally (Producer/Director) & J. Katz & J. Earp (Writers). (1999), *Tough Guise* [DVD]. (Available from the Media Education Foundation at http://www.mediaed.org/videos/MediaGenderAndDiversity/ToughGuise).

ORGANIZATIONS

American Men's Studies Association, http://mensstudies.org

American Psychological Association Division for the Psychological Study of Men and Masculinity (SPSMM), http://www.apa.org/about/division/div51.html

Gay, Lesbian, and Straight Education Network (GLSEN), http://www.glsen.org/cgi-bin/iowa/all/home/index.html

GLBT National Help Center, http://www.glnh.org/index2.html

Men's Health Network, http://www.menshealthnetwork.org/

National Organization for Men Against Sexism (NOMAS), http://www.nomas.org

National Men's Resource Center ("Menstuff"), http://www.menstuff.org

Parents, Families, and Friends of Lesbians and Gays, http://community.pflag.org/NETCOMMUNITY/Page.aspx?pid=194&srcid=-2

JOURNALS

Fathering: A Journal of Theory and Research about Men as Parents (Men's Studies Press)
International Journal of Men's Health (Men's Studies Press)
Men and Masculinities (Sage)
Psychology of Men and Masculinity (American Psychological Association)
The Journal of Men's Studies (Men's Studies Press)
The Men's Bibliography (15th ed. April, 2006), http://mensbiblio.xyonline.net/
THYMOS: Journal of Boyhood Studies (Men's Studies Press)

REFERENCES

Addis, M. E., & Mahalik, J. R. (2003). Men, masculinity, and the contexts of help seeking. *American Psychologist, 58*, 5–14.

Americans with Disabilities Act of 1990, Public Law 101-336, 42 U.S.C. 12111, 12112.

Albee, G. W. (1983). Psychopathology, prevention, and the just society. *Journal of Primary Prevention, 4*, 5–40.

Albee, G. W. (2005). Call to revolution in the prevention of emotional disorders. *Journal of Primary Prevention, 24*, 37–44.

Alberti, R., & Emmons, M. (2001). *Your perfect right: Assertiveness and equality in your life and relationships* (8th ed.). Atascadero, CA: Impact Publishers.

Allen, M., & Burrell, N. (1996). Comparing the impact of homosexual and heterosexual parents on children: Meta-analysis of existing research. *Journal of Homosexuality, 32*, 19–35.

American Psychiatric Association. (2002). *Diagnostic and statistical manual of mental disorders* (4th ed.). Washington, DC: American Psychiatric Association.

American Psychological Association, Division 12 Task Force on Promotion and Dissemination of Psychological Procedures. (1995). Training in and dissemination of empirically validated psychological treatments: Report and recommendations. *The Clinical Psychologist, 48 (1)*, 3–23.

American Psychological Association, Division 44. (2000). Guidelines for Psychotherapy with Lesbian, Gay, and Bisexual Clients. *American Psychologist, 55*, 1440–1451.

American Psychological Association, Division of Exercise and Sport Psychology. Retrieved March 4, 2009, from http://www.apa.org/about/division/div47.html

Ammerman, R. T., & Hersen, M. (Eds.). (1993). *Handbook of behavior therapy with children and adults: A developmental and longitudinal perspective*. Boston: Allyn & Bacon.

Andronico, M. (Ed.). (1996). *Men in groups: Insights, interventions, & psychoeducational work*. Washington, DC: American Psychological Association.

Andronico, M. (2001). Mythopoetic and weekend retreats to facilitate men's growth. In G. R. Brooks & G. E. Good (Eds.), *The new handbook of counseling and psychotherapy with men*. (pp. 464–480). San Francisco, CA: Jossey Bass.

Arbona, C., & Coleman, N. (2008). Risk and resilience. In S. D. Brown & R. W. Lent (Eds.), *Handbook of counseling psychology* (4th ed., pp. 483–499). New York, NY: Wiley.

Arcaya, J. (1999). Hispanic American boys and adolescent males. In A. M. Horne & M. S. Kiselica (Eds.), *Handbook of counseling boys and adolescent males* (pp. 101–116). Thousand Oaks, CA: Sage.

Arias, E. (2005). United States life tables 2002. National Vital Statistics Reports, Center for Disease Control, retrieved August 19, 2009, from http://www.cdc.gov/nchs/data/nvsr/nvsr53/nvsr53_06.pdf

Arkowitz, H. (1984). Historical perspective on the integration of psychoanalytic therapy and behavioral therapy. In H. Arkowitz & S. B. Messer (Eds.). *Psychoanalytic therapy and behavior therapy: Is integration possible?* (pp. 1–30). New York, NY: Plenum.

Ashton, W. A., & Fuehrer, A. (1993). Effects of gender and gender role identification of participant and type of social support resources on support seeking. *Sex Roles, 28,* 461–476.

Atkinson, D. R., Kim, B. S. K., & Caldwell, R. (1998). Ratings of helper roles by multicultural psychologists and Asian American students: Initial support for the three dimensional model of multicultural counseling. *Journal of Counseling Psychology, 45,* 414–423.

Atkinson, D. R., Thompson, C. E., & Grant, S. K. (1993). A three-dimensional model for counseling racial/ethnic minorities. *Counseling Psychologist, 21,* 257–277.

Attneave, C. (1982). American Indian and Alaska Native families. In M. McGoldrick, J. K. Pearce, & J. Giordano (Eds.), *Ethnicity and family therapy* (pp. 55–83). New York, NY: Guilford Press.

Ballou, M., & Brown, L. S. (Eds.). (2002). *Rethinking mental health and disorder: Feminist perspectives.* New York, NY: Guilford.

Balswick, J. O. (1988). *The inexpressive male.* Lexington, MA: Lexington Books.

Bank, B. J. (1995). Friendships in Australia and the United States: From feminization to a more heroic image. *Gender and Society, 9,* 79–98.

Barber, J. S., & Mobley, M. (1999). Counseling gay adolescents. In A. M. Horne & M. S. Kiselica (Eds.), *Handbook of counseling boys and adolescent males* (pp. 161–178). Thousand Oaks, CA: Sage.

Barnett, R. C., & Baruch, G. K. (1987). Social roles, gender, and psychological distress. In R. C. Barnett, L. Biener, & G. K. Baruch (Eds.), *Gender and stress* (pp. 122–143). New York, NY: The Free Press.

Barrett, D. B., & Johnson, T. M. (1998). Religion: World religious statistics. In *Encyclopedia Britannica book of the year.* Chicago, IL: Encyclopedia Britannica, Inc.

Bechtoldt, H., Norcross, J., Wyckoff, L. A., Pokrywa, M. L., & Campbell, L. F. (2001). Theoretical orientations and employment settings of clinical and counseling psychologists: A comparative study. *The Clinical Psychologist, 54,* 3–6.

Beitman, B. D., & Yue, D. (1999). *Learning psychotherapy: A time-efficient, research-based, and outcome measured psychotherapy training program.* New York, NY: Norton.

Bepko, C., & Krestan, J. (1990). *Too good for her own good: Searching for self and intimacy in important relationships.* New York, NY: Harper Perennial.

Berger, R., & Kelly, J. (1996). Gay men and lesbians grown older. In R. J. Cabaj & T. Stein (Eds.), *Textbook of homosexuality and mental health* (pp. 305–316). Washington, DC: American Psychiatric Press.

Bergman, S. J. (1995). Men's psychological development: A relational perspective. In R. H. Levant & W. S. Pollack (Eds.), *A new psychology of men* (pp. 68–90). New York, NY: Basic.

Bernard, J. (1981). The good provider role: Its rise and fall. *American Psychologist, 36,* 1–12.

Betcher, R. W., & Pollack, W. S. (1993). *In a time of fallen heroes: The re-creation of masculinity.* New York, NY: Ateneum.

Beutler, L. E. & Harwood, M. (2000). *Prescriptive psychotherapy: A practical guide to systematic treatment selection.* New York, NY: Oxford.

Bierman, K. L., Coie, J. D., Dodge, K. A., Greenberg, M. T., Lochman, J. E., McMahon, R. J., & Pinderhughes, E. E. (1999, October). Initial impact of the fast track prevention trial for conduct problems: I. The high-risk sample. *Journal of Consulting and Clinical Psychology, 67,* 631–347.

Bieschke, K. J., Perez, R. M., & DeBord, K. A. (Eds.). (2007). *Handbook of counseling and psychotherapy with lesbian, gay, bisexual, and transgender clients* (2nd ed.). Washington, DC: American Psychological Association.

Bingenheimer, J. B., Repetto, P. B., Zimmerman, M. A., & Kelly, J. G. (2003). A brief history and analysis of health promotion. In T. P. Gullotta & M. Bloom (Eds.), *Encyclopedia of primary prevention and health promotion* (pp. 15–26). New York, NY: Kluwer.

Blackmon, L. (2004). Self-help, media cultures and the production of female psychopathology. *European Journal of Cultural Studies, 7(2),* 219–236.

Bloom, M. (2008). Principles and approaches to primary prevention. In T. P. Gullotta & G. M. Blau (Eds.), *Handbook of childhood behavioral issues: Evidence-based approaches to prevention and treatment* (pp. 107–122). New York, NY: Routledge.

Bly, R. (1990). *Iron John: A book about men.* New York, NY: Vintage Books.

Bohart, A. C., Elliott, R., Greenberg, L. S. & Watson, J. C. (2002). Empathy. In J. C. Norcross (Ed.), *Psychotherapy relationships that work* (pp. 89–108). New York, NY: Oxford University Press.

Bordin, E. S. (1994). Theory and research on the therapeutic working alliance: New directions. In A. O. Horvath & L. S. Greenberg (Eds.), *The working alliance: Theory, research, and practice* (pp. 13–37). New York, NY: Wiley.

Borkovec, T. D., Crnic, K. A., & Costello, E. (1993). Generalized anxiety disorder. In R. T. Ammerman & M. Hersen (Eds.), *Handbook of behavior therapy with children and adults* (pp. 202–216). Boston, MA: Allyn & Bacon.

Bowlby, J. (1969). *Attachment and loss.* New York, NY: Basic Books.

Boyd-Franklin, N. (2003). *Black families in therapy: Understanding the African American experience.* New York, NY: Guilford.

Boyd-Franklin, N., Franklin, A. J., & Toussaint, P. (2001). *Boys into men: Raising our African American teenage sons*. New York, NY: Plume.

Brannon, L., & Feist, J. (2000). *Health psychology: An introduction to behavior and health*. Belmont, CA: Thomson Cole.

Brehm, S. (1985). *Intimate relationships*. New York, NY: Random House.

Brenton, M. (1966). *The American male*. New York, NY: Coward-McCann.

Brickman, J. (1984). Feminist, non-sexist, and traditional models of therapy: Implications for working with incest. *Women and Therapy, 3,* 49–67.

Brooks, G. R. (1992). Gender-sensitive family therapy in a violent culture. *Topics in family psychology and counseling, 1,* 24–36.

Brooks, G. R. (1995). *The centerfold syndrome: How men can overcome objectification and achieve intimacy with women*. San Francisco, CA: Jossey-Bass.

Brooks, G. R. (1996). Treatment for therapy-resistant men. In M. Andronico (Ed.), *Men in groups: Insights, interventions, & psychoeducational work* (pp. 7–19) .Washington, DC: American Psychological Association.

Brooks, G. R. (1997). The centerfold syndrome. In R. F. Levant & G. R. Brooks (Eds.), *Men and sex: New psychological perspectives* (pp. 28–57). New York, NY: Wiley.

Brooks, G. R. (1998). *A new psychotherapy for traditional men*. San Francisco, CA: Jossey Bass.

Brooks, G. R. (2003). Helping men embrace equality. In L. B. Silverstein & T. J. Goodrich (Eds.), *Feminist Family Therapy: Empowerment in Social Context* (pp. 163–176). Washington, DC: American Psychological Association.

Brooks, G. R. (2005). Counseling and psychotherapy for male military veterans. In G. E. Good & G. R. Brooks (Eds.), *A new handbook of counseling and psychotherapy with men* (pp. 104–118). San Francisco, CA: Jossey Bass.

Brooks, G. R., & Gilbert, L. A. (1995). Men in families: Old constraints, new possibilities. In R. F. Levant & W. S. Pollack (Eds.), *A new psychology of men* (pp. 252–279). New York, NY: Basic Books.

Brooks, G. R., & Good, G. E. (Eds.). (2001). *The new handbook of counseling and psychotherapy with men: A Comprehensive guide to settings, problems, and treatment approaches*. San Francisco, CA: Jossey Bass.

Brooks, G. R., & Silverstein, L. B. (1995). Understanding the dark side of masculinity: An integrative systems model. In R. H. Levant & W. S. Pollack (Eds.), *A new psychology of men* (pp. 280–336). New York, NY: Basic.

Brooks, G. R., & Willoughby, F. W. (2004, August). Masculinity as diathesis: User-friendly therapies for male substance abusers. Symposium conducted at the American Psychological Association Convention, Honolulu, HI.

Brooks-Harris, J. E. (2008). *Integrative multitheoretical psychotherapy*. Boston, MA: Lahaska Press.

Broverman, I., Broverman, D., Clarkson, F., Rosencrantz, P., & Vogel, S. (1970). Sex role stereotypes and clinical judgements of mental health. *Journal of Consulting and Clinical Psychology, 34,* 1–7.

Brown, L. (1989). Lesbians, gay men, and their families: Common clinical issues. *Journal of Gay and Lesbian Psychotherapy, 1(1),* 65–77.

Brown, L. S. (1986). Gender-role analysis: A neglected component of psychological assessment. *Psychotherapy, 23,* 243–248.

Brown, L. S. (1994). *Subversive dialogues: Theory in feminist therapy.* New York, NY: Basic Books.

Brown, G. W., & Harris, T. (1978). *The social origins of depression: A study of psychiatric disorder in women.* London, England: Tavistock.

Bruch, M. A. (1978). Holland's typology applied to client-counselor interaction: Implications for counseling men. *The Counseling Psychologist, 7,* 26–32.

Buhrke, R. (1989). Female student perspectives on training in lesbian and gay issues. *Counseling Psychologist, 17,* 629–636.

Burda, P. C., & Vaux, A. C. (1987). Social support processes in men: Overcoming sex-role obstacles. *Human Relations, 40,* 31–43.

Buss, D. M. (1994). *The evolution of desire: Strategies of human mating.* New York, NY: Basic Books.

Caldwell, L. D., & White, J. L. (2005). African-centered therapeutic and counseling interventions for African American males. In G. E. Good & G. R. Brooks (Eds.). *A new handbook of counseling and psychotherapy with men* (pp. 323–336). San Francisco, CA: Jossey Bass.

Carlson, N. (1987). Woman therapist: Male client. In M. Scher, M. Stevens, G. Good, & G. Eichenfield (Eds.), *Handbook of counseling and psychotherapy with men* (pp. 39–50). Newbury Park, CA: Sage.

Carpenter, K. M., Addis, M. E. (2000). Alexithymia, gender, and responses to depressive symptoms. *Sex Roles, 43,* 363–378.

Casas, J. M., Turner, J. A., & Ruiz De Esparza, C. A. (2005). Machismo revisited in a time of crisis: Understanding and counseling Hispanic men: In G. E. Good & G. R. Brooks (Eds.), *A new handbook of counseling and psychotherapy with men* (pp.337–356). San Francisco, CA: Jossey Bass.

Chambless, D. L., & Hollon, S. D. (1998). Defining empirically validated therapies. *The Clinical Psychologist, 64,* 497–504.

Charmaz, K. (1995). Identity dilemmas of chronically ill men. In D. Sabo & D. Gordon (Eds.), *Men's health and illness: Gender, power, and the body* (pp. 266–291). Thousand Oaks, CA: Sage.

Chen, C. L., & Yang, D. C. Y. (1986). The self image of Chinese-American adolescents: A cross-cultural comparison. *International Journal of Social Psychiatry, 32,* 19–26.

Chesler, P. (1972). *Women and madness.* Garden City, NY: Doubleday.

Chodorow, N. (1978). *The reproduction of mothering.* Berkeley: University of California Press.

Clark, W. M., & Serovich, J. M. (1997). Twenty years and still in the dark? Content analysis of articles pertaining to gay, lesbian, and bisexual issue in marital and family therapy. *Journal of Marriage and Family Therapy, 23,* 239–253.

Clatterbaugh, K. (1990). *Contemporary perspectives on masculinity: Men, women, politics in modern society*. Boulder, CO: Westview Press.

Clatterbaugh, K. (1997). *Contemporary perspectives on masculinity: Men, women, politics in modern society* (2nd ed.). Boulder, CO: Westview Press.

Cochran, S. V. (2001). Assessing and treating depression in men. In G. R. Brooks & G. E. Good (Eds.), *The new handbook of counseling and psychotherapy with men* (pp. 229–245). San Francisco, CA: Jossey Bass.

Cochran, S. V., & Rabinowitz, F. E. (2000). *Men and depression: Clinical and empirical perspectives*. San Diego, CA: Academic Press.

Cohen, T. (1992). Men's families, men's friends: A structural analysis of constraints on men's social ties. In P. M. Nardi (Ed.), *Men's friendships* (pp. 115–131). Newbury Park, CA: Sage.

Consason, J., Ross, A., & Cokorinos, L. (1996, October 7). The Promise Keepers are coming: The third wave of the religious right. *The Nation*, pp. 11–19.

Connell, R. W. (1995). *Masculinities*. Berkeley: University of California Press.

Conyne, R. (1987). *Primary preventive counseling: Empowering people and systems*. Muncie, IN: Accelerated Development.

Cooper, C. C. (2001). Men and divorce. In G. R. Brooks & G. E. Good (Eds.), *The new handbook of counseling and psychotherapy with men: A comprehensive guide to settings, problems, and treatment approaches* (pp. 335–354). San Francisco, CA: Jossey Bass.

Cooper, M. L., Russell, M., Skinner, J. B., Frone, M. R., & Mudar, P. (1992). Stress and alcohol use: Moderating effects of gender, coping and alcohol expectancies. *Journal of Abnormal Psychology, 101*, 139–152.

Copenhaver, M. M., & Eisler, R. M. (1996). Masculine gender role stress: A perspective on men's health. In P. M. Kato & T. Mann (Eds.), *Handbook of diversity issues in health psychology* (pp. 219–235). New York, NY: Plenum.

Courtenay, W. H. (2000). Engendering health: A social constructionist examination of men's health beliefs and behaviors. *Psychology of men and masculinity, 1*, 4–15.

Courtenay, W. H. (2005). Counseling men in medical settings: A six-point HEALTH plan. In G. E. Good & G. R. Brooks (Eds.), *A new handbook of counseling and psychotherapy with men* (pp. 29–53). San Francisco, CA: Jossey Bass.

Cross, W. E. (1995). The psychology of Nigresence: Revising the Cross model. In J. G. Poneterotto, J. M. Casas, L. A. Suzuki, & C. M. Alexander (Eds.), *Handbook of multicultural counseling* (pp. 93–122). Thousand Oaks, CA: Sage.

Cuellar, I., & Paniagua, F. A. (2000). *Handbook of multicultural mental health*. San Diego, CA: Academic Press.

Cullen, D. (2009) *Columbine*. New York, NY: Twelve.

D'Augelli, A., & Garnets, L. (1995). Lesbian, gay, and bisexual communities. In A. D'Augelli & C. Patterson (Eds.), *Lesbian, gay, and bisexual identities over the lifespan: Psychological perspectives* (pp. 293–320). New York, NY: Oxford University Press.

D'Augelli, A. R., Hershberger, S. L., & Pilkington, N. W. (1998). Lesbian, gay, and bisexual youth and their families. *American Journal of Orthopsychiatry, 68*(3), 361–371.

Danish, S. J., & Forneris, T. (2008). Promoting positive development and competence across the life span. In S. D. Brown & R. W. Lent (Eds.), *Handbook of counseling psychology* (4th ed., pp. 500–516). New York, NY: Wiley.

David, D. S., & Brannon, R. (1976). *The forty-nine percent majority: The male sex role*. Reading, MA: Addison-Wesley.

Davidson, M. G. (2000). Religion and spirituality. In P. S. Richards & A. Bergin (Eds.), *Handbook of psychotherapy and religious diversity* (pp. 409–433). Washington, DC: American Psychological Association.

Davis, D., & Padesky, C. (1989). Enhancing cognitive therapy with women. In A. D. Freeman, K. M. Simon, L. E. Beutler, & H. Arkowitz (Eds.), *Comprehensive handbook of cognitive therapy* (pp. 535–557). New York, NY: Plenum Press.

Dawson, D. (1996). Gender differences in the risk of alcohol dependence: United States, 1992. *Addiction, 91*, 1831–1842.

DeBord, K. A., & Perez, R. M. (2000). Group counseling theory and practice with lesbian, gay, and bisexual clients. In R. M. Perez, K. A. DeBord, & K. J. Bieschke (Eds.), *Handbook of counseling and psychotherapy with lesbian, gay, and bisexual clients* (pp. 183–206). Washington, DC: American Psychological Association.

Diamond, J. (1987). Counseling male substance abusers. In M. Scher, M. Stevens, G. Good, & G. Eichenfield (Eds.), *Handbook of counseling and psychotherapy with men* (pp. 332–342). Newbury Park, CA: Sage.

Dickstein, L. J., Stephenson, J. J., & Hinz, L. D. (1990). Psychiatric impairment in medical students. *Academic Medicine, 65*, 588–593.

Dillard, D. A., & Manson, S. M. (2000). Assessing and treating American Indians and Alaska natives. In I. Cuellar & F. A. Paniagua (Eds.), *Handbook of multicultural mental health* (pp. 226–249). San Diego, CA: Academic Press.

Dimidjian, S., Martell, C. R., & Addis, M. E. (2008). Behavioral activation for depression. In D. Barlow (Ed.), *Clinical Handbook of Psychological Disorders*. New York, NY: Guilford.

Dolgin, K. G. (2001). Men's friendships: Mismeasured, demeaned, and misunderstood? In T. F. Cohen (Ed.), *Men and masculinity* (pp. 103–117). Belmont, CA: Wadsworth.

Doyle, J. A. (1995). *The male experience* (3rd. ed.). Dubuque, IA: Brown.

Dufrene, P. M., & Coleman, V. D. (1992). Counseling Native Americans: Guidelines for group process. *Journal for Specialists in Group Work, 17*, 229–234.

Dworkin, S. H. (2000). Individual therapy with lesbian, gay, and bisexual clients. In R. M. Perez, K. A. DeBord, & K. J. Bieschke (Eds.), *Handbook of counseling and psychotherapy with lesbian, gay, and bisexual clients* (pp. 157–181). Washington, DC: American Psychological Association.

Eisler, R. M. (1995). The relationship between masculine gender role stress and men's health risk: The validation of a construct. In R. H. Levant & W. S. Pollack (Eds.), *A new psychology of men* (pp. 207–228). New York, NY: Basic.

Ellis, A. E. (1988). *How to stubbornly refuse to make yourself miserable about anything, yes anything.* New York, NY: Lyle Stuart.

Ellis, T. (2005). *The rantings of a single male: Losing patience with feminism, political correctness . . . and basically everything.* Austin, TX: Rannenberg.

Engel, G. (1980). Clinical application of the biopsychosocial model. *American Journal of Psychiatry, 135,* 535–544.

Erickson, B. M. (1993). *Helping men change: The role of the female therapist.* Newbury Park, CA: Sage.

Espiritu, Y. L. (1999). Gender and labor in Asian immigrant families. *American Behavioral Scientist, 42,* 628–634.

Everett, F., Proctor, N., & Cortmell, B. (1989). Providing psychological services to American Indian children and families. In D. R. Atkinson, G. Morten, & D. W. Sue (Eds.), *Counseling American Minorities* (3rd. ed., pp. 53–71). Dubuque, IA: Brown.

Faludi, S. (1991). *Backlash: The undeclared war against American women.* New York, NY: Crown Publishers.

Faludi, S. (1999). *Stiffed: The betrayal of the American man.* New York, NY: Morrow.

Farr, K. A. (1986). Dominance bonding through the good old boys socializing group. *Sex Roles, 18,* 259–277.

Farrell, W. T. (1975). *The liberated man.* New York, NY: Bantam.

Farrell, W. T. (1986). *Why men are the way they are.* New York, NY: McGraw-Hill.

Farrell, W. T. (1993). *The myth of male power.* New York, NY: Simon & Schuster.

Farrell, W., Svoboda, S., & Sterba, J. P. (2007). *Does feminism discriminate against men? A debate (Point/Counterpoint).* New York, NY: Oxford University Press.

Fassinger, R. E. (2000). Applying counseling theories to lesbian, gay, and bisexual clients: Pitfalls and possibilities. In R. M. Perez, K. A. DeBord, & K. J. Bieschke (Eds.), *Handbook of counseling and psychotherapy with lesbian, gay, and bisexual clients* (pp. 107–132). Washington, DC: American Psychological Association.

Fasteau, M. F. (1975). *The male machine.* New York, NY: Dell.

Firestein, B. (Ed.). (2007). *Becoming visible: Counseling bisexuals across the lifespan.* New York, NY: Columbia University Press.

Fisch, R., Weakland, J., & Segal, L. (1982). *The tactics of change: Doing therapy briefly.* San Francisco, CA: Jossey Bass.

Fitzhugh-Craig, M. (1996, February 21). Local churches start men's groups. *Oakland Tribune.* Retrieved July 7, 2006, from http://findarticles.com/p/articles/mi_qn4176/1s_20060707/ai_n16529349/print

Fleming, M. C., & Englar-Carlson, M. (2008). Examining depression and suicidality in boys and male adolescents: An overview and clinical considerations. In M. S. Kiselica, M. Englar-Carlson, & A. M. Horne (Eds.), *Counseling troubled boys: A guidebook for professionals* (pp. 125–162). New York, NY: Routledge.

Flood, M. (2006). Changing men—Best practice in sexual violence education. *Women against violence, 18,* 26–36.

Frank, J. L. (1961). *Persuasion and healing: A comparative study of psychotherapy.* New York, NY: Schocken.

Franklin, A. J. (2004). *From brotherhood to manhood: How Black men rescue their relationships and dreams from the invisibility syndrome.* New York, NY: Wiley.

Freeman, J. (1989). Introduction. In J. Freeman (Ed.), *Women: A feminist perspective* (pp. xi–xiv). Mountain View, CA: Mayfield.

Friedan, B. (1963). *The feminine mystique.* New York, NY: Norton.

Fuhriman, A., & Burlingame, G. M. (2001). Group psychotherapy training and effectiveness. *Journal of Group Psychotherapy Special Issue, 51,* 399–416.

Fukuyama, M. A., & Ferguson, A. D. (2000). Lesbian, gay, and bisexual people of color: Understanding cultural complexity and managing multiple oppressions. In R. M. Perez, K. A. DeBord, & K. J. Bieschke (Eds.), *Handbook of counseling and psychotherapy with lesbian, gay, and bisexual clients* (pp. 81–106). Washington, DC: American Psychological Association.

Gabbard, G. O., & Gabbard, K. (1999). *Psychiatry and the cinema* (2nd. ed.). Washington, DC: American Psychiatric Press.

Gallup Organization. (January 28, 2009). "State of the States," retrieved August 19, 2009, from http://www.gallup.com/poll/114022/State-States-Importance-Religion.aspx?version=print

Garbarino, J. (1999). *Lost boys: Why our sons turn violent and how we can save them.* New York, NY: The Free Press.

Garcia-Preto, N. (2005). Puerto-Rican families. In M. McGoldrick, J. Giordano, & N. Garcia-Preto (Eds.), *Ethnicity and family therapy* (3rd ed., pp. 242–255). New York, NY: Guilford Press.

Garfield, S. L. (1973). Basic ingredients or common factors in psychotherapy? *Journal of Consulting and Clinical Psychology, 41,* 9–12.

Garfield, S. L. (1980). *Psychotherapy: An eclectic approach.* New York, NY: Wiley.

Garfield, S. L. (1994). Research on client variables in psychotherapy. In A. E. Bergin & S. L. Garfield (Eds.), *Handbook of psychotherapy and behavior change.* New York, NY: John Wiley & Sons.

Garnets, L., Hancock, K. A., Cochran, S. D., Goodchilds, J., & Peplau, L. A. (1991). Issues in psychotherapy with lesbians and gay men. *American Psychologist, 91,* 964–972.

Garnets, L., & Kimmel, D. (1993). Lesbian and gay male dimensions in the psychological study of human diversity. In L. Garnets & D. Kimmel (Eds.), *Psychological perspectives on lesbian and gay male experiences* (pp. 1–51). New York, NY: Columbia University Press.

Garrett, M. T., & Osborne, W. C. (1995). The Native American sweat lodge as metaphor for group work. *Journal for Specialists in Group Work, 20*, 33–39.

Garwick, A. G., & Auger, S. (2000). What do providers need to know about American Indian culture? Recommendations from urban Indian family caregivers. *Family, Systems & Health, 18*, 177–190.

Gauron, E. F., Steinmark, S. W., & Gersh, F. S. (1977). The orientation group in pre-therapy training. *Perspectives in psychiatric care, 15*, 32–37.

Gelso, C. J., & Hayes, J. A. (2002). The management of countertransference. In J. C. Norcross (Ed.), *Psychotherapy relationships that work* (pp. 267–284). New York, NY: Oxford University Press.

Gerschick, T. J., & Miller, A. S. (1997). Gender identities at the crossroads of masculinity and physical disability. In M. Gergen & S. Davis (Eds.), *Toward a new psychology of gender* (pp. 455–475). New York, NY: Routledge.

Gilbert, J. (2005). *Men in the middle*. Chicago, IL: University of Chicago Press.

Gilbert, L. A. (1993). *Two careers/One family: The promise of gender equality*. Newbury Park, CA: Sage.

Gilbert, L. A., & Scher, M. (1999). *Gender and sex in counseling and psychotherapy*. Boston, MA: Allyn & Bacon.

Gim, R. H., Atkinson, D. R., & Whitely, S. (1990). Asian-American acculturation, severity of concerns, and willingness to see a counselor. *Journal of Counseling Psychology, 37*, 281–285.

Glassgold, J. M., Fitzgerald, J., & Haldeman, D. C. (2002). Letter to the Editor. *Psychotherapy: Theory, Research, Practice, Training, 39*, 376–378.

Glicken, M. D. (2005). *Working with troubled men: A contemporary practitioner's guide*. Mahwah, NJ: Erlbaum.

Goldberg, H. (1976). *The hazards of being male*. New York, NY: New American Library.

Gold, J. R. (1993). The sociohistorical context of integrative therapy. In G. Stricker & J. R, Gold (Eds.), *Comprehensive handbook of psychotherapy integration* (pp. 3–8). New York, NY: Plenum.

Goldberg, H. (1976). *The hazards of being male*. New York, NY: New American Library.

Goldenberg, I., & Goldenberg, H. (2004). *Family therapy: An overview* (6th ed.). Pacific Grove, CA: Brooks Cole.

Goldner, V. (1985). Feminism and family therapy. *Family Process, 24*, 31–47.

Goldner, V. (1988). Generation and gender: Normative and covert hierarchies. *Family Process, 27*, 17–32.

Good, G. E., & Brooks, G. R. (Eds.). (2005). *The new handbook of counseling and psychotherapy with men: A Comprehensive Guide to settings, problems, and treatment approaches*. (Rev. ed.). San Francisco, CA: Jossey Bass.

Good, G. E., Gilbert, L. A., & Scher, M. (1990). Gender aware therapy: A synthesis of feminist therapy and knowledge about gender. *Journal of Counseling and Development, 68*, 376–380.

Good, G. E., & Mintz, L. B. (2005). Integrative therapy for men. In G. E. Good & G. R. Brooks (Eds.), *A new handbook of counseling and psychotherapy with men* (pp. 248–263). San Francisco, CA: Jossey Bass.

Goodman, L. A., Koss, M. P., Fitzgerald, L. F., Russo, N. F., & Keita, G. P. (1993). Male violence against women. Current research and future directions. *American Psychologist, 48*, 1054–1058.

Gottman, J. M. (1994). *Why marriages succeed or fail.* New York, NY: Simon & Schuster.

Gottman, J. M. (2000). *Marital therapy: A research-based approach (clinician's manual).* Seattle, WA: The Gottman Institute.

Gottman, J. M., Ryan, K. D., Carrere, S., & Erly, A. M. (2002). Toward a scientifically based marital therapy. In H. A. Liddle, D. A. Santisteban, R. F. Levant, & J. H. Bray (Eds.), *Family psychology: Science-based interventions* (pp. 147–174). Washington, DC: American Psychological Association.

Gove, W. R. (1972). The relationship between sex roles, marital status, and mental illness. *Social Forces, 51*, 34–44.

Gove, W. R. (1984). Gender differences in mental and physical illness: The effects of fixed roles and nurturant roles. *Social Science and Medicine, 19*, 77–84.

Greene, B. (1994). Ethnic minority lesbians and gay men: Mental health and treatment issues. *Journal of Consulting and Clinical Psychology, 62*, 243–251.

Greenley, J. R., & Mechanic, D. (1976). Social selection in seeking care for psychological problems. *Journal of Health and Social Behavior, 17*, 249.

Greenson, R. (1968). Disidentifying from mother. *International Journal of Psychoanalysis, 49*, 370–374.

Greif, G. L. (2009). *Buddy system: Understanding male friendships.* New York, NY: Oxford University Press.

Grucza, R. A., Norberg, K., Bucholz, K. K., & Bierut, L. J. (2008). Correspondence between secular changes in alcohol dependence and age of drinking onset among women in the United States. *Alcoholism: Clinical & Experimental Research, 32*, 1493–1501.

Grucza, R. A., Norberg, K. E., & Bierut, L. J. (2009). Binge drinking among youths and young adults in the United States: 1979–2006. *Journal of the American Academy of Child & Adolescent Psychiatry, 48*(7), 692–702.

Gullotta, T. P., & Bloom, M. (Eds.). (2003). *The encyclopedia of primary prevention and health promotion.* New York, NY: Klewer Academic/Plenum.

Gurian, M. (1999). *The good son: Shaping the moral development of boys and young men.* New York, NY: Tarcher/Putnam.

Gurian, M. (2006). *The wonder of boys: What parents, mentors, and educators can do to shape boys into exceptional men.* New York, NY: Tarcher/Putnam.

Gurian, M., & Stevens, K. (2005). *The minds of boys: Saving our sons from falling behind in school and life.* San Francisco, CA: Jossey Bass.

Habben, C., & Petiprin, G. (1997, August). *The new psychology of men and the graduate school experience.* Symposium conducted at the APA Convention, Chicago, IL.

Haldeman, D. C. (1994). The practice and ethics of sexual orientation conversion therapy. *Journal of Consulting and Clinical Psychology, 62,* 221–227.

Haldeman, D. C. (2001). Therapeutic antidotes: Helping gay and bisexual men recover from conversion therapies. *Journal of Gay & Lesbian Psychotherapy, 5,* 117–130.

Haldeman, D. C. (2001). Psychotherapy with gay and bisexual men. In G. R. Brooks & G. E. Good (Eds.), *The new handbook of counseling and psychotherapy with men* (pp. 796–815). San Francisco, CA: Jossey Bass.

Haldeman, D. C. (2005). Psychotherapy with gay and bisexual men. In G. R. Brooks & G. E. Good (Eds.), *The new handbook of counseling and psychotherapy with men* (pp. 369–383). San Francisco, CA: Jossey Bass.

Halgin, R. P., & Whitbourne, S. K. (1993). *Abnormal psychology.* Philadelphia: Harcourt Brace Jovanovich.

Hall, R. L. (1998). Mind and body: Toward the holistic treatment of African American women. *The Psychotherapy Patient, 10,* 81–100.

Hammond, L. A. (2008). Women and self-help books. *Dissertation Abstracts International: Section B: The Sciences and Engineering, 68(7-B),* 4826.

Hare-Mustin, R. T. (1989). The problem of gender in family therapy theory. In M. McGoldrick, C. M. Anderson & F. Walsh (Eds.), *Women in families: A framework for family therapy* (pp. 61–77). New York, NY: Norton.

Harrison, J. (1978). Warning: The male sex-role may be hazardous to your health. *Social Issues, 34,* 65–86.

Hawkins, R. L. (1992). Therapy with the male couple. In S. H. Dworkin & F. J. Gutierrez (Eds.), *Counseling gay men and lesbians: Journey to the end of the rainbow* (pp. 81–94). Alexandria, VA: American Counseling Association.

Heartfield, J. (2002). There is no masculinity crisis. *Genders, 35.* Retrieved June 18, 2008, from http://www.genders.org/g35/g35_heartfield.html

Hedges-Goett, L., & Tannenbaum, M. (2001). Navigating the social landscape: A rationale and method for interpersonal group therapy with pre-adolescent boys. *Journal of Child and Adolescent Group Therapy, 11,* 135–146.

Heesacker, M., & Prichard, S. (1992). In a different voice, revisited: Men, women, and emotion. *Journal of Mental Health Counseling, 14,* 274–290.

Heilman, R. (1973). *Early recognition of alcoholism and other drug dependence.* Center City, MN: Hazelden.

Heinrich, R. K., Corbin, J. L., & Thomas, K. R. (1990). Counseling Native Americans. *Journal of Counseling and Development, 69,* 128–133.

Helms, J. E. (1995). An update of Helms's White and people of color racial identity models. In J. G. Poneterotto, J. M. Casas, L. A. Suzuki, & C. M. Alexander (Eds.), *Handbook of multicultural counseling* (pp. 181–191). Thousand Oaks, CA: Sage.

Herdt, G., & deVries, B. (2004). *Gay and lesbian aging: Research and future directions.* New York, NY: Springer.

Herek, G. (1991). Stigma, prejudice and violence against lesbians and gay men. In J. Gonsiorek & J. Weinrich (Eds.), *Homosexuality: Research implications for public policy* (pp. 60–80). Newbury Park, CA: Sage.

Herek, G. (1992). The social construction of hate crimes: Notes on cultural heterosexism. In G. Herek & K. Berrill (Eds.), *Hate crimes: Confronting violence against lesbians and gay men* (pp. 89–104). Newbury Park, CA: Sage.

Hernandez, R. (2002). *Fatherwork in the crossfire: Chicano teen fathers struggling to take care of business* (Report No. JSRI-WP-58). East Lansing: Michigan State University, Julian Samoa Research Institute. (ERIC Document Reproduction Services No. ED471 926).

Herring, R. D. (1999). *Counseling with Native American Indians and Alaskan natives.* Thousand Oaks, CA: Sage.

Hershberger, S. L., & D'Augelli, S. R. (2000). Issues in counseling lesbian, gay, and bisexual adolescents. In R. M. Perez, K. A. DeBord, & K. J. Bieschke (Eds.), *Handbook of counseling and psychotherapy with lesbian, gay, and bisexual clients* (pp. 225–248). Washington, DC: American Psychological Association.

Highlen, P. S. (1994). Racial/ethnic diversity in doctoral programs of psychology: Challenges for the twenty-first century. *Applied and preventive psychology, 3,* 91–108.

Hill, C. E., & Williams, E. N. (2000). The process of individual therapy. In S. D. Brown & R. W. Lent (Eds.), *Handbook of counseling psychology* (3rd ed., pp. 670–710). New York, NY: Wiley.

Hills, H. I., Carlstrom, A., & Evanow, M. (2005). Consulting with men in business and industry. In G. E. Good & G. R. Brooks (Eds.), *The new handbook of counseling and psychotherapy with men: A Comprehensive Guide to settings, problems, and treatment approaches* (Rev. ed., pp. 54–69). San Francisco, CA: Jossey Bass.

Hines, P. M., & Boyd-Franklin, N. (2005). African American families. In M. McGoldrick, J. Giordano, & N. Garcia-Preto (Eds.), *Ethnicity and family therapy* (3rd. ed., pp. 87–100). New York, NY: Guilford Press.

Hochschild, A. (1989). *The second shift.* New York, NY: Viking.

Hochschild, A., & Machung, A. (2001). Men who share the 'second shift." In J. M. Heslin (Ed.), *Down to earth sociology* (pp. 395–409). New York, NY: Free Press.

Holahan, W., & Gibson, S. A. (1994). Heterosexual therapists leading lesbian and gay therapy groups: Therapeutic and political realities. *Journal of Counseling and Development, 72,* 591–594.

Hong, G. K., & Ham, D. C. (2001). *Psychotherapy and counseling with Asian-American clients*. Thousand Oaks, CA: Sage.

Horne, A., Jolliff, D., and Roth, E. (1996). Men mentoring men in groups. In M. Andronico (Ed.), *Men in groups: Insights, interventions, psychoeducational work* (pp. 97–112). Washington, DC: American Psychological Association.

Horne, A. M., & Kiselica, M. S. (Eds.). (1999). *Handbook of counseling boys and adolescent males*. Thousand Oaks, CA: Sage.

Horrocks, R., & Campling, J. (1994). *Masculinity in crisis: Myths, fantasies, and realities*. London, England: McMillan Press.

Horvath, A. O., & Bedi, R. P. (2002). The alliance. In J. C. Norcross (Ed.), *Psychotherapy relationships that work* (pp. 37–70). New York, NY: Oxford University Press.

Hossain, Z., & Roopnarine, J. L. (1993). Division of household labor and child care in dual-earner African American families with infants. *Sex Roles, 29*, 571–583.

Huang, L. N. (1994). An integrative approach to clinical assessment and intervention with Asian-American adolescents. *Journal of Clinical Child Psychology, 23*, 23–31.

Huang, L. N., & Ying, Y. W. (1991). Chinese children and adolescents. In J. T. Gibbs & L. N. Huang (Eds.), *Children of color: Psychological interventions with minority youth* (pp. 30–66). San Francisco, CA: Jossey Bass.

Hyde, J. S., & Oliver, M. B. (2000). Gender differences in sexuality: Results from meta-analysis. In C. B. Travis & J. White (Eds.), *Sexuality, society, and feminism* (pp. 57–77). Washington, DC: American Psychological Association.

Imbesi, R. (2007). Engaging young people in leadership roles in the prevention of sexual assault. *Primary and Middle School Educator, 5*, 21–25.

Isenhart, C. (2005). Treating substance abuse in men. In G. E. Good & G. R. Brooks (Eds.), *A new handbook of counseling and psychotherapy with men* (pp. 134–146). San Francisco, CA: Jossey Bass.

Jackson, L. C., & Greene, B. (2000). *Psychotherapy with African American women: Innovations in psychodynamic perspectives and practice*. New York, NY: Guilford.

Jakupcak, M., Osborne, T. L., & Scott, M. (2006). Implications of masculine gender role stress in male veterans with posttraumatic stress disorder. *Psychology of Men and Masculinity, 7*, 203–211.

Jensen, R. (2005). *Getting off: Pornography and the end of masculinity*. Cambridge, MA: South End Press.

Johnson, N. G. (2001). Women helping men: Strengths and barriers to women therapists working with men clients. In G. R. Brooks & G. E. Good (Eds.), *The new handbook of counseling and psychotherapy with men* (pp. 696–718). San Francisco, CA: Jossey Bass.

Johnson, T. W. & Keren, M. S. (1996). Creating and maintaining boundaries in male couples. In J. Laird & R. Green (Eds.), *Lesbians and gays in couples and families* (pp. 231–250). San Francisco, CA: Jossey Bass.

Jolliff, D. (1994). Guest editorial: Group work with men. *Journal for Specialists in Group Work, 19,* 50–51.

Jolliff, D., & Horne, A. M. (1999). Growing up male: The development of mature masculinity. In A. M. Horne & M. S. Kiselica (Eds.), *Handbook of counseling boys and adolescent males* (pp. 3–24). Thousand Oaks, CA: Sage.

Kantrowitz, R. E., & Ballou, M. (1992). A feminist critique of cognitive-behavior therapy. In L. S. Brown & M. Ballou (Eds.), *Personality and psychopathology: Feminist reappraisals* (pp. 70–87). New York, NY: Guilford.

Kapalka, G. M. (2008). Improving self-control: Counseling boys with attention-deficit hyperactivity disorder. In M. S. Kiselica, M. Englar-Carlson, & A. M. Horne (Eds.), *Counseling troubled boys: A guidebook for professionals* (pp. 163–192). New York, NY: Routledge.

Kaplan, H. S. (1974). *The new sex therapy.* New York, NY: Brunner/Mazel.

Kaplan, R. S., O'Neil, J. S., & Owen, S. V. (1993, August). *Misogynous, normative, progressive masculinity and sexual assault: Gender role conflict, hostility toward women and hypermasculinity.* Paper presented at the annual convention of the American Psychological Association, Toronto, Canada.

Katz, J. (1999). *Tough guise: Violence, media, and the crisis in masculinity.* [Motion picture]. (Available from Media Education Foundation, http://www.mediaed.org).

Katz, J. (2006). *The macho paradox: Why some men hurt women and how all men can help.* Naperville, IL: Sourcebooks, Inc.

Katz, J., & Jhally, S. (1999, May 2). Focus section. *Boston Globe,* p. E1.

Katz, J. H. (1985). The sociopolitical nature of counseling. *The Counseling Psychologist, 13,* 615–624.

Kauth, M. R., Hartwig, M. J., & Kalichman, S. C. (2000). Healthy behavior relevant to psychotherapy with lesbian, gay, and bisexual clients. In R. M. Perez, K. A. DeBord, & K. J. Bieschke (Eds.), *Handbook of counseling and psychotherapy with lesbian, gay, and bisexual clients* (pp. 435–456). Washington, DC: American Psychological Association.

Kazdin, A. E. (1994). Methodology, design, and evaluation in psychotherapy research. In S. L. Garfield & A. E. Bergin (Eds.), *Handbook of psychotherapy and behavior change* (4th ed., pp. 19–71). New York, NY: Wiley.

Keel, M. (2005). Prevention of sexual assault: Working with adolescents in the education system. *Aware, 8,* 16–25.

Kellner, D. (2008). *Guys and guns amok: Domestic terrorism and school shootings from the Oklahoma City bombing to the Virginia Tech massacre.* Boulder, CO: Paradigm Publishers.

Kersting, K. (2005, June 6). Men and depression: Battling depression through public education. *APA Monitor, 36,* 66.

Kessler, R. C., Brown, R. L., & Boman, C. L. (1981). Sex differences in psychiatric help-seeking: Evidence from four large-scale surveys. *Journal of Health and Social Behavior, 22,* 49–64.

Kieser, D. J. (1983). The 1982 interpersonal circle: A taxonomy for complementarity in human transactions. *Psychological Review, 90,* 185–214.

Kilburg, R. R. (2007). Toward a conceptual understanding and definition of executive coaching. In R. R. Kilburg & R. C. Diedrich (Eds.), *The wisdom of coaching: Essential papers in consulting psychology for a world of change* (pp. 21–30). Washington, DC: American Psychological Association.

Kilgore, H., Sideman, L., Amin, K., Baca, L., & Bohanske, B. (2005). Psychologists' attitudes and therapeutic approaches towards gay, lesbian, and bisexual issues continue to improve: An update. *Psychotherapy: Theory Research, Practice, Training, 42,* 395–400.

Kilmartin, C. T. (2007). *The masculine self* (3rd ed.). Cornwall-on-the Hudson, NY: Sloan.

Kimmel, M. S. (Ed). (1990). *Men confront pornography.* New York, NY: Crown.

Kimmel, M. S. (1994). Masculinity as homophobia. In H. Brod & M. Kaufman (Eds.), *Theorizing masculinities* (pp. 119–141). Newbury Park, CA: Sage.

Kimmel, M. (1996). *Manhood in America: A cultural history.* New York: New York Free Press.

Kimmel, M. S., & Messner, M. A. (1989). *Men's lives.* New York, NY: MacMillan.

Kindlon, D., & Thompson, M. (2000). *Raising Cain: Protecting the emotional life of boys.* New York, NY: Ballantine.

Kiselica, M. S. (1995). *Multicultural counseling with teenage fathers: A practical guide.* Newbury Park, CA: Sage.

Kiselica, M. S. (2003). Transforming psychotherapy in order to succeed with boys: Male-friendly practices. *Journal of Clinical Psychology: In Session, 59,* 1225–1236.

Kiselica, M. S. (2005). *A male-friendly therapeutic process with school-age boys.* In G. E. Good & G. R. Brooks (Eds.), *The new handbook of counseling and psychotherapy with men: A comprehensive guide to settings, problems, and treatment approaches* (Rev. ed., pp. 17–28). San Francisco, CA: Jossey Bass.

Kiselica, M. S., & Englar-Carlson, M. (2008). Establishing rapport with boys in individual counseling and psychotherapy. In M. S. Kiselica, M. Englar-Carlson, & A. M. Horne (Eds.), *Counseling troubled boys: A guidebook for professionals* (pp. 49–65). New York, NY: Routledge.

Kiselica, M. S., Englar-Carlson, M., & Horne, A. M. (Eds.). (2008). *Counseling troubled boys: A guidebook for professionals.* New York, NY: Routledge.

Kiselica, M. S., Englar-Carlson, M., Horne, A. M., & Fisher, M. (2008). A positive psychology perspective on helping boys. In M. S. Kiselica, M. Englar-Carlson, & A. M. Horne (Eds.), *Counseling troubled boys: A guidebook for professionals* (pp. 31–48). New York, NY: Routledge.

Kiselica, M. S., & Look, C. T. (1993). Mental health counseling and prevention: Disparity between philosophy and practice? *Journal of Mental Health Counseling, 15,* 3–14.

Kiselica, M. S., Mule, M., & Haldeman, D. C. (2008). Finding inner peace in a homophobic world: Counseling gay boys and boys who are questioning their sexual identity. In M. S. Kiselica, M. Englar-Carlson, & A. M. Horne (Eds.), *Counseling troubled boys: A guidebook for professionals* (pp. 243–272). New York, NY: Routledge.

Kiselica, M. S., & O'Brien, S. (2001, August). Are attachment disorders and alexithymia characteristic of males? In M. S. Kiselica (Chair), *Are males really emotional mummies? What do the data indicate?* Symposium conducted at the annual convention of the American Psychological Association Convention, San Francisco.

Kizer, K. W. (1996). *Prescription for change.* Washington, DC: U.S. Department of Veterans Affairs.

Klerman, G. L., Weissman, M. M., Rounsaville, B. J., & Chevron, E. S. (1984). *Interpersonal psychotherapy of depression.* New York, NY: Basic Books.

Koocher, G. P. (1976). Civil liberties and aversive conditioning for treatment with children. *American Psychologist, 35,* 94–95.

Koss, M. P. (1993). Rape. Scope, impact, interventions, and public policy responses. *American Psychologist, 48,* 1062–1069.

Koss, M. P., & Cook, S. L. (1998). Facing the fact: Date and acquaintance rape are significant problems for women. In R. K. Bergen (Ed.), *Issues in intimate violence* (pp. 147–156). Thousand Oaks, CA: Sage.

Kravetz, D. (1978). Consciousness-raising groups in the 1970's. *Psychology of Women Quarterly, 3,* 168–186.

Kruger, P. (1999, June). A leader's journey. *Fast Company, 25,* 116–129.

Kupers, T. (1999). *Prison Madness.* San Francisco, CA: Jossey Bass.

Kupers, T. A. (2001). Psychotherapy with men in prison. In G. R. Brooks & G. E. Good (Eds.), *The new handbook of counseling and psychotherapy with men: A comprehensive guide to settings, problems, and treatment approaches* (pp. 170–184). San Francisco, CA: Jossey Bass.

Lambert, M. J., & Barley, D. E. (2002). Research summary on the therapeutic relationship and psychotherapy outcome. In J. C. Norcross (Ed.), *Psychotherapy relationships that work* (pp. 17–36). New York, NY: Oxford University Press.

Lambert, M. J., & Ogles, B. M. (2004). The efficacy and effectiveness of psychotherapy. In M. J. Lambert (Ed.), *Handbook of psychotherapy and behavior change* (5th ed., pp. 139–193). New York, NY: Wiley.

Laws, D. R., & Marshall, W. L. (2003). A brief history of behavioral and cognitive approaches to sexual offenders: The modern era. *Sexual Abuse: A Journal of Research and Treatment, 15,* 193–220.

Lazarus, A. A. (1976). *Multimodal behavior therapy.* New York, NY: Springer.

Lazarus, A. A. (1989). *The practice of multimodal therapy.* Baltimore, MD: Johns Hopkins.

Leary, T. (1957). *Interpersonal diagnosis of personality*. New York, NY: Ronald Press.

Lee, C. C. (1992). *Empowering young black males*. Ann Arbor, MI: Eric Clearinghouse.

Lee, C. C. (1999). Counseling African American men. In L. E. Davis (Ed.), *Working with African American males: A guide to practice* (pp. 39–53). Thousand Oaks, CA: Sage.

Lee, C. C. (2007). *Counseling for social justice* (2nd ed.) Alexandria, VA: American Counseling Association.

Lee, E., & Mock, M. R. (2005). Asian families: An overview. In M. McGoldrick, J. Giordano, & N. Garcia-Preto (Eds.), *Ethnicity and family therapy* (33rd. ed., pp. 269–289). New York, NY: Guilford Press.

Leonard, S., Lee, C., & M. S. Kiselica (1999). Counseling African American male youth. In A. M. Horne & M. S. Kiselica (Eds.), *Handbook of counseling boys and adolescent males* (pp.75–86). Thousand Oaks, CA: Sage.

Lemle, R., & Mishkind, M. E. (1989). Alcohol and masculinity. *Journal of Substance Abuse Treatment, 6, 213–222.*

Leszcz, M. (1992). The interpersonal approach to group psychotherapy. *International Journal of Group Psychotherapy, 42, 37–62.*

Levant, R., & Kelly, J. (1989). *Between father and child*. New York, NY: Viking.

Levant, R. F. (1990). Psychological services designed for men: A psychoeducational approach. *Psychotherapy, 27, 309–315.*

Levant, R. F. (1998). Desperately seeking language: Understanding, assessing, and treating normative male alexithymia. In W. S. Pollack & R. F. Levant (Eds.), *New psychotherapy for men* (pp. 35–56). New York, NY: John Wiley and Sons.

Levant, R. F. (2001a). The crises of boyhood. In G. R. Brooks & G. E. Good (Eds.), *The new handbook of counseling and psychotherapy with men: A comprehensive guide to settings, problems, and treatment approaches* (pp. 355–368). San Francisco, CA: Jossey Bass.

Levant, R. F. (2001b). Desperately seeking language: Understanding, assessing, and treating normative male alexithymia. In G. R. Brooks & G. E. Good (Eds.), *The new handbook of counseling and psychotherapy with men: A comprehensive guide to settings, problems, and treatment approaches* (pp. 424–443). San Francisco, CA: Jossey Bass.

Levant, R. F., & Brooks, G. R. (Eds.). (1997). *Men and sex: New psychological perspectives*. New York, NY: Wiley.

Levant, R. F., & Kopecky, G. (1995). *Masculinity reconstructed: Changing the rules of manhood—at work, in relationships, and in family life*. New York, NY: Dutton.

Levant, R. F., & Pollack, W. S. (Eds.). (1995). *A new psychology of men*. New York, NY: Basic Books.

Levant, R. H. (1997). Nonrelational sexuality in men. In R. H. Levant & G. R. Brooks (Eds.), *Men and sex: New psychological perspectives* (pp. 9–27). New York, NY: Wiley.

Levant, R. H. (2003). Treating male alexithymia. In T. J. Goodrich & L. B. Silverstein, (Eds.), *Feminist family therapy: Empowerment in social context* (pp. 177–188). Washington, DC: American Psychological Association.

Levant, R. H., & Fischer, J. (1998). The male role norms inventory. In C. M. Davis, W. H. Yarber, R. Bauserman, G. Schreer, & S. L. Davis (Eds.), *Sexuality-related measures: A compendium* (pp. 469–472). Newbury Park, CA: Sage.

Levant, R. L. (1995). Toward the reconstruction of masculinity. In R. L. Levant & W. S. Pollack (Eds.), *A new psychology of men* (pp. 229–251). New York, NY: Basic Books.

Levinson, D., Darrow, C., Klein, E., Levinson, M., & McKee, B. (1978). *The seasons of a man's life*. New York, NY: Knopf.

Levit, D. (1991). Gender differences in ego defenses in adolescence: Sex roles as one way to understand the differences. *Journal of Abnormal and Social Psychology, 61*, 992–999.

Levy, D. P. (2005). Hegemonic complicity, friendship, and comradeship: Validation and causal processes among White, middle-class, middle-aged men. *Journal of Men's Studies, 13*, 199–224.

Liddle, B. (1996). Therapist sexual orientation, gender, and counseling practices as they relate to ratings of helplessness by gay and lesbian clients. *Journal of Counseling Psychology, 43*, 394–401.

Lisak, D. (2001a). Homicide, violence, and male aggression. In G. R. Brooks & G. E. Good (Eds.), *The new handbook of counseling and psychotherapy with men* (pp. 278–292). San Francisco, CA: Jossey Bass.

Lisak, D. (2001b). Male survivors of trauma. In G. R. Brooks & G. E. Good (Eds.), *The new handbook of counseling and psychotherapy with men* (pp. 263–277). San Francisco, CA: Jossey Bass.

Long, D. (1987). Working with men who batter. In M. Scher, M. Stevens, G. Good, & G. A. Eichenfield (Eds.), *Handbook of counseling and psychotherapy with men* (pp. 306–320). Newbury Park, CA: Sage.

Lowen, A. (1975). *Bioenergetics*. New York, NY: Penguin.

Luepnitz, D. A. (1988). *The family interpreted: Feminist theory in clinical practice*. New York, NY: Basic Books.

Lusterman, D-D. (1989). Empathic interviewing. In G. Brooks, D-D. Lusterman, R. Nott, & C. Philpot (Chairs), Men and women relating: The carrot or the stick. Symposium conducted at the Annual Conference of the American Association of Marital and Family, San Francisco, CA.

Mahalik, J. R. (2000). Men's gender role conflict in men as a predictor of self-rating of behavior on the Interpersonal Circle. *Journal of Social and Clinical Psychology, 19*, 276–292.

Mahalik, J. (2001). Cognitive therapy for men. In G. R. Brooks & G. E. Good (Eds.), *The new handbook of counseling and psychotherapy with men: A comprehensive guide to settings, problems, and treatment approaches* (pp. 544–564). San Francisco, CA: Jossey Bass.

Mahalik, J. R. (2005a). Cognitive therapy for men. In G. E. Good & G. R. Brooks (Eds.), *A new handbook of counseling and psychotherapy with men* (pp. 217–233). San Francisco, CA: Jossey Bass.

Mahalik, J. R. (2005b). Interpersonal therapy for men. In G. E. Good & G. R. Brooks (Eds.), *A new handbook of counseling and psychotherapy with men* (pp. 234–247). San Francisco, CA: Jossey Bass.

Mahalik, J., R., Locke, B. D., Ludlow, L. H., Diemer, M., Scott, R. P. J., Gottfried, M., et al., (2003). Development of the conformity to masculine norms inventory. *Psychology of Men and Masculinity, 4*, 3–25.

Majors, R., & Billson, J. M. (1992). *Cool Pose: The dilemmas of black manhood in America*. New York, NY: Lexington Books.

Malley, M., & McCann, D. (2002). Family therapy with lesbian and gay clients. In A. Coyle & C. Kitzenger (Eds.), *Lesbian and gay psychology* (pp. 198–218). Malden, MA: Blackwell.

Maples, M. R., & Robertson, J. M. (2005). Counseling men with religious affiliations. In G. E. Good & G. R. Brooks, (Eds.) *The new handbook of counseling and psychotherapy with men: A comprehensive guide to settings, problems, and treatment approaches* (Rev. ed., pp. 384–404). San Francisco, CA: Jossey Bass.

Maracek, J. (1997). Disappearances, silences, and anxious rhetoric: Gender in abnormal psychology textbooks. In M. M. Gergen & S. N. Davis (Eds.), *Toward a new psychology of gender* (pp. 543–552). New York, NY: Routledge.

Maracek, J. (2001). Disorderly constructs: Feminist frameworks for clinical psychology. In R. K. Unger (Ed.), *Handbook of the psychology of women and gender* (pp. 303–316). New York, NY: Wiley.

Marini, I. D. (2005). Issues of males with physical disabilities in rehabilitation settings. In G. R. Brooks & G. E. Good (Eds.), *The new handbook of counseling and psychotherapy with men* (pp. 88–103). San Francisco, CA: Jossey Bass.

Mason, G. (2001). *The spectacle of violence: Homophobia, gender, and knowledge*. London, England: Routledge.

Masters, W. H., & Johnson, V. E. (1970). *Human sexual inadequacy*. Boston, MA: Little, Brown.

Matthee, I. (1997, Sept. 9). Anti-Asian hate crimes on the rise in the U.S. but state sees decline in such offenses. *Seattle Post-Intelligencer*, p. A3.

Matthews, C. R., & Lease, S. H. (2000). Focus on lesbian, gay, and bisexual families. In R. M. Perez, K. A. DeBord, & K. J. Bieschke (Eds.), *Handbook of counseling and psychotherapy with lesbian, gay, and bisexual clients* (pp. 249–274). Washington, DC: American Psychological Association.

Mauer, M., & Hurling, T. (1995). Young black Americans and the criminal justice system. Washington, DC: Sentencing Press.

McCrady, B. S., & Morgenstern, J. (1993). Psychoactive substance abuse disorders. In R. T. Ammerman & M. Hersen (Eds.), *Handbook of behavior therapy with children and adults* (pp. 361–374). Boston, MA: Allyn & Bacon.

McGill, M. E. (1985). *The McGill report on male intimacy*. New York, NY: Harper and Row.

McGoldrick, M., Anderson, C. M., & Walsh, F. (1989). *Women in families: A framework for family therapy*. New York, NY: Norton.

McHenry, S. S., & Johnson, J. W. (1993). Homophobia in the therapist and gay or lesbian client: Conscious and unconscious collusions in self-hate. *Psychotherapy, Research, Practice, Training, 30*, 141–151.

McKinnon, J. (2003). *The Black population in the United States: March 2002*. Current Population Reports, Series P20-541. Washington, DC: U.S. Bureau of the Census.

McLean, C. (1996). The politics of men's pain. In C. McLean, M. Carey, & C. White (Eds.), *Men's ways of being* (pp. 11–28). Boulder, CO: Westview Press.

Meyer, A. (1957). *Psychobiology: A science of men*. Springfield, IL: Charles C. Thomas.

Meyer, I. (1995). Minority stress and mental health in gay men. *Journal of Health and Social Behavior, 7*, 9–25.

Miller, W. R., & Rollnick, S. (2002). *Motivational interviewing: Preparing people to change* (2nd ed.). New York, NY: Guilford.

Mirande, A. (1997). *Hombres y machos: Masculinity and Latino culture*. Boulder, CO: Westview Press.

Modell, A. H. (1976). The "holding environment" and the therapeutic action of psychoanalysis. *Journal of the American Psychoanalytic Association, 24*, 285–308.

Moody, A. J. (1984). The effect of clients' choice of therapist and pre-therapy training on outcome in psychotherapy. *Dissertation Abstracts International, 45*(6-B), 1902.

Mooney, T. F. (1998). Cognitive behavior therapy for men. In W. S. Pollack & R. F. Levant (Eds.), *New psychotherapy for men* (pp. 57–82). Hoboken, NJ: Wiley.

Morrow, S. L. (2000). First do no harm: Therapist issues in psychotherapy with lesbian, gay, and bisexual clients. In R. M. Perez, K. A. DeBord, & K. J. Bieschke (Eds.), *Handbook of counseling and psychotherapy with lesbian, gay, and bisexual clients* (pp. 137–156). Washington, DC: American Psychological Association.

Muehlenhard, C., & Linton, M. A. (1987). Date rape and sexual aggression in dating situations: Incidence and risk factors. *Journal of Counseling Psychology, 34*, 186–196.

Murphy, R. F. (1990). *The body silent*. New York, NY: Norton.

Myers, H. F., Echemendia, R. J., & Trimble, J. E. (1991). The need for training ethnic minority psychologists. In H. Myers, P. Wohlford, L. P. Guzman, & R. Echemendia (Eds.), *Ethnic minority perspectives on clinical training and services in psychology* (pp. 3–11). Washington, DC: American Psychological Association.

Nardi, P. M. (1992). "Seamless souls": An introduction to men's friendships. In P. M. Nardi (Ed.), *Men's friendships* (pp. 1–14). Newbury Park, CA: Sage.

Neligh, G. (1990). Mental health programs for American Indians: Their logic, structure, and function. *The Journal of the National Center Monograph Series, 3*,(3), 1–279.

Neff, J. A., & Hoppe, S. K. (1993). Race/ethnicity, acculturation, and psychological distress: Fatalism and religiosity as cultural resources. *Journal of Community Psychology, 21*, 3–20.

Newman, G. & Muzzonigro, P. (1993). The effects of traditional family values on the coming out process of gay male adolescents. *Adolescence, 28*, 212–226.

Newton, J. L. (2005). *From panthers to promise keepers: Rethinking the men's movement.* Lanham, MD: Rowman & Littlefield.

Newton, F., Rathbun, A., & Arck, W. (1999). *Leadership training syllabus* (Available from F. N. Newton, University Counseling Services, Kansas State University, Manhattan, Kansas 66506).

Nichols, J. (1975). *Men's liberation: A new definition of masculinity.* New York, NY: Penguin Books.

Nichols, S. L., & Good, T. L. (2004). Why today's young people are viewed so negatively. *Education Week*, 4/14/2004, 23 (31), 42.

Nicolisi, J. (1997). *Reparative therapy of male homosexuality: A new clinical approach.* Northvale, NJ: Jason Aronson.

Niednagel, J. P. (1997). *Your key to sports success.* Laguna, CA: Laguna Press.

Niiya, B. (1996, June 8). The Rafu Shampoo: New definitions of masculinity: Asian men never had the John Wayne option. *Los Angeles Times*, p. 7.

Nock, S. L. (1998). *Marriage in men's lives.* New York, NY: Oxford University Press.

Nolen-Hoeksema, S. (1990). *Sex differences in depression.* Stanford, CA: Stanford University Press.

Norcross, J. C. (2005). A primer on psychotherapy integration. In J. C. Norcross & M. R. Goldfried (Eds.), *Handbook of psychotherapy integration* (2nd ed.). New York, NY: Oxford University Press.

Norcross, J. C. & Goldfried, M. R. (2005). *Handbook of psychotherapy integration* (2nd ed.). Oxford, England: Oxford University Press.

Norcross, J. C., Karpiak, C. P., & Lister, K. M. (2005). What's an integrationist? A study of self-identified integrative and (occasionally) eclectic psychologists. *Journal of Clinical Psychology, 61*, 1587–1594.

Novaco, R. (1995). Clinical problems of anger and its assessment and regulation through a stress coping skills approach. In W. O'Donohue & L. Krasner (Eds.), *Handbook of psychological skills training* (pp. 320–338). Boston, MA: Allyn & Bacon.

Odell, M., & Quinn, W. H. (1998). Therapist and client behaviors in the first interview: Effects on session impact and treatment duration. *Journal of Marital & Family Therapy, 24 (3)*, 369–388.

Okazaki, S. (2000). Treatment delay among Asian-American patients with severe mental illness. *American Journal of Orthopsychiatry, 70*, 58–64.

Olkin, R. (1999). *What psychotherapists should know about disability.* New York, NY: Guilford.

Olufson, M., Marcus, S. C., Druss, B., & Pincus, H. A. (2002). National trends in the use of outpatient psychotherapy. *American Journal of Psychiatry, 159*, 1914–1920.

O'Neil, J. M. (1982).Gender-role conflict and strain in men's lives. In K. Solomon & N. Levy (Eds.), *Men in transition: Theory and therapy* (pp. 5–44). New York, NY: Plenum.

O'Neil, J. M. (1996). The gender role journey workshop: Exploring sexism and gender role conflict in a coeducational setting. In M. Andronico (Ed.), *Men in groups: Insights, interventions, & psychoeducational work* (pp. 193–214). Washington, DC: American Psychological Association.

O'Neil, J. M. (2008). Summarizing 25 years of research on men's gender role conflict using the Gender Role Conflict Scale: New research paradigms and clinical implications. *The Counseling Psychologist, 36*(3), 358–445.

O'Neil, J. M., & Carroll, M. R. (1988). A gender role workshop focused on sexism, gender role conflict, and the gender role journey. *Journal of Counseling and Development, 67*, 193–197.

O'Neil, J. M., Helms, B., Gable, R., David, L., & Wrightman, L. (1986). Gender Role Conflict Scale: College men's fear of femininity. *Sex Roles, 31*, 517–531.

Orchowski, L. M., Spickard, B. A., & McNamara, J. R. (2006). Cinema and the valuing of psychotherapy: Implications for clinical practice. *Professional Psychology: Research and Practice, 37*, 506–514.

Orlinsky, D. E., Ronnestad, M. H., & Willutzki, U. (2004). Fifty years of psychotherapy process-outcome research: Continuity and change. In M. J. Lambert (Ed.), *Bergin and Garfield's handbook of psychotherapy and behavior change* (5th ed., pp. 307–390). New York, NY: John Wiley.

Orpinas, P., Horne, A. M., & Staniszewski, D. (2003). School bullying: Changing the problem by changing the school. *School Psychology Review, 32*, 431–444.

Osbourne, J. W. (1997). Race and academic disidentification. *Journal of Educational Psychology, 89*, 728–735.

Osherson, S. (1986). *Finding our fathers: The unfinished business of manhood.* New York, NY: Free Press.

Osherson, S., & Krugman, S. (1990). Men, shame, and psychotherapy. *Psychotherapy, 27*, 327–339.

Ossana, S. M. (2000). Relationship and couples counseling. In R. M. Perez, K. A. DeBord, & K. J. Bieschke (Eds.), *Handbook of counseling and psychotherapy with lesbian, gay, and bisexual clients* (pp. 275–302). Washington, DC: American Psychological Association.

Owen, C. L. (2005). Working together as culture brokers by building trusting alliance with bilingual and bicultural newcomer paraprofessionals. *Child Welfare, 84*, 669–688.

Paniagua, F. A. (1998). *Assessing and treating culturally diverse clients: A practical guide.* Thousand Oaks, CA: Sage.

Parham, T. A. (1999). Invisibility syndrome in African descent people: Understanding cultural manifestations of the struggle for self-affirmation. *The Counseling Psychologist, 2* (6), 794–801.

Parham, T. A. (2002). *Counseling persons of African descent: Raising the bar of practitioner competence.* Thousand Oaks, CA: Sage.

Pedersen, P. (1999). *Multiculturalism as a fourth force.* Philadelphia, PA: Brunner/Mazel.

Perez, R. M., DeBord, K. A., & Bieschke, K. J. (2000). *Handbook of counseling and psychotherapy with lesbian, gay, and bisexual clients.* Washington, DC: American Psychological Association.

Petitpas, A. J., Giges, B., & Danish, S. J. (1999). The sport psychologist-athlete relationship: Implications for training. *Professional Practice, 13,* 344–357.

Phelps, R. E., Taylor, J. D., & Gerard, P. A. (2001). Cultural mistrust, ethnic identity, racial identity, and self-esteem, among ethnically diverse Black university students. *Journal of Counseling and Development, 79,* 209–216.

Phillips, F. B. (1990). NTU psychotherapy: An Afrocentric approach. *Journal of Black Psychology, 17,* 55–74.

Phillips, S. P. (2005, July 14). Defining and measuring gender: A social determinant whose time has come. *International Journal for Equity in Health,4,* retrieved August 19, 2009, from http://www.equityhealthj.com/content/4/1/11

Phillips, J., & Fischer, A. (1998). Graduate students: Training experiences with lesbian, gay, and bisexual issues. *The Counseling Psychologist, 26,* 712–734.

Philpot, C. L., Brooks, G. R., Lusterman, D., & Nutt, R. L. (1997). *Bridging separate gender worlds.* Washington, DC: American Psychological Association.

Pilkington, N., & Cantor, J. (1996). Perceptions of heterosexual bias in professional psychology programs: A survey of graduate students. *Professional Psychology: Research and Practice, 27,* 604–612.

Pinsof, W. M. (1995). *Integrative IPCT: A synthesis of biological, individual and family therapies.* New York, NY: Basic.

Pipher, M. (1994). *Reviving Ophelia: Saving the selves of adolescent girls.* New York, NY: Putnam.

Pittman, F. (1990). The masculine mystique. *Family Therapy Networker, 14,* 40–52.

Pleck, J. H. (1980). Men's power with women, other men, and society: A men's movement analysis. In E. Pleck & J. H. Pleck (Eds.), *The American man* (pp. 417–433). Englewood Cliffs, NJ: Prentice-Hall.

Pleck, J. H. (1987). American fathering in historical perspective. In M. S. Kimmel (Ed.), *Changing men* (pp.83–97). Newbury Park, CA: Sage.

Pleck, J. H. (1995). The gender role strain paradigm: An update. In R. H. Levant & W. S. Pollack (Eds.), *A new psychology of men* (pp. 11–32). New York, NY: Basic.

Pleck, J. H. (1997). Paternal involvement: Levels, sources, and consequences. In M. E. Lamb (Ed.), *The role of the father in child development* (pp. 66–103). New York, NY: John Wiley & Sons.

Pleck, J. H. (1999). Balancing work and family. *Scientific American Presents, 1999,* 38–43.

Pleck, J. H., & Masciadrelli, B. P. (2004). Paternal involvement by U.S. residential fathers: Levels, sources, and consequences. In M. E. Lamb (Ed.), *The role of the father in child development* (4th ed., pp. 222–271). New York, NY: John Wiley & Sons.

Pleck, J. H. (2007). From the editor. *Fathering, 5 (1),* 3.

Pleck, J. H. (2007). Why could father involvement benefit children? Theoretical perspectives. *Applied Developmental Science, 11,* 196–202.

Pollack, W. S. (1990). Men's development and psychotherapy: A psychoanalytic perspective. *Psychotherapy, 27,* 316–321.

Pollack, W. S. (1995). Deconstructing disidentification: Rethinking psychoanalytic concepts of male development. *Psychoanalysis and psychotherapy, 12,* 30–45.

Pollack, W. S. (1998). *Real boys: Rescuing our sons from the myths of boyhood.* New York, NY: Random House.

Pollack, W. S. (2005). "Masked men": New psychoanalytically oriented treatment models for adult and young adult men. In G. E. Good & G. R. Brooks (Eds.), *A new handbook of counseling and psychotherapy with men* (pp. 203–216). San Francisco, CA: Jossey Bass.

Pollack, W. S., & Levant, R. F. (1998). *New psychotherapy for men.* New York, NY: Wiley.

Portwood, S. G. & Waris, R. G. (2003). Violence prevention, childhood. In T. P. Gullotta & M. Bloom (Eds.), *Encyclopedia of primary prevention and health promotion* (pp. 1130–1136). New York, NY: Kluwer.

Prochaska, J. O. (1979). *Systems of psychotherapy: A transtheoretical analysis* (1st ed.). Homewood, IL: Dorsey Press.

Prochaska, J. O., & DiClemente, C. C. (1982). Transtheoretical therapy: Toward a more integrative model of change. *Psychotherapy, 19,* 276–288.

Prochaska, J. O. & DiClemente, C. C. (2005). The transtheoretical approach. In J. C. Norcross & M. R. Goldfried (Eds.), *Handbook of psychotherapy integration* (pp. 147–171). New York, NY: Oxford University Press.

Prochaska, J. O., & Norcross, J. C. (2003a). *Systems of psychotherapy* (5th ed.). Pacific Grove, CA: Brooks/Cole.

Prochaska, J. O. & Norcross, J. C. (2003b). States of change. In J. C. Norcross (Ed.), *Psychotherapy relationships that work: Therapist contributions and responsiveness to patients* (pp. 303–314). New York, NY: Oxford University Press.

Prochaska, J. O., & Norcross, J. C. (2007). *Systems of psychotherapy: A transtheoretical analysis.* Belmont, CA: Thomson.

Rabinowitz, F. E. (2005). Group therapy for men. In G. E. Good & G. R. Brooks (Eds.), *The new handbook of psychotherapy and counseling with men approaches* (Rev. ed., pp. 264–277). San Francisco, CA: Jossey Bass.

Rabinowitz, R. E., & Cochran, S. V. (2002). *Deepening psychotherapy with men.* Washington, DC: American Psychological Association.

Rawlings, E. I., & Carter, D. K. (1977). *Psychotherapy for women: Treatment toward equality.* Springfield, IL: Thomas.

Reese, L. F., Vera, E. M., Simm, T. R., & Ikeda, R. M. (2000). The role of families and caregivers as risk and protective factors in preventing youth violence. *Clinical Child and Family Psychology, 3,* 61–77.

Reich, W. (1973). *The function of the orgasm.* New York, NY: Pocket Books (Original work published 1942)

Reid, H. M., & Fine, G. A. (1992). Self-disclosure in friendships. In P. M. Nardi (Ed.), *Men's friendships* (pp. 132–152). Newbury Park, CA: Sage.

Reynolds, A. L., & Hanjorgiris, W. F. (2000). Coming out: Lesbian, gay, and bisexual identity development. In R. M. Perez, K. A. DeBord, & K. J. Bieschke (Eds.), *Handbook of counseling and psychotherapy with lesbian, gay, and bisexual clients* (pp. 35–55). Washington, DC: American Psychological Association.

Rice, J. D., & Rice, J. K. (1973). Implications of the women's liberation movement for psychotherapy. *American Journal of Psychiatry, 130,* 1911–1916.

Richards, P. S., & Bergin, A. E. (2000). Toward religious and spiritual competency for mental health professionals. In P. S. Richards & A. Bergin (Eds.), *Handbook of psychotherapy and religious diversity* (pp. 1–26). Washington, DC: American Psychological Association.

Ridley, C. R. (1995). *Overcoming unintentional racism in counseling and therapy: A practitioner's guide to intentional intervention.* Thousand Oaks, CA: Sage.

Robertson, J. M. & Newton, F. B. (2001). Working with men in sports settings. In G. R. Brooks & G. E. Good (Eds.), *The new handbook of counseling and psychotherapy with men* (pp. 92–125). San Francisco, CA: Jossey Bass.

Robertson, J. M., & Shepard, D. S. (2008). The psychological development of boys. In M. S. Kiselica, M. Englar-Carlson, & A. M. Horne (Eds.), *Counseling troubled boys: A guidebook for professionals* (pp. 3–30). New York, NY: Routledge.

Rochlen, A. B., & Hoyer, W. D. (2005). Marketing mental health to men: Theoretical and practical considerations. *Journal of Clinical Psychology, 61,* 675–684.

Rodriguez, O. (1987). *Hispanics and human services: Help-seeking in the inner city.* (Monograph No. 14). New York, NY: Fordham University. Hispanic Research Center.

Rosenberg, S. D., Rosenberg, H. J., & Farrell, M. P. (1999). The midlife crisis revisited. In S. L. Willis & J. D. Reid (Eds.), *Life in the middle: Psychological and social development in middle age* (pp. 47–73). San Diego, CA: Academic Press.

Rotheram-Borus, M. J., Luna, G. C., Marotta, T., & Kelly, H. (1994). Going nowhere fast: Methamphetamine and HIV infection. In F. J. Battles, A. Sloboda, & W. C. Grace (Eds.), *The context of HIV use among drug users and their sexual partners* (NIH Pub. No. 94–3750, pp. 155–182). Washington, DC: Government Printing Office.

Russell, D. E. H. (1982). The prevalence and incidence of forcible rape and attempted rape of females. *Victimology: An International Journal, 7*, 81–93.

Sandhu, D. S. (1997). Psychocultural profiles of Asian and Pacific Islander Americans: Implications for counseling and psychotherapy. *Journal of Multicultural Counseling and Development, 25*, 7–22.

Sattel, J. W. (1976). The inexpressive male: Tragedy or sexual politics? *Social Problems, 23*, 469–477.

Savin-Williams, R. C. (2001). *Mom, dad. I'm gay.* Washington, DC: American Psychological Association.

Sawyer, J. (1970). On male liberation. *Liberation, 15*, 6.

Sax, L. (2007). *Boys adrift: The five factors driving the growing epidemic of unmotivated boys and underachieving young men.* New York, NY: Basic.

Schacht, A. N., Tafoya, N., Mirabla, K. (1989). Home-based therapy with American Indian families. *American Indian and Alaska Native Mental Health Research, 3*, 27–42.

Schnieder, I. (1987). The theory and practice of movie psychiatry. *American Journal of Psychiatry, 144*, 996–1002.

Schwartzberg, S., & Rosenberg, L. G. (1998). Being gay and being male: Psychotherapy with gay and bisexual men. In W. S. Pollack & R. F. Levant (Eds.), *New psychotherapy for men* (pp. 259–281). Hoboken, NJ: Wiley.

Scher, M. (1990). Effect of gender-role incongruities on men's experience as clients in psychotherapy. *Psychotherapy, 27*, 322–326.

Sears, J. T. (1991). *Growing up gay in the South: Race, gender, and journeys of the spirit.* New York, NY: Harrington Park.

Seligman, L. (2006). *Theories of counseling and psychotherapy: Systems, strategies, and skills* (2nd ed.). Columbus, OH: Pearson.

Sellers, S. L., Bonham, V., Neighbors, H. W., & Amell, J. W. (2009). Effects of racial discrimination and health behaviors on mental and physical health of middle-class African American men. *Health Education and Behavior, 36*(1), 31–44.

Shapiro, J. L. (2001). Therapeutic interventions with fathers. In G. R. Brooks & G. E. Good (Eds.), *The new handbook of counseling and psychotherapy with men* (pp. 403–423). San Francisco, CA: Jossey Bass.

Shay, J. J. (1996). Okay, I'm here but I'm not talking: Psychotherapy with the reluctant male. *Psychotherapy, 33*, 503–513.

Simmons, R., & Rosenberg, M. (1975). Sex, sex roles, and self-image. *Journal of Youth and Adolescence, 4*, 229–258.

Simonds, W. (1992). *Women and self-help culture: Reading between the lines.* New Brunswick, NJ: Rutgers.

Silverberg, R. (1986). *Psychotherapy for men: Transcending the masculine mystique.* Springfield, IL: C. C. Thomas.

Silverstein, L. B. (2003). Classic texts and early critiques. In L. B. Silverstein & T. J. Goodrich (Eds.), *Feminist family therapy: Empowerment in social context* (pp. 17–36). Washington, DC: American Psychological Association.

Silverstein, L. B., & Auerbach, C. F. (1999). Do Promise Keepers dream of feminist sheep? *Sex Roles, 40*(9/10), 665–688.

Silverstein, L. B., & Goodrich, T. J. (Eds.). (2003). *Feminist family therapy: Empowerment in social context.* Washington, DC: American Psychological Association.

Skovholt, T. M. (1978). Feminism and men's lives. *The Counseling Psychologist, 7,* 3.

Sleek, S. (1995). Psychology and society: The media isn't always kind to mental health providers. *Monitor on Psychology, 26,* 7.

Solomon, K. (1982). The masculine gender role: Description. In K. Solomon & N. Levy (Eds.), *Men in transition: Theory and therapy* (pp. 45–76). New York, NY: Plenum Press.

Sommers, C. H. (1995). *Who stole feminism?* New York, NY: Touchstone.

Sommer, C. H. (2000). *The war against boys: How misguided feminism is harming our young men.* New York, NY: Touchstone.

Smith, M. H., Glass, G. V., & Miller, T. (1980). *The benefits of psychotherapy.* Baltimore, MD: Johns Hopkins.

Sprinthall, N. A. (1990). Counseling psychology from Greystone to Atlanta: On the road to Armageddon? *Counseling Psychologist, 18,* 455–463.

Stanford, M. S. (2008). *Grace for the afflicted: A clinical and biblical perspective.* Carlisle, CA: Authentic Press.

Stanley, A. (2008, January 28). Four days, a therapist: Fifth day, a patient. *New York Times.* Retrieved February 26,2008, from http://www.nytimes.com/2008/01/28/arts/television/28stan.html?_r=1&oref=slogin

Stanton, G. T., & Maier, B. (2004). *Marriage on trial: The case against same-sex marriage and parenting.* Downers Grove, IL: InterVarsity Press.

Stark, E. (1990). Rethinking homicide: Violence, race, and the politics of gender. *International Journal of Health and Services, 20*(1), 3–26.

Stephenson, J. (1991). *Men are not cost-effective.* Napa, CA: Diemer, Smith.

Sternbach, J. (1992). A men's studies approach to group treatment with all-male groups. *Men and Mental Health (Special Issue). Men's Studies Review, 9,* 14–22.

Sternbach, J. (2001). Counseling with the young older man. In G. R. Brooks & G. E. Good (Eds.), *The new handbook of counseling and psychotherapy with men* (pp. 464–480). San Francisco, CA: Jossey Bass.

Stricker, G., & Gold, J. (2005). Assimilative psychodynamic psychotherapy. In J. C. Norcross & M. R. Goldfried (Eds.), *Handbook of psychotherapy integration* (2nd ed., pp. 221–240). New York, NY: Oxford.

Substance Abuse and Mental Health Services Administration, Office of Applied Studies. (2008). *Results from the 2007 National Survey on Drug Use and Health: National Findings* (NSDUH Series H-34, DHHS Publication No. SMA 08-4343). Rockville, MD: Author.

Sue, D. (1999). Counseling Asian American boys and adolescent males. In A. M. Horne & M. S. Kiselica (Eds.), *Handbook of counseling boys and adolescent males* (pp. 87–100). Thousand Oaks, CA: Sage.

Sue, D. (2005). Asian American masculinity and therapy: The concept of masculinity in Asian American males. In G. E. Good & G. R. Brooks (Eds.), *A new handbook of counseling and psychotherapy with men* (pp. 357–368). San Francisco, CA: Jossey Bass.

Sue, D. W., & Sue, D. (1990). *Counseling the culturally different: Theory and practice* (3rd ed.). New York, NY: John Wiley & Sons.

Sue, D. W. & Sue, D. (2003). *Counseling the culturally diverse: Theory and practice* (4th ed.). New York, NY: Wiley.

Sue, D. W. & Sue, D. (2008). *Counseling the culturally diverse: Theory and practice* (5th ed.). New York, NY: Wiley.

Sullivan, H. S. (1953). *The interpersonal theory of psychiatry*. New York, NY: Norton.

Sutton, C. T. & Broken Nose, M. A. (2005). American Indian families: An Overview. In M. McGoldrick, J. Giordano, & N. Garcia-Preto (Eds.), *Ethnicity and family therapy* (3rd. ed., pp. 43–54). New York, NY: Guilford Press.

Sweeny, T. J. (1998). *Adlerian counseling: A practitioner's approach* (4th ed.). Bristol, PA: Accelerated Development.

Sweet, H. (2006). Finding the person behind the persona: Engaging men as a female therapist. In M. Englar-Carlson & M. A. Stevens (Eds.), *In the room with men: A casebook of therapeutic change* (pp. 69–90). Washington, DC: American Psychological Association.

Tannen, D. (1990). *You just don't understand: Women and men in conversation*. New York, NY: Morrow.

Task Force on Promotion and Dissemination of Psychological Procedures (1995). Training in dissemination of empirically validated psychological treatments: Report and recommendations. *The Clinical Psychologist, 48*, 3–23.

Thomason, T. C. (1991). Counseling Native Americans: An introduction for non-Native American counselors. *Journal of Counseling and Development, 69*, 321–327.

Thompson, E. H., & Pleck, J. H. (1995). Masculinity ideologies: A review of research instrumentation on men and masculinities. In R. H. Levant & W. S. Pollack (Eds.), *A new psychology of men* (pp. 129–163). New York, NY: Basic Books.

Thorpe, G. L., & Olson, S. L. (1997). *Behavior therapy*. Needham Heights, MA: Allyn & Bacon.

Tiger, L. (1969). *Men in groups*. New York, NY: Random House.

Tolson, A. (1977). *The limits of masculinity*. London, England: Tavistock.

Toomer, J. E. (1978). Males in psychotherapy. *The Counseling Psychologist, 7*, 22–25.

Tracey, T. J. G., & Schneider, P. L. (1995). An evaluation of the circular structure of the checklist of interpersonal transactions and the checklist of psychotherapy interactions. *Journal of Counseling Psychology, 42*, 496–507.

Trimble, J. E., Fleming, C. M., Beauvais, F., & Jumper–Thurman, P. (1996). Essential cultural and social strategies for counseling Native American Indians. In P. B. Pederson, J. G. Draguns, W. J. Lonner, & J. E. Trimble (Eds.), *Counseling across cultures* (4th ed., pp. 177–209). Thousand Oaks, CA: Sage.

Tryon, G. S. (1986). Client and counselor characteristics and engagement in counseling. *Journal of Counseling Psychology, 33,* 471–474.

Tyler, F. B., Sussewell, D. R., & Williams-McCoy, J. (1985). Ethnic validity in psychotherapy. *Psychotherapy, 22,* 311–320.

Umbarger, C. C. (1983). *Structural family therapy: Theory, practice, and technique.* New York, NY: Grune Stratton.

Unitarian Universalist Men's Network (2008). UUMen mission and objectives. Retrieved August 19, 2009, from http://www.uumen.org/mission_goals.htm

Urschel, J. K. (2000). Men's studies and women's studies: Commonalities, dependence, and independence. *Journal of Men's Studies, 8,* 407–411.

U.S. Census Bureau (2004). *We are the people: Asians in the United States.* Washington, DC: U.S. Government Printing Office.

Velasquez, R. J., Arellano, L. M., & McNeill, B. W. (2004). *The handbook of Chicana/o psychology and mental health.* Mahweh, NJ: Erlbaum.

Vera, E. M., & Reese, L. E. (2000). Preventive interventions with school-age youth. In S. D. Brown & R. W. Lent (Eds.), *Handbook of counseling psychology* (3rd ed.; pp. 411–434). Hoboken, NJ: Wiley.

Verbrugge, L. M. (1985). Gender and health: An update on hypothesis and evidence. *Journal of Health and Social Behavior, 26,* 156–182.

Vessey, J. T., & Howard, K. I. (1993). Who seeks psychotherapy? *Psychotherapy, 30,* 546–553.

Wachtel, P. L. (1977). *Psychoanalysis, behavior therapy and the relational world.* Washington, DC: American Psychological Association.

Watkins, D. C., & Neighbors, H. W. (2007). An initial exploration of what "mental health" means to young black men. *Journal of Men's Health and Gender, 4*(3), 271–282.

Walters, M., Carter, B., Papp, P., & Silverstein, O. (1988). *The invisible web: Gender patterns in family relationships.* New York, NY: Guilford.

Watson, S. T., & Gresham, F. M. (Eds.). (1998). *Handbook of child behavior therapy.* New York, NY: Plenum Press.

Wedding, D., & Niemiec, R. M. (2003). The clinical use of films in psychotherapy. *Journal of Clinical Psychology, 59,* 207–215.

Weikel, W. J., & Palmo, A. J. (1989). The evolution and practice of mental health counseling. *Journal of Mental Health Counseling, 11,* 7–25.

Weston, K. (1994). Building gay families. In G. Handel & G. G. Whitchurch (Eds.), *The psychosocial interior of the family* (pp. 525–533). New York, NY: Harrington Press.

White, J. L., & Cones, J. H. (1999). *Black man emerging: Facing the past and seizing the future in America*. New York, NY: Freeman.

White, J. W., & Kowalski, R. M. (1998). Male violence toward women: An integrated perspective. In R. G. Green & E. Donnerstein (Eds.), *Human aggression: Theories, research, and implications for social policy* (pp. 203–228). San Diego, CA: Academic Press.

Whitehurst, C. (1977). *Women in America: The oppressed majority*. Santa Monica, CA: Goodyear.

Wierzbicki, M. & Pekarik, G. (1993). A meta-analysis of psychotherapy dropout. *Professional Psychology: Research and Practice, 24,* 190–195.

Wilchins, R. (2008, April 8). An invisible war. *Advocate, 1005,* 33.

Wilcox, D. W., & Forrest, L. (1992). The problems of men and counseling: Gender bias or gender truth. *Journal of Mental Health Counseling, 14,* 291–304.

Wilcox, W. B., & Nock, S. L. (2006). What's love got to do with it? Equality, equity, commitment and women's marital quality. *Social Forces, 84,* 1321–1345.

Williams, J. (1977). *The psychology of women: Behavior in a biosocial context*. New York, NY: Norton.

Winnicott, D. W. (1974). *The maturational process and the facilitating environment*. New York, NY: International Universities Press.

Wisch, A. F., Mahalik, J. R., Hayes, J. A., & Nutt, E. A. (1995). The impact of gender role conflict and counseling technique on psychological help-seeking in men. *Sex Roles, 33,* 77–89.

Wood, J. T. (1994). *Gendered lives: Communication, gender, and culture*. Belmont, CA: Wadsworth.

Worell, J., & Johnson, D. (2001). Therapy with women: Feminist frameworks. In R. K. Unger (Ed.), *Handbook of the psychology of women and gender* (pp. 317–329). New York, NY: Wiley.

Worell, J., & Remer, P. (1992). *Feminist perspectives in therapy*. New York, NY: Wiley.

Wrenn, C. G. (1962). The culturally-encapsulated counselor. *Harvard Educational Review, 32,* 444–449.

Wyche, K. F., & Rice, J. K. (1997). Feminist therapy: From dialogue to tenets. In J. Worell and M. Johnson (Eds.), *Shaping the future of feminist psychology: Education, research, and practice* (pp. 57–71). Washington, DC: American Psychological Association.

Yalom, I. D. (2005). *The theory and practice of group psychotherapy* (5th ed.). New York, NY: Basic Books.

Yarhouse, M. A. (2005). Christian explorations in sexual identity. *Journal of Psychology & Christianity, 24,* 291–291.

Zabos, G. R., & Trinh, C. (2001). Bringing the mountain to Mohammed: A mobile dental team serves a community-based program for people with HIV/AIDS. *American Journal of Public Health, 91,* 1187–1189.

Zins, J. E., & Erchul, W. P. (2002). Best practices in school consultation. In A. Thomas & J. Grimes (Eds.), *Best practices in school psychology* (pp. 625–643). Washington, DC: National Association of School Psychologists.

Zakrzewski, P. (2005, June, 19). Daddy, what did you do in the men's movement? The *Boston Globe*. Retrieved August 19, 2009, from http://www.boston.com/news/globe/ideas/articles/2005/06/19/daddy_what_did_you_do_in_the_mens_movement/

Zur, O. (2001). Out-of-office experience: When crossing office boundaries and engaging in dual relationships are clinically beneficial and ethically sound. *Independent Practitioner, 21* (1), 96–100.

Zur, O. (2008). *Beyond the office walls: Home visits, celebrations, adventure therapy, incidental encounters, and other encounters outside the office walls.* Retrieved August 6, 2009, from Zur Institute Web site: http://www.zurinstitute.com/outofoffice experiences.html

INDEX

Danish, S. J., 55, 62–63
Dark side of masculinity. *See* Masculinity
Darrow, C., 22
David, D. S., 19, 20, 30, 31
Davis, D., 92
DeBord, K. A., 128
Deepening Psychotherapy With Men
　　(R. E. Rabinowitz and
　　S. V. Cochran), 103
Defensive autonomy, 88, 90
Delphi poll, 53
Depth therapy, 90
Descriptive beliefs, 31
Desensitization interventions, 97
Developmental perspective, 87–88
Diagnostic assessment, male-specific, 71
Diagnostic and Statistical Manual of
　　Mental Disorders (DSM-IV), 9,
　　14, 128
Diamond, J., 15
DiClemente, C. C., 142, 144, 147, 150
Diffuse physiological arousal, 97
Disability community, 134
Disability experience, The, 134
Disadvantages, cultural, 41–42, 45
Disidentification, 88
Diverse masculinities, 113–138, 173
　　African Americans, 118–120
　　Asian Americans, 125–127
　　and ethnocentric monoculturalism,
　　　117–118
　　gay and bisexual, 128–134
　　Hispanics/Latinos, 120–122
　　Native Americans, 122–125
　　physical disabilities, men with,
　　　134–137
　　and racism/oppression, 115–117
Diversity issues, for boys and adolescents,
　　55–56
Dominance, 38–39
Doyle, J. A., 19, 20, 31
Dramatic relief, 145, 148, 152
DSM-IV. See Diagnostic and Statistical
　　Manual of Mental Disorders

Earth mother, 20
Eclectic models of psychotherapy,
　　141–142
Educational orientation, 119
Elliott, R., 81

Emotional abandonment, 88–90
Emotional inexpressiveness, 40, 88
Emotional isolation, 22–23
Empathic interview technique, 109
Empathy, 81–82
Empirically supported treatments
　　(ESTs), 79
Empowerment, women's, 9, 45, 108
Encyclopedia of Primary Prevention and
　　Health Promotion, 55
Engaging men, 69–84
　　and drop rates, 70–71
　　with initial assessment, 71–73
　　and motivational pressures, 73–76
　　by surmounting motivational
　　　hurdles, 76–79
　　with therapeutic alliance, 79–84
Englar-Carlson, M., 23, 78, 111–112,
　　162, 166
Environmental reevaluation, 148
Epic male, 14
Erchul, W. P., 60
Espiritu, Y. L., 126
Essentialism, 28–29
ESTs (empirically supported
　　treatments), 79
Ethnic diversity. *See* Diverse
　　masculinities
Ethnic validity model, 168
Ethnocentric monoculturalism, 43,
　　117–118, 123
Evanow, M., 62
Executive coaching, 62
Existential therapies, 103, 153
Experiential therapies, 101–104
Expressive power, 22
Extended family, 122
Eye contact, 166

Facial expression, 166
Faludi, Susan, 24, 26
Family, 122, 126, 132
Family therapy, for males, 109
Farr, K. A., 165–166
Farrell, M. P., 22, 106
Farrell, Warren, 82
Fassinger, R. E., 131
Fasteau, M. F., 14
FAST Track program, 54

Fatherhood
    and African American males,
        118–119
    and masculinity, 19–20
Father hunger, 19
"Father loss," 27
Female therapists, 163, 167–169
The Feminine Mystique (Betty Friedan),
    25
Feminism. *See also* Feminist approach
    and cultural variables, 114–115
    First Wave of, 24
    and marital and family therapies, 107
    Second Wave of, 24–25
Feminist approach
    impact on psychotherapy, 41–45
    as male-friendly psychotherapy,
        104–105
    models for family therapy, 109
Finding Our Fathers (Samuel
    Osherson), 19
Fine, G. A., 23
First Wave, of feminism, 24
Fisch, R., 73
Fischer, M., 78, 162
Fisher, M., 23
Fitzgerald, J., 131
Forensic settings, 66
Forneris, T., 55
Frank, J. L., 142
Frank, Jerome, 79, 144
Freeman, J., 24–25
Freud, Sigmund, 82
Freudian therapists, 87
Friedan, Betty, 25–26
Friendship patterns, 22

Garbarino, J., 17
Garcia-Preto, N., 122
Garfield, Sol, 79, 144
Gay, Lesbian, and Straight Education
    Network (GLSEN), 56
Gay, Lesbian, Bisexual, and Transsexual
    (GLBT) National Help Center,
    56, 133
Gay-affirming therapy, 131, 134
Gay and bisexual males, 128–134
    as adolescents, 132–134
    barriers to treatment for, 129–130

and churches, 64
    lives of, 128–129
    psychotherapy processes for, 131–132
    special content areas with, 130–131
    therapeutic interventions with,
        128–134
Gay cultural literacy, 130
Gelso, C. J., 82
Gender, of therapist, 163, 167–169
Gender aware therapy, 45
Gender blindness, 53
Gender expectations, traditional, 8
Gender inquiry technique, 109
Gender-neutral therapy, 45
Gender role, male. *See* Male role
    socialization
Gender role analysis, 71–73
Gender role conflict, 93–94, 99–100
Gender Role Conflict Scale (GRCS),
    31, 32
Gender role identity paradigm, 31
"Gender role journey," 59, 154, 158
Gender role strain paradigm. *See also*
    Male gender role strain
    context of, 98
    and male development, 87–88
    and masculinity, 31–32
    on pathologizing males, 163–164
Gender role stress, 93–94
Gender scripts, 156
Gender sensitive therapy, 45
Gerschick, T. J., 135–136
Gestalt therapy, 102–103
Giges, B., 62–63
Gilbert, J., 25, 99
Gilmore, David, 39
"Give 'Em Hell," 30
Glassgold, J. M., 131
GLBT National Help Center, 56, 133
Glicken, M. D., 82, 165
GLSEN (Gay, Lesbian, and Straight
    Education Network), 56
Goals, client, 80, 96
Goals for Health, 55
Going for the Goal program, 55
Goldenberg, H., 107
Goldenberg, I., 107
Goldfried, M. R., 141–142, 150
Good, G. E., 142
Good-provider role, 19

"Model minority," 125
Monoculturalism, ethnocentric,
    117–118
Mooney, T. F., 92–94
Motivational interviewing, 77
Motivational factors, 73–79
MRNI (Male Role Norms Inventory),
    31, 32
Mule, M., 56, 134
Multicultural competence, 43, 159–169
    and awareness, 161–164
    and knowledge, 160–161
    and skills, 164–169
    and transtheoretical model, 160
Multicultural counseling and therapy
    (MCT), 160, 163–164
Multiculturalism
    aspects of, 140–141
    as fourth force in psychotherapy, 160
    and masculinities, 173
Multimodal therapy (MMT), 142,
    145–147, 156
Murphy, R. F., 134
Mythopoetic men's movement, 27,
    163–165

Narcissism, 90
National Advocacy Youth Coalition,
    133–134
National Black Lesbian and Gay
    Leadership Forum, 134
National Fellowship of Catholic Men, 64
National Institute of Mental Health
    (NIMH), 60
National Organization for Changing
    Men, 28
National Organization of Men Against
    Sexism, 28, 57
The National Youth Advocacy
    Center, 56
Native American males, 19
    in prison population, 66
    social issues related to, 116
    and storytelling techniques, 165
    therapeutic interventions with,
        122–125
Nature of masculinity, 5–7
New fathers, 20
"New sexism," 161

New psychology of men, 11
Newsweek (magazine), 132
Newton, F. B., 63
New York Times, 37
Niemiec, R. M., 37
NIMH (National Institute of Mental
    Health), 60
Nonblaming approach, 92–93
Non-relational sexuality, 41
Non-sexist therapy, 45
Norcross, John, 12, 53, 58, 74, 76,
    85–86, 98, 141, 142, 144–146,
    149, 150, 153–156, 158
Normative male alexithymia, 21
"No Sissy Stuff," 20, 30
Nutt, E. A., 92
Nutt, R. L., 109

Object relations therapies, 86–91
Oliver, M. B., 21
Olkin, Rhoda, 135
O'Neil, J. M., 15, 31, 39, 59, 154
Operant reinforcement, 97
Oppression, racial, 115–118
Orchowski, L. M., 37
Ordinary People (film), 71
Origins, of masculinity crisis, 3, 24–26
Orpinas, P., 54
Osherson, S., 19
Ossana, S. M., 107, 132
Outdoor/adventure therapy, 57
Out-of-office interventions. *See* Primary
    prevention
Outproud, 56
Overgeneralization, 123
Owen, C. L., 15

PACT (Positive Adolescents Choices
    Training), 54
Padesky, C., 92
Paniagua, F. A., 119, 122
Paradox of male power, 39
Parents and Friends of Lesbians and
    Gays (PFLAG), 133
Parham, Thomas, 119–120
Pathologizing culture, 163
PATHS (Providing Alternative Think-
    ing Strategies), 54
Patients, behavior toward, 43–44
Patriarchy, 20, 39

Racism, 115–118
Rape/sexual assault, 16
Rapidity of effect feature, 93
Real Boys (William Pollack), 17
Real Men, Real Depression campaign, 60
Reese, L. E., 54
Rehabilitation settings, 65–66
Reichian body work, 104
Reid, H. M., 23
Relational bond, 80
Relationship counseling, for gay men, 132
Relationships, 20–24
Relaxation interventions, 97
Religious accommodations
    for African American males, 119
    with gay and bisexual males, 131
    for Hispanic males, 122
    for Native American males, 123
Religious settings, 63–64
Remedial intervention, 51
Reparative therapy, 130
Repetto, P. B., 59
Resilience, building, 54–56
Resistance, to psychotherapy, 36–37,
    76–77, 156
Respected Elders training program, 120
"Respeto," 121
Reviving Ophelia (Mary Pipher), 17
Rice, J. K., 42
Richards, P. S., 64
Rites of passage, 55
Robertson, J. M., 19, 63
Rochlen, A. B., 59–60
Rogerian therapy, 81, 101–102
Role socialization. *See* Male role
    socialization
Rollnick, S., 77
Rosenberg, H. J., 22
Rosenberg, L. G., 131
Rosenberg, M., 136
Rosenberg, S. D., 22
Roth, E., 105
Rowan, John, 27
Ruiz De Esparza, C. A., 116, 121

Sattel, J. W., 36
Sawyer, J., 26
Sax, L., 17–18
Schacht, A. N., 124

Scher, M., 39, 99
Schneider, I., 37
School shootings, 18
Schwartzberg, S., 131
Scrivner, Roy, 130
Secondary prevention, 51
Second Wave, of feminism, 24, 161–162
Segal, L., 73
Self-confrontation, 118
Self-disclosure, 106, 166–167
Self-evaluation, 148
Self-help, 58
Self-interrogation, 118
Self-liberation, 146, 153
Self-listening, 106
Seligman, L., 93, 102
"Sequence of change," 157
Serovich, J. M., 107
Setting-specific primary prevention,
    60–67
Sex therapy, 97
Sexual dysfunction, 31
Sexuality, 21, 40–41, 54
Sexual orientation, 129–130. *See also*
    Gay and Bisexual males
Sexual violence, 15–16, 36, 54
Shame, 93, 105–106
Shame attacking exercise, 94
Shapiro, J. L., 19
Shepard, D. S., 19
Shifting levels, 156
Silverberg, R., 89
Silverstein, L. B., 14, 82–83, 107
Simba Wachanga program, 120
Simmons, R., 136
Skills, and multicultural competence,
    164–169
Sleek, S., 37
Social change, 23–24
Social construction, of masculinity, 8–9
Social constructionism, 29
Socialization. *See* Male role socialization
Social liberation, 146
Social movements, of 1960s, 26
Society for the Psychological Study of
    Men and Masculinity, 162
Sociocultural contexts, 142, 159
Softened start-up, 97
Solomon, K., 31
Somerset Institute's Modern Men's
    Weekend, 57

Wachtel, P. L., 142
Warrior male, 14, 65
Watson, J. C., 81
Weakland, J., 73
Wedding, D., 37
Welcoming space, 112
Weston, K., 132
Whitbourne, S. K., 99
White, J. L., 118, 119
White American men, 19, 160
White culture, 117–118
Wilderness therapy, 57
Williams, J., 20
Williams-McCoy, J., 168
Willoughby, F. W., 66
Window shopper, 74
Winnicott, D. W., 90
Wisch, A. F., 92
Women and Madness (Phyllis Chesler), 41

Women's empowerment, 9, 45, 108
Women's Liberation Movement, 24
Women's Veterans Program Office, 65
Wood, J. T., 29
Worell, J., 45, 104
Work, and masculinity, 19
Working alliance, 80
Wyche, K. F., 42

Yalom, I. D., 105, 106
Young Lions program, 120
Yue, D., 142

Zabos, G. R., 60
Zakrzewski, Paul, 57
Zimmerman, M. A., 59
Zins, J. E., 60
Zur, O., 50, 52

ABOUT THE AUTHOR

Gary R. Brooks, PhD, is a professor of psychology at Baylor University's Department of Psychology and Neuroscience in Waco, Texas, and a core faculty member in the graduate clinical program there. He was staff psychologist (1976–1996) and chief of psychological services (1996–2000) at the Veterans Administration Center in Temple, Texas. He is also a licensed psychotherapist specializing in men and masculinity issues. Dr. Brooks is the author or editor of a variety of books on the male experience with psychotherapy, including *The New Handbook of Psychotherapy and Counseling With Men: A Comprehensive Guide to Settings, Problems, and Treatment Approaches* (with Glenn E. Good); *The Centerfold Syndrome: How Men Can Overcome Objectification and Achieve Intimacy With Women*; and *Men and Sex: New Psychological Perspectives* (coedited with Ronald F. Levant). He is a former president of the American Psychological Association's Division 51 (Society for the Psychological Study of Men and Masculinity).